INTRODUCTION TO
LOGICAL THEORY

Introduction to
LOGICAL THEORY

by

P. F. STRAWSON
Fellow of University College, Oxford

METHUEN & CO LTD
11 NEW FETTER LANE . LONDON . EC4

First published 1 October 1952
Reprinted 1960, 1963 and 1964
Printed in Great Britain by
Jarrold & Sons Ltd, Norwich
Catalogue No 2/5401/41
1.4

PREFACE

THERE are in existence many text-books and technical treatises on formal logic, and I have not sought in this book to add to their number. Many such books, excellent as they often are in their expositions of the technical and systematic aspects of logic, deal comparatively sketchily, and often rather mis-leadingly, with the relations between the formal systems they expound and the logical features of ordinary discourse. As a result of this omission, the true character of formal logic itself is apt to be left obscure. So this book has two complementary aims : one is to bring out some points of contrast and of con-tact between the behaviour of words in ordinary speech and the behaviour of symbols in a logical system; the other is to make clear, at an introductory level, the nature of formal logic itself. I have included enough of the elementary material of formal logic to provide a basis for the philosophical discussion of its nature, and to serve, if desired, as an introduction to more advanced technical treatises. Since the book is designed to be used as a general introduction to logic, I have added a concluding chapter on induction and probability.

I wish to acknowledge my great indebtedness to the many Oxford colleagues from whose discussions of the topics of this book I have profited; and among these, in particular, to Mr. H. P. Grice, from whom I have never ceased to learn about logic since he was my tutor in the subject; and to Professor Gilbert Ryle, Mr. G. A. Paul and Miss Ruby Meager, all of whom read the book either in manuscript or in proof and saved me from many inelegancies and mistakes.

P. F. S.

Oxford,
 May, 1952.

CONTENTS

CONTENTS

Chapter 3.   TRUTH-FUNCTIONS

Chapter 4.   CLASSES : AN ALTERNATIVE INTERPRETATION OF THE TABULAR SYSTEM

CONTENTS

CHAPTER 1

LOGICAL APPRAISAL

1. WHEN a man says or writes something, there are many different ways in which his performance may be judged. Among other things, we may question his truthfulness or criticize his style, we may assess the morality of what he says, or we may appraise its logic; though not all these types of assessment are appropriate to all kinds of utterance. The words 'logical' and 'illogical' are themselves among the words of logical appraisal. If you call a discourse logical, you are in some degree commending it. If you call it illogical, you are, so far, condemning it. Words and phrases which go with 'logical' are 'consistent','cogent', 'valid', 'it follows'; words and phrases which go with 'illogical' are 'inconsistent', 'self-contradictory', 'invalid', 'a *non sequitur*'. Part of our problem is to see what sort of appraisal these words are used for, to what kind of standards we appeal in using them. It is easy to see that these are not moral or aesthetic standards; that logical criticism is not, say, a kind of literary criticism. A slightly more difficult distinction is that between the criticism we offer when we declare a man's remarks to be untrue and the criticism we offer when we declare them to be inconsistent. In the first case we criticize his remarks on the ground that they fail to square with the facts; in the second case we criticize them on the ground that they fail to square with one another. The charge of untruth refers beyond the words and sentences the man uses to that in the world about which he talks. We deny his assertion, and, in doing so, make a counter-assertion of our own about the subject of his discourse. We contradict him. But the charge of inconsistency does not in this way refer to anything outside the statements that the man makes. We simply consider the way his statements hang together. Just from considering the sentences themselves, as they are used, we can, perhaps, see that not all the statements he makes can be true together. It is not that we contradict him, and in doing so, make a counter-assertion about the subject of his remarks;

we assert that he has contradicted himself, and, in doing this, we make no appeal to the facts and express no opinion about them.   It is this kind of internal criticism that is appraisal of the logic of a piece of discourse.

I. INCONSISTENCY

2. Words of logical appraisal have connected meanings.   To be clear about the meaning of one such word is to be clear about the meanings of the others.   For example, in a proof or argument, one statement (the conclusion) is said to follow logically from, or to be logically implied by, others (the premises), if the argument is valid; and an argument is valid only if it would be inconsistent (or self-contradictory) to assert the premises while denying the conclusion; or, in other words, only if the truth of the premises is inconsistent with the falsity of the conclusion. A deductive argument is a sort of threat, which takes the form : if you accept these premises as true, then you must accept this conclusion as true as well, on pain of self-contradiction.   From among the various concepts of logical appraisal, I shall select this notion of <u>inconsistency</u> or <u>self-contradiction</u> for detailed discussion.   Other choices could have been made, but there are reasons, which will emerge as we go on, for making this choice.

3. What is inconsistency?   It is better to approach this question indirectly, by asking a series of others.   One might ask first : Why bother to avoid inconsistency?   What is wrong with contradicting yourself?   There is nothing morally wrong about it.   It may not even be entirely pointless.   Suppose a man sets out to walk to a certain place; but, when he gets half-way there, turns round and comes back again.   This may not be pointless.   He may, after all, have wanted only exercise.   But, from the point of view of a change of position, it is as if he had never set out.   And so a man who contradicts himself may have succeeded in exercising his vocal chords.   But from the point of view of imparting information, of communicating facts (or falsehoods) it is as if he had never opened his mouth.   He utters words, but does not say anything.   Or he might be compared with a man who makes as if to give something away and then takes it back again.   He arouses expectations which he does not

fulfil; and this may have been his purpose. Similarly, it may have been the purpose of a man who contradicts himself just to create puzzlement. The point is that the *standard* purpose of speech, the intention to communicate something, is frustrated by self-contradiction. Contradicting oneself is like writing something down and then erasing it, or putting a line through it. A contradiction cancels itself and leaves nothing. Consequently one cannot explain what a contradiction is just by indicating, as one might be tempted to do, a certain form of words. One might be tempted to say that a contradiction was anything of the form ' X is the case and X is not the case '. But this will not do. If someone asks you whether you were pleased by something, you may reply : ' Well, I was and I wasn't ', and you will communicate perfectly well. Or there might be a convention that when one said anything of this form, the second part of the sentence was to be neglected. Then the minimum requirement for such a contradiction would be to say, first, ' X is the case and X is not the case ' and, after that, ' X is not the case and X is the case '. Nevertheless, the temptation to explain a contradiction as anything of this form is, we shall see, not without point.

4. The next two questions to ask are more difficult. They are : (*a*) when we use these words of logical appraisal, what is it exactly that we are appraising ? and (*b*) how does logical appraisal become possible ? That is, we shall ask : what is it exactly that we declare to be inconsistent ? and : what makes inconsistency possible ? I have spoken of *statements* as being inconsistent with each other; and there is a temptation to think that in this context we mean by a statement the same thing as a sentence of a certain kind; or, perhaps, the meaning of such a sentence. But suppose I write on the blackboard the following two pairs of sentences : (i) ' I am under six foot tall ' and ' I am over six foot tall '; (ii) ' The conductor is a bachelor ' and ' The conductor is married '. In writing the sentences on the blackboard, I have, of course, not contradicted myself; for I may have written them there with a purely illustrative intention, in giving an English lesson. Someone might say : Nevertheless, the sentences in each pair *are* inconsistent with each other. But what would this mean ? Would it mean that if they were

ever uttered with the intention of making a statement, an inconsistency would result? But suppose the first two sentences
were uttered by different people, or by the same person at an
interval of years; and that the second two sentences were
uttered in different omnibuses, or in the same omnibus, but on
different days. Then there would be no inconsistency. Earlier,
I paraphrased ' seeing that two statements are inconsistent ' as
' seeing that they cannot both be true together '. And it is
clear that that of which we can say that it is true or false is also
that of which we can say that it is consistent or inconsistent with
another of its kind. What these examples show is that we cannot identify that which is true or false (the statement) with the
sentence used in making it; for the same sentence may be used
to make quite different statements, some of them true and some
of them false. And this does not arise from any ambiguity in
the sentence. The sentence may have a single meaning which
is precisely what, as in these cases, allows it to be used to make
quite different statements. So it will not do to identify the
statement either with the sentence or with the meaning of the
sentence. A particular statement is identified, not only by
reference to the words used, but also by reference to the circumstances in which they are used, and, sometimes, to the
identity of the person using them. No one would be tempted
to say that the sentence ' I am over six foot tall ' was inconsistent with the sentence ' You are under six foot tall '. But
plainly they can be used, in certain circumstances, to make
statements which are inconsistent with each other; i.e., in the
case where the second sentence is addressed to the man by
whom the first sentence is uttered.

It is easy to see why one is tempted to think of the sentence
' I am over six foot tall ' as being inconsistent with the sentence
' I am under six foot tall '. One thinks of both sentences as
being uttered, in the same breath, by the same person. In this
case we should ordinarily regard that person as having contradicted himself, i.e., we should regard him as having said something and then unsaid it; and so as having said nothing. The
important assumption is that the two expressions ' over six
foot tall ' and ' under six foot tall ' are applied to the same
person at the same time. Let us give the name ' incompatible
predicates ' to any pair of expressions the application of which

to the same person or thing at the same time results in an inconsistency. Thus we can say that one of the ways in which it is
possible to say something inconsistent is by applying incompatible
predicates to the same person or thing at the same time.

5. But must a language have incompatible predicates in it?
And what makes predicates incompatible? I want to answer
the first question by saying, not that a language must have incompatible predicates in it; only that it is very natural that it
should. And I want to answer the second question by saying
that it is we, the makers of language, who make predicates incompatible. One of the main purposes for which we use language
is to report events and to describe things and persons. Such
reports and descriptions are like answers to questions of the
form : what was it like? what is it (he, she) like? We describe
something, say what it is like, by applying to it words that we
are also prepared to apply to other things. But not to all other
things. A word that we are prepared to apply to everything
without exception (such as certain words in current use in
popular, and especially military, speech) would be useless for
the purposes of description. For when we say what a thing is
like, we not only compare it with other things, we also distinguish
it from other things. (These are not two activities, but two
aspects of the same activity.) Somewhere, then, a boundary
must be drawn, limiting the applicability of a word used in
describing things; and it is we who decide where the boundaries
are to be drawn.

This metaphor of drawing boundaries is in some ways misleading. I do not mean by it that we often make conscious
decisions of this kind (though we sometimes do); nor that our
boundary-drawing is a quite arbitrary matter; nor that the
boundaries are fixed and definite; nor that the decisions we
make when we make them, are purely verbal decisions. The
boundaries are more like areas of indeterminate ownership than
frontier-lines. We show ourselves to be near such a boundary,
and we show also its indeterminacy, when, in reply to such a
question as ' Was it red? ', we give such an answer as ' Well, I
suppose you could call it red '. We show ourselves on the point
of making a boundary-decision when, with all the facts before
us, we hesitate over the application of a certain word. Does

such and such an act constitute an act of aggression or not?
This case shows, too, how our decision is not a purely verbal
matter; for important consequences may follow from our deciding that it is, or is not, an act of aggression.   What makes our
decisions, for a word already in use, non-arbitrary, is this : that
our normal purpose will be defeated if the comparison implicit
in the use of the word is too unnatural, if the similarity is too
tenuous.

non-arbitrary

We may say : two predicates are incompatible when they lie
on different sides of a boundary we have drawn : ' under six
foot tall ' and ' over six foot tall '; ' red ' and ' orange '; ' aggressive ' and ' pacific '.   But this needs some explanation.
Suppose you draw a closed figure on a piece of paper and then
someone indicates a point on the ceiling and says : ' Does this
point lie inside or outside the boundaries of the figure? '   Of
course, one might answer by imagining the boundaries of the
figure extended in another dimension, up to the ceiling.   But
you might refuse to answer the question, by saying that you
were drawing the boundary line only in the plane of the paper.
Whatever lay outside the line in the plane of the paper was
excluded from the figure.   Things lying in a different plane were
not excluded from it, but neither were they included in it.   The
figure has a certain plane of exclusiveness.   And so with a word :
it has a certain range of incompatibilities.   ' Under six foot tall '
is incompatible with ' over six foot tall '; but neither is incompatible with ' aggressive '.   The last expression has a different
incompatibility-range from the other two.   There may sometimes be objections of a logical kind to applying expressions
with different incompatibility-ranges to the same thing; but
these will not be the objection that inconsistency will result from
doing so.

When we apply a predicate to something, we implicitly exclude from application to that thing the predicates which lie
outside the boundaries of the predicate we apply, but in the
same incompatibility-range.   By this I mean that if we go on to
apply to the thing, in the same breath, one of the predicates
which lie outside those boundaries, we shall be taken to have
contradicted ourselves and said nothing.   (This might be taken
as a definition of ' incompatible predicates '.)   But there is a
qualification to be made here.   Just as we might reply to the

query ' Were you pleased ? ' with the words ' Well, I was and I wasn't ' without inconsistency, so we might apply to the same thing, in the same breath, two predicates, which would ordinarily be regarded as incompatible, without contradicting ourselves.   If we do this, we invite the question ' What do you mean ? '; and if we can explain what we mean, or show the point of saying what we say, then we have not contradicted ourselves.   But if there is no way of doing this, we are inconsistent.   Thus we might say, in answer to a question, ' He is both over six foot tall and under six foot tall', and then explain that he has a disease which makes him stoop, but that if he were cured and were able to stand upright, he would top the six-foot mark.   This shows again that one cannot fully explain what self-contradiction is, just by reference to groupings of words.

6. So long as we bear this qualification in mind, we can safely speak of incompatible predicates and can safely say that, when we apply a predicate to something by way of describing it, we implicitly exclude from application to it any predicates incompatible with that which we apply.   (We should be said to have contradicted anyone who had just applied any of those predicates to the thing.)   When we notice that this function of exclusion is implicit in all descriptive uses of language, we should not find it surprising that language contains devices for rendering the function explicit; devices of which, in English, the word ' not ' is the most prominent.   There are many very different kinds of occasion on which our primary concern is with the explicit exclusion of a predicate; e.g., when we wish to contradict a previous assertion; or to correct a possible false impression; or to express the contrast between what had been expected, feared, suggested, or hoped, and the reality; sometimes, when we are answering a direct question; sometimes, when we grope towards the right description by eliminating the wrong ones. What is common to such cases is that they create a need or a motive for emphasizing a difference rather than a resemblance. It is instructive to compare the use of ' not ' with the use of those words which begin with negative prefixes; like ' intolerable ', ' unpretentious ', ' impolite ', ' non-aggressive '.   These words bear their incompatibilities on their faces as surely as any

phrase containing ' not '; but one would hardly say of them that they have the same function of explicitly rejecting a suggested description. They do not point more emphatically to differences than to likenesses; they rather serve to underline the fact that the two are complementary. One might ask why some words have such manifest incompatibles (viz., words which are the same except for a negative prefix), while others do not; why we do not speak of things as ' unblue ', for example. One might be inclined to suggest that it is because ' not being blue ' is relatively so indeterminate; i.e., that, where there is a wide range of incompatible predicates, like colour-words, it is unnatural to have a single word expressly excluding one of them. But I do not think this is a complete answer. There is a wide range of races and nationalities, but we have words (e.g., ' foreign ', ' non-English ', ' non-European ') to indicate ' not being of a particular nationality (or range of races) '. I think the answer is, rather, that if we had a constant and persistent interest in things not being blue, as opposed to such a temporary interest as may arise from, e.g., wishing to correct a false impression, then we *should* have a word for this. Then we might say that in calling a thing ' unblue ' we should be as much emphasizing its likeness to other unblue things as its difference from blue things. (It was characteristic of those formal logicians who framed unnatural-looking negative terms, like ' nonblue ', not to concern themselves with questions and differences of this kind.)

This discussion of the function of ' not ' helps us to see part of the point of the saying, incorrect though it is, that a contradiction is simply something of the form ' X is the case and X is not the case '. The standard and primary use of ' not ' is specifically to contradict or correct; to cancel a suggestion of one's own or another's. And there is no restriction on the sphere in which it may exercise this function. Not all predicates have corresponding negatively prefixed terms, and not all statements are of the kind in which we simply apply a descriptive predicate to some person or thing. But any statement, whether or not it is of this simple kind, can be contradicted by the use of ' not '. So we are strongly inclined to regard a statement involving something of the form ' X is the case and X is not the case ' as a self-contradiction; though always the indeterminacy of the verbal boundaries we draw, the different points of view which may tempt us both to apply and to withhold an expression, allow of the possibility of a consistent meaning being given to something of this form.

7. It is, then, our own activity of making language through using it, our own determination of the limits of the application of words, that makes inconsistency possible; and it is no accident that, when we want to form for ourselves a general pattern or type of inconsistency, we employ the two words ' and ' and ' not ', together with a repetition of some one phrase or expression. Since all concepts of logical appraisal may be explained in terms of inconsistency, it is not surprising that these two words should play an important role in logic.

But we can create the possibility of inconsistency in statement, and hence of validity in argument, in a way more deliberate and self-conscious than those I have so far discussed. We can deliberately fix the boundaries of some words in relation to those of other words. This is what we do when we *define* [1] words or phrases. To introduce or to accept a definition [1] is to announce or to agree that conjoining the defined (or defining) expression with the defining (or defined) expression by the words ' and ' and ' not ' in their standard use (or in any equivalent way), and referring this conjunction to one and the same situation, is to count as an inconsistency. Accepting a definition is agreeing to be bound by a rule of language of this kind.

8. Let us now return to the questions we asked earlier : namely, what is it to which we apply words of logical appraisal ? and : what makes logical appraisal possible ? We saw that the answer to the first question was not ' sentences or groups of words ', but ' statements or groups of statements '. It is statements and not sentences that are inconsistent with one another, follow from one another, etc. We see that the answer to the second question is : the boundaries of application that we draw between one expression and another, the rules we come to

---

[1] The words ' define ' and ' definition ' have many connected, though distinguishable, uses, of some of which what I say here is not true. I use the words here in a ' strict ' sense.

observe for using expressions of all kinds.[1] And the answer to the second question shows the full point of the temptation to answer the first by talking of sentences (groups of words) as being inconsistent. Behind inconsistencies between statements, stand rules for the use of expressions. If one understands this relationship, a lot of things which have puzzled people become clear. One sees how a linguistic rule for expressions in a particular language can lead to a general statement of logical appraisal which transcends individual languages altogether. Suppose someone says : ' A statement to the effect that a certain person is someone's son-in-law is inconsistent with the statement that he has never been married.' Let us call the statement he makes in saying this a general statement of logical appraisal or, for short, a logical statement. Now suppose someone says : ' In English the words " son-in-law of " mean the same as the words " married to the daughter of ".' Let us call the statement he makes in saying this a linguistic statement. Now what is the relation between the logical statement and the linguistic statement? Well, suppose we translate into French the sentence used to make the logical statement. We shall obtain a sentence with no English words in it. If we also translate into French the sentence used to make the linguistic statement (i.e., the sentence beginning ' In English '), we shall obtain a French sentence, beginning ' En anglais ', in which the expressions ' " son-in-law of " ' and ' " married to the daughter of " ' reappear unchanged. It seems that, whereas we are inclined to say that the French and English versions of the logical statement mean the same thing, or are used to make the same statement, we are not inclined to say that the English sentence used to make the linguistic statement means the same as the French sentence : ' En français les mots " gendre de " veulent dire la même chose que les mots " marié avec la fille de " '. For we are inclined to say that anyone uttering *this* sentence would be talking about a rule of French, whereas anyone uttering the English sentence used to make the linguistic statement would be talking about

---

[1] But we must notice that, as far as ordinary speech is concerned, and apart from the introduction of words by *definition*, this talk of ' rules ' may mislead us. We do not *generally* (in ordinary speech) draw up rules and make our practice conform to them ; it is rather that we extract the rules from our practice, from noticing when we *correct* one another, when we are inclined to say that something is *inconsistent*, and so on.

a rule of English.   So these sentences are used to make quite different statements about quite different things, namely French words and English words.   And if one says this, as one is strongly inclined to do, and also says that the French and English versions of the logical statement mean the same (are versions of the same statement), then, of course, it would seem to follow that the logical statement is not about what the linguistic statements are about, that the truth of the logical statement is independent of the truth of the linguistic statements; and from here it is an easy step to thinking of logical facts as independent of linguistic facts, and to adopting an attitude of reverence to logical facts. But to take this step is to forget that the fact that the English and French versions of the logical statement mean the same is itself in part the linguistic fact that ' son-in-law of ' and ' married ' in English mean the same as ' gendre de ' and ' marié ' in French.   We might express this by saying that there is, after all, an alternative translation of the English sentence used for making the linguistic statement; namely the French sentence quoted above, beginning ' En français . . .' We might say that these were really different versions of the same rule; that in laying down inconsistency-rules in one language, we were implicitly laying down inconsistency-rules for the corresponding expressions in all languages; and that thus a linguistic statement *of the kind quoted* transcends the language of the words which it mentions.   Only it is less natural to say this than to say that a logical statement transcends the language in which it is framed.

We see that there are difficulties in identifying logical statements with linguistic statements; in saying that sentences used to make logical statements mean the same as corresponding sentences used to make linguistic statements; and seeing this is apt to give us the illusion of an independent realm of logical facts, of which linguistic rules are merely the adventitious verbal clothing. We feel that, while it is a mere matter of linguistic history, which could easily have been different, that the expression ' son-in-law ' means what it does mean, the statement we make when we say ' The statement that a man is a son-in-law is inconsistent with the statement that he has never been married ' is one that could not be false, even though it is an historical accident that we make it in these words. But when we voice this feeling we are voicing the truism that a word could not both have the sense it in fact has (the sense in which we use it in making statements) and not have that sense.

The important thing is to see that when you draw the boundaries of the applicability of words in one language and then connect the words of that language with those of another by means of translation-rules, there is no need to draw the boundaries again for the second language. They are already drawn. (I am not suggesting that this is the order in which things are done; though it is the order in which things are learned.) This is why (or partly why) logical statements framed in one language are not just about that language.

It is important also to notice that this reason for not regarding statements of logical appraisal as about particular groups of words (e.g., sentences) is different from, though connected with, that which we have discussed earlier. Earlier we pointed out that it is not sentences which we say are inconsistent with one another, follow from one another, etc., but statements; the question of what statement is made, and of whether a statement is made at all, depends upon other things than simply what words are used. But rules about words lie behind all statements of logical appraisal; and it remains to be seen whether we can best do logic in terms of rules directly about representative expressions, or in terms of logical relations between statements.

II. REASONING

9. People often say that logic is the study of the principles of deductive reasoning. But this is too narrow, and includes irrelevant suggestions. Arguing, proving, inferring, concluding, solving a mathematical problem, might all be said to be kinds of reasoning. Their aims and purposes are different. The aim of argument is conviction; one tries to get someone to agree that some statement is true or false. You may get a man to agree that a statement is true by showing him that it follows from other statements which he already accepts. You may get him to agree that a statement is false because from it there follows another which he rejects. Proving is different : a man may argue successfully, and even validly, without proving; for an invalid argument may convince, and the premises of a

valid argument may be false. Moreover, a man may prove something without arguing, without seeking to convince. When you prove a mathematical theorem in an examination, you are not trying to convince the examiner of its truth; your object is to exhibit your mathematical knowledge by writing down a set of statements of which the last is the theorem to be proved and of which each follows from the ones written down already, together with earlier theorems. Inferring, drawing conclusions, is different again. Here you know some facts or truths already, and are concerned to see what further information can be derived from them; to find out their logical consequences. Though inferring, proving, arguing have different purposes, they seem usually [1] to have also the common purpose of connecting truths with truths. The validity of the steps is, in general, prized for the sake of the truth of the conclusions to which they lead. But neither the common purpose, nor the different purposes, of arguing, proving, inferring, are a logical concern. The logical question, of the validity of the steps, is one that can be raised and answered independently of the question of whether these purposes are achieved. The validity of the steps does not alone guarantee the truth of the conclusion, nor their invalidity, its falsity. For to say that the steps are valid, that the conclusion follows from the premises, is simply to say that it would be inconsistent to assert the premises and deny the conclusion; that the truth of the premises is inconsistent with the falsity of the conclusion. The assessment of the reasoning as valid rules out a certain *combination* of truth and falsity; viz., truth in the premises and falsity in the conclusion. But it leaves open the possibility of other combinations : falsity with falsity and falsity with truth, as well as truth with truth. We are not told, when we are told that the reasoning is valid, that it would be inconsistent to deny both premises and conclusion or to assert the conclusion and deny the premises.

10. We often signalize a claim to be making a valid step in reasoning by the use of certain expressions to link one statement,

---

[1] Not always. A child solves problems in applied arithmetic. What he aims at is not the *true* answer but the *right* answer. And what he is given marks for is not the answer, but the way he gets it.

or set of statements, and another.   These are words and phrases like ' so ', ' consequently ', ' therefore ', ' since ', ' for ', ' it follows that ', &c.   And other expressions are sometimes used to signalize steps, which we should rightly hesitate to call steps in reasoning, but which are of no less interest to the logician. I have in mind such expressions as ' that is to say ', ' in other words ', ' more briefly ', ' I mean '.   These are expressions which we sometimes (though not always or only) use on occasions on which we should describe ourselves, not as inferring or arguing, but rather as, say, putting into other words something that has already been said, or repeating it with something left out, or summarizing it, or making a *précis*.   There is no sharply definite line separating those steps which we should call steps in reasoning, and those steps which we should describe in one of the alternative ways I have listed.   Obviously, there are extremes, which we should classify without hesitation.   Where the steps are numerous and intricate, we unhesitatingly apply such words as ' inference ', or ' argument ';   where something that has been said is simply repeated, in whole or in part, we unhesitatingly withhold these words.   But there are borderline cases.   A man who linked one part of his discourse with another by the phrase, ' in other words ', thus disclaiming anything so portentous as an inference, might be met with the rejoinder ' But that doesn't follow ', which imputes, and disallows, the claim to have validly inferred.   <u>The differences between the steps which are steps in reasoning and the steps we should not so describe are, from some points of view, important.</u> From our present point of view, they are less important than the resemblances.   What is common to all the cases I refer to is the claim, signalized by the linking expressions,[1] that it would be inconsistent to assert what precedes those expressions and to deny what follows them.   The logician interests himself in cases in which this relationship holds between statements, irrespective of whether or not the transition from one statement to another so related to it is a transition which we should dignify by the name ' step in reasoning ';   irrespective even of whether it is something we should acknow-

---

[1] Of course, the linking expressions I listed are not always used to make just this claim.   Cf. Chapter 2, p. 37, and Chapter 9.

ledge as a transition. (Later, we shall see the reason for his catholicity of interest.) This explains why ' study of the principles of valid deductive reasoning ' is too narrow a description of logic. A man who repeats himself does not reason. But it is inconsistent to assert and deny the same thing. So a logician will say that a statement has to itself the relationship he is interested in.

III. THE LOGICIAN'S SECOND-ORDER VOCABULARY

11. Most of the statements we make are not themselves about statements but about people or things. Statements which are not themselves about statements we shall call first-order statements; statements about first-order statements we shall call second-order statements; and so on. Since words of logical appraisal are used for talking about statements, the statements we make in using such words must at least be of the second order. We shall say that such words constitute a part of the logician's second-order vocabulary. Later, we shall speak analogously of first-order sentences (i.e., sentences used for making statements not about sentences or statements), and second-order sentences (i.e., sentences used for making statements about first-order sentences or first-order statements).

The phrases ' follows from ' and ' logically implies ' carry with them a suggestion of those mind-exercising situations in which we are prepared to talk of reasoning being carried on, of inferences being made, &c. The word ' valid ', applied to a group of statements linked by some expression (e.g., ' therefore ') signalizing the claim that one of the statements follows from the others, carries the same suggestion. We want a word, to signify that one statement is so related to another that it would be inconsistent to assert the first and deny the second, which does not carry this suggestion. It is customary to use the word ' entails ' for this purpose. But, when it is convenient to do so, I shall license myself also to use ordinary words and phrases of logical appraisal in a manner which disregards the suggestion that reasoning-situations are involved. Such a departure from ordinary usage need not be misleading, if it is self-conscious.

12. I want now to discuss the relations to one another of some words of the logician's second-order vocabulary. First we must discriminate between two kinds of inconsistency, between a wider and a narrower sense of ' contradiction '.

Suppose someone says of a certain man that he is over six foot tall, and someone else says of the same person that he is under six foot tall. Let us say that the first speaker makes the statement that o; and then let us abbreviate the phrase ' the statement that o' to ' S_o'. And let us say that the second speaker makes the statement that u; and then let us abbreviate the phrase ' the statement that u' to ' S_u'. Then, unless explanations are produced to show that the contradiction is only apparent, we shall properly say that the second speaker has contradicted the first, that S_u is inconsistent with S_o. A third speaker may say, of the man discussed, that he is just six foot tall; and in doing so he contradicts both previous speakers. Let us say that he makes S_j (the statement that the man under discussion is just six foot tall); and that S_j is inconsistent both with S_o and with S_u.

But now let us suppose that the second speaker, instead of making S_u, had made S_{not-o} (the statement that the man under discussion was not over six foot tall). Again, unless explanations were produced to show that the contradiction was only apparent, we should say that he had contradicted the first speaker, that S_{not-o} was inconsistent with S_o. But the relation between S_o and S_{not-o} is not quite the same as the relation between S_o and S_u. For whereas a statement, viz., S_j, could be made, that was inconsistent with both S_o and S_u, there is no way of making a statement that is inconsistent with both S_o and S_{not-o}. We express this by saying that S_o and S_{not-o} are contradictories, whereas S_o and S_u are only contraries. To say of two statements that they are contradictories is to say that they are inconsistent with each other and that no statement is inconsistent with both of them. To say of two statements that they are contraries is to say that they are inconsistent with each other, while leaving open the possibility that there is some statement inconsistent with both. (This may be taken as a definition of ' contradictory ' and ' contrary ' in terms of ' inconsistent '.) But we say of a man that he ' contradicts ' another (or himself) when they (or he) make (or makes) statements which are inconsistent with each other, whether or not they are contradictories.[1]

We have already discussed the question of how inconsistency is possible; and the same discussion helps us to see how contradiction, in the narrower sense, is possible; and how this sense underlies the natural choice of ' X is the case and X is not the case ' as the general form of a contradiction. We compared the incompatibility-range of a predicate with the plane of a closed figure. Two predicates were incompatible when they lay on different sides of a boundary we had drawn in a certain range of incompatibilities. Suppose two predicates lying on different sides of such a boundary are applied to the same thing, so that two inconsistent statements are made. Then we can make a statement inconsistent with both these by applying to that thing a predicate lying outside the boundaries of both these predicates, but in the same incompatibility-range. But suppose, between them, the predicates exhaust this range. Then there is no way of making a statement inconsistent with both the previous statements. (If half of the surface of a sheet of paper is coloured red and the other half blue, there is no way of finding a point on the surface of the paper which is in neither the blue nor the red area.) We saw that we had, in language, besides predicates which were incompatible, devices (like ' not ') for explicitly excluding (rejecting, withholding) a predicate from application to something. Where such devices exist, it is easy to see how the range of incompatibilities can be exhausted, how it is possible for contradictory statements to be made. Where two inconsistent statements are made by the application of merely incompatible predicates to something, there remains open the possibility of making a statement inconsistent with both, by the application of a third predicate belonging to the same incompatibility-range. But where one statement is inconsistent with another because it explicitly rejects (withholds, excludes) the predicate which the other applies, this possibility vanishes. To say that a thing neither has nor has not a certain property (i.e., to attempt to say something inconsistent both with the statement that it has, and with the statement that it has not,

---

[1] I shall continue to use ' contradiction ', ' self-contradictory ', ' contradict ' sometimes in the wider sense; but shall restrict ' contradictory ' to the narrower.

that property) is like saying that it both has, and has not, that property. One would not know what it meant, unless an explanation were given; though the indeterminacy of the boundaries of words, or the different points of view from which we may be tempted to apply and to withhold expressions, may allow of our giving a meaning to such a form of words. One might say : two statements are contradictories when a man who asserts both and a man who denies both, will both be taken to have contradicted themselves and said nothing.

But there is another way in which we can understand someone who says that a thing neither has nor has not a certain property. E.g., ' Does he care about it ? ' ' He neither cares nor doesn't care; he's dead.' The answer shows that the question is inappropriate to the circumstances, that some assumption which the questioner is making is untrue. It does not show that the statement that he cared and the statement that he did not care would both be false; it shows rather that the question of which is true does not arise, because the conditions of its arising are not fulfilled. Many statements are made in this way, against a background of assumption which is not called in question when their truth or falsity is discussed, and the calling in question of which prohibits discussion of their truth or falsity. Comment on the logical relations of statements occurs against the same background, at the same level of assumption, as discussion of their truth or falsity.

Contradictory statements, then, have the character of being both logically exclusive and logically exhaustive. It is perhaps easier to imagine a language in which contradictory statements could not be made than a language in which merely inconsistent statements could not be made. If there were only two kinds of four-footed animals, namely lions and tigers, one would have less need of the word ' not ' in discussing the identity of an animal. If people felt less impulse to talk with inadequate information, to ask certain kinds of questions, to approach experience with doubts, fears, hopes, and expectations, one would have less need of the word. But the occasions on which the need is felt for the explicit exclusion of a predicate, or the explicit rejection of a statement or suggestion, are in fact, many. And so we have contradictory statements. We rightly associate with contradiction (in the narrow sense) the following pairs of antithetical expressions or notions : ' Yes ' and ' No '; assertion and denial; truth and falsity; ' it is the case ' and ' it is not the case '; affirmation and negation. This association is harmless so long as we remember that ' Yes and no ' may not be a self-contradictory answer; that ' it is and it isn't ' (the conjunction of affirmation and negation) may be used to make a genuine statement; that we may hesitate to call a statement either true or false. ' Assertion ' and ' denial ' are in a slightly different position. They have contradictory opposition as part of their meaning. Though a man may say ' It is and it isn't ' without self-contradiction, we should hesitate to describe this as asser-tion and denial of the same thing. We would not say that a man could, in the same breath, assert and deny the same thing without self-contradiction. Of these pairs of antithetical expressions, ' assert ' and ' deny ', ' affirmative ' and negative ', ' true ' and ' false ' belong, like the word ' statement ' itself, to the logician's second-order vocabulary, though they are not words of logical appraisal; whereas ' yes ' and ' no ', ' it is ' and ' it is not ' belong to the first-order vocabulary, though they may figure in second-order contexts.

13. We are now in a position to deploy more systematically the logician's interrelated vocabulary of logical appraisal. For this purpose it is convenient to introduce certain abbreviatory devices. To begin with we shall make a new extension of an abbreviatory device we have used already. In discussing the relation between the statement, made with regard to a certain person, that he was over six foot tall, and the statement, with regard to the same person, that he was under six foot tall, we referred to the first statement by means of the expression ' S_o ' and to the second statement by means of the expression ' S_u '. But when we discuss, in a general way, the inter-rela-tions of the vocabulary of logical appraisal, we shall want to refer to statements in general rather than to particular state-ments. For example, we introduced the word ' entails ', ex-plaining its meaning roughly as follows : to say that one state-ment entails another is to say that it would be inconsistent to make the first and deny the second. This explanation, which refers not to particular statements, but to statements in general, we shall express as follows : to say that S_1 entails S_2 is to say

that it would be inconsistent to make S_1 and deny S_2. Here the subscripts play the role of the words ' one ', ' another ', ' first ', and ' second ' in the original explanation.

This explanation can be paraphrased further. The notion of denial is, as we have seen, closely linked with that of contradictoriness. To deny a statement has the same logical force as to assert its contradictory; the differences are here irrelevant. So we may paraphrase our explanation as follows : to say that S_1 entails S_2 is to say that it would be inconsistent both to assert S_1 and to assert the contradictory of S_2. Now the negative form of a statement (say, a form which includes the word ' not ') is not always its contradictory, as we have seen. But it is so sufficiently often to justify us in abbreviating the phrase ' the contradictory of S_2 ' to ' not-S_2 '. So we can re-paraphrase : to say that S_1 entails S_2 is to say that it would be inconsistent both to assert S_1 and to assert not-S_2. If it would be inconsistent to make a certain pair of statements, it would be inconsistent to make the conjunctive statement (employing, say, the word ' and ') of which they were the conjuncts. So, abbreviating ' the conjunctive statement of which S_1 and not-S_2 are the conjuncts ' to ' S_1 and not-S_2 ', we shall reparaphrase : to say that S_1 entails S_2 is to say that S_1 and not-S_2 is inconsistent.

This explanation of entailment is like a definition of ' entails '. We are giving a rule for the use of the word. We may emphasize this character of the proceeding by using inverted commas and writing :

' S_1 entails S_2 ' may be defined as ' S_1 and not-S_2 is inconsistent ' and this can be abbreviated to :

$$\text{' } S_1 \text{ entails } S_2 \text{ '} =_{Df} \text{ ' } S_1 \text{ } and \text{ } not\text{-}S_2 \text{ is inconsistent '.}$$

When we use inverted commas, we emphasize the fact that we are giving a rule for the use of a certain expression in a certain language. When we refrain from using them, we emphasize the fact that implicit in such a rule are rules for all synonymous expressions in all languages. The definition is related to the explanation somewhat as linguistic statement to logical statement. There are other differences between the explanation of entailment and the definition.[1] These will emerge later.

---

[1] The symbol ' S_1 ' changes its character (see below Chapter 2, pp. 28 ff, for discussion of formulae and variables).

14. Variants on ' is inconsistent ' are ' is self-contradictory ', ' is logically impossible ', ' is logically false '. Now suppose we deny, or assert the contradictory of, an inconsistent statement. We saw that a man who *makes* an inconsistent statement says, in a manner, nothing at all. His statement cancels itself. So what is said by a man who *denies* an inconsistent statement? It seems that he says nothing either : he, too, leaves things where they were. (Of course, one can separately deny two statements which are inconsistent with each other, provided they are not contradictories, and succeed in saying something : to the speakers who respectively make S_o and S_u we can say ' You are both wrong ' and in saying this, we implicitly make S_j. But to deny the single statement, S_o *and* S_u, is to say nothing about the height of the man discussed ; for to make S_o *and* S_u is to say nothing about his height.) Nevertheless, there may be a point in asserting the contradictory of an inconsistent statement. It may serve, for example, to remind someone of the rule that is broken in making it. It may show him he has got into a tangle in making it. It may help him to show us how he was not really making an inconsistent statement at all, but trying to describe an unusual situation or a borderline case. Or it may serve to remind *ourselves* of the rules, to help us to work something out, or to correct tangles of our own. It may have other purposes as well. When we assert the contradictory of an inconsistent statement, we are said to make a logically necessary statement. Variants on ' logically necessary statement ' are ' analytic statement ', ' necessary truth ', ' logically true statement '.

It is evident that the purposes which I have said might be served by making a logically necessary statement in the form of a contradiction of an inconsistent statement could be served equally well by making it in the form of a second-order statement of logical appraisal. These would, in fact, be different ways of saying the same thing, or of making the same appraisal. Instead of saying ' He is not both over and under six foot tall ', we could say ' The statement that he is over six foot tall is inconsistent with the statement that he is under six foot tall ', or ' The statement that he is over six foot tall entails the statement that he is not under six foot tall '. Or we might adopt a form of words intermediate between the quoted first-order form and the quoted second-order forms. We might say : ' He *can't*

be both over and under six foot tall ' or ' It's *impossible* for him
to be both over and under six foot tall '.   Of these forms of
words, those which employ the logical-appraisal words ' entails '
and ' inconsistent ' are the least apt to be philosophically misleading.   The first form is too reminiscent of the form of words
in which we give information about the height of a man, and
is apt to make us think that anyone using this sentence would be
giving very reliable information of this kind.   The last two
forms are too reminiscent of those sentences in which we discuss
the physical and practical impossibilities of life, and are apt to
make us think that we have here an instance of laws more
adamant than even Nature gives, though of that kind.

   To say that a statement is necessary, then, is to say that it is
the contradictory of an inconsistent statement.   We should
notice that there is an oddity in using the word ' statement ' at
all in this connexion, and that we only do so by a kind of analogy.
When a man makes an ordinary statement (ordinary statements,
i.e., statements which are neither inconsistent nor logically
necessary, are sometimes called ' contingent ' or ' synthetic '),
there is, or may be, a question as to whether what he says is
true or false; and to determine the answer to it, we must turn
our attention from the words he uses to the world, towards
whatever it is that he is talking about.   We may have to conduct
experiments.   But when a man makes a necessary or self-
contradictory statement, there is no comparable question and no
comparable procedure.   We should not know where to look,
or what experiments to conduct.   How could we determine
the truth or falsity of an inconsistent statement, when a man
who makes such a statement says nothing?   Of course, there
are resemblances between the man who makes an inconsistent,
and the man who makes an ordinary, statement.   They both
utter (or write) words; and they both use words which *can* be
used to inform (or to misinform).   The difference is that the
man who makes an inconsistent statement arranges these words
in such a way that we regard him as having said something
which cancels itself.   This is an unsatisfactory way of using
words, and we compare this with the unsatisfactoriness of the
way in which we use words when we make a false statement.
For the general and standard purpose of making statements is to
communicate information, to state facts.   This purpose is

frustrated when something false is said. It is also frustrated, though in a quite different way, when a man contradicts himself. So we compare the two ways of failing to state facts; and by analogy with the case of a man who makes a false statement, we say, of the man who contradicts himself, that he too, makes a false statement, only a *logically* false statement. And since we say that the man who asserts the contradictory of a false statement makes a true statement, we easily take the step of talking of a man who negates the form of words used in making the inconsistent statement as having uttered a true statement, only a *logically* (or *necessarily*) true statement. And then we are misled by the analogy : either into thinking of a special set of extralinguistic facts or realities (logical necessities) described by logically true statements; or, when we see that what lie behind logical appraisals are rules of language, into thinking of necessary statements as, straightforwardly, statements *about* words. But they are neither; it is a corrective to both views to say, from time to time : the word ' statement ' is misapplied in this connexion.

But there is no need to say it all the time. So I shall continue to talk of necessary statements. This conception enables us to give a further explanation of entailment, this time in terms of logical necessity. To say that S_1 entails S_2 is to say that the contradictory of S_1 *and not*-S_2 is logically necessary. Using the convention of abbreviating ' the contradictory of ' to ' *not*-', and using brackets to indicate that it is the contradictory of the single statement, S_1 *and not*-S_2, that we are talking of, we have : to say that S_1 entails S_2 is to say that *not*-$(S_1$ *and not*-$S_2)$ is logically necessary. By analogy with a practice of logicians which will be discussed later, the expression ' *not*-$(S_1$ *and not*-$S_2)$ ' may be abbreviated by the use of the symbol ' $\supset$ ' to ' $S_1 \supset S_2$ '. Writing the explanation as a definition, we have

' S_1 entails S_2 ' $=_{Df}$ ' $S_1 \supset S_2$ is logically necessary '.

If we eliminate all the abbreviations and write the latest form of the explanation in full, we have : to say that one statement entails another is to say that the contradictory of the conjunction of the first statement with the contradictory of the second is a necessary statement.

2

15. These two definitions of ' S_1 entails S_2 ' as ' S_1 *and not*-S_2 is inconsistent ' and as ' $S_1 \supset S_2$ is logically necessary ' raise a problem. Suppose we have two statements, of which one is inconsistent and the other synthetic. We might, say, have the statement with regard to a certain person, that he both was and was not over six foot tall (we will refer to this as S_t) and the statement that Xmas Day, 1900, was a fine day (we will refer to this as S_f). Are we, on the strength of the fact that S_t is inconsistent, to say that anyone who makes S_t *and not*-S_f makes an inconsistent statement? If we say this, and adhere to our definition of ' entails ', we shall have to say that S_t entails S_f. But we wanted to give a meaning to ' entails ' such that saying that one statement entailed another meant the same as saying that the second statement followed logically from the first; except that the suggestion of mind-exercising processes of inference which perhaps adheres to ' follows from ' was to be omitted. But we should certainly not say that S_f followed from S_t. ' He is and is not over six foot tall; therefore (so, consequently, in other words, that is to say) Xmas Day, 1900, was a fine day ' strikes us as nonsensical, and the use of any of the linking expressions as quite unjustified. Generally, if we *both* adhere to our definition of ' entails ' *and* agree to call any conjunctive statement inconsistent simply on the ground that one or both of its conjuncts is inconsistent, we shall be committed to saying that an inconsistent statement entails any statement whatever (whether synthetic or not) and that a necessary statement is entailed by any statement whatever (whether synthetic or not). Equally, we can avoid these consequences either by making it a rule for the use of ' inconsistent ' that no conjunctive statement is to be called inconsistent simply on the ground that one or both of its conjuncts is inconsistent; or by adding to our definition of ' S_1 entails S_2 ' as ' S_1 *and not*-S_2 is inconsistent ' the proviso that the inconsistency of the conjunctive statement does not result simply from the inconsistency of one or both of its conjuncts. Between these alternatives we are free to choose.

16. And now to conclude the catalogue of words of logical appraisal. First, we may note that, allowing ourselves the terminological licence claimed at the beginning of this part of the chapter, we shall have as variants on ' S_1 entails S_2 ' the

following expressions : ' S_1 logically implies S_2 '; ' S_2 follows from S_1 '; ' the step from S_1 to S_2 is valid '; ' S_2 is deducible from S_1 '.   Second, we shall introduce and define the notion of logical equivalence as follows : ' S_1 is logically equivalent to S_2 ' $=_{Df}$ ' S_1 entails S_2 and S_2 entails S_1 '.   An alternative definition would be : ' S_1 and *not*-S_2 are contradictories '.   It is evident that the introduction of any *definition* leads to a statement of logical equivalence.   The definition of ' S_1 entails S_2 ' as ' S_1 is inconsistent with the contradictory of S_2 ' for example, leads to the following statement of equivalence : the statement that one statement entails another is logically equivalent to the statement that the first is inconsistent with the contradictory of the second.   Third, we may define ' S_1 is the subcontrary of S_2 ' as follows : ' *not*-S_1 is inconsistent with *not*-S_2 '.   This may be compared with the definition of ' S_1 is the contrary of S_2 ' as ' S_1 is inconsistent with S_2 '.   Two statements are contraries when it is logically impossible for them both to be true ; subcontraries when it is logically impossible for them both to be false.   These definitions of ' contrary ' and ' subcontrary ' leave it open whether statements which stand in either of these relations to each other are contradictories or not.   Finally, two very useful additions to the logician's vocabulary are the phrases ' necessary condition ' and ' sufficient condition '.   When one statement entails another, the truth of the first is a sufficient condition of the truth of the second, and the truth of the second a necessary condition of the truth of the first.

CHAPTER 2

FORMAL LOGIC

1. THERE is no limit to the number of logical appraisals that could correctly be made. If the task of the formal logician were to compile lists of all possible correct appraisals, it would be an endless task; even if he confined himself to appraisals expressed as entailment-statements, on the ground that all logical relations could be so expressed, it would still be endless. But it is not the task of the formal logician to compile exhaustive lists of entailments. His task is limited by three factors which I shall try to make clear in this chapter.

I. GENERALITY. THE USE OF FORMULAE

2. Suppose a lunatic embarked on the task of recording every entailment. He hears one man, A, say of another, B, that B is a younger son; and he records that the statement that B is a younger son entails the statement that B has a brother. Later he hears someone, C, say of someone, D, that D is a younger son; and he records that the statement that D is a younger son entails the statement that D has a brother. So long as he thus confines himself to recording *particular entailments*, i.e., entailments between individual statements, he will never exhaust even the set of particular entailments which resemble these two as closely as they resemble each other. It is obvious that the reason why all the particular entailments of this set hold, can be given in one *general* entailment-statement, as follows : any statement to the effect that a certain person (certain persons) is a younger son (are younger sons) entails a statement to the effect that that person (those persons) has a brother (have brothers). Let us refer to the general entailment-statement made in these words as ES 1. And let us call the particular entailments belonging to this set, exemplifications of the general entailment. The general entailment-statement entails any of its exemplifications ; e.g., it would be inconsistent to make ES 1 and to deny that A's statement that B was a younger son entailed the statement that B had a brother.

The first factor limiting the logician's task is that he confines himself to making general entailment-statements. One sees how it is that he can do this if one remembers how logical appraisal becomes possible. Every particular entailment-statement is an exemplification of a general entailment-statement; for behind every particular statement of logical appraisal stands a general rule for the use of words.

3. Before we consider the second factor limiting the logician's task, we must make a decision on a question of technique which was left open in the last chapter, viz., the question of whether it would be more convenient to do logic in terms of rules about representative expressions, or in terms of logical relations between statements. An attempt to continue the discussion solely in terms of the latter would in fact make it progressively more unwieldy. By opting for the former alternative, we are able to introduce several convenient devices of abbreviation. These I proceed to illustrate for the case of ES 1.

The first step is to make the transition from ES 1 to the statement (ES 2) that any statement in making which the predicate ' is a younger son ' is applied to a certain person entails a statement in making which the predicate ' has a brother ' is applied to that person. (I omit here the complications which allow for the cases of talking of more than one person.) ES 2 is a statement (or rule) overtly about the quoted expressions. We have already discussed the relation between statements like ES 1 and statements like ES 2. In making ES 1 in the words I used to make it, the expressions ' is a younger son ' and ' has a brother ' are simply used to identify the class of pairs of statements (*which could be made without the use of these expressions*) between which the entailment is said to hold. ES 2 is narrower than ES 1 in that it confines our attention to those cases in which the statements are made by the actual use of these expressions. But we can perfectly well allow the linguistic statement, ES 2, to stand as the *representative* of the logical statement, ES 1. Behind every logical statement that can be made stands a linguistic statement (or rule). ES 2 has to ES 1 the relation which the definition we gave of ' entails ' has to the explanation we gave of entailment.

ES 2, like ES 1, is both cumbersome and vague. It asserts

that any statement in which the predicate ' is a younger son '
is applied to a certain person entails *some* (actual or possible)
statement in which the predicate ' has a brother ' is applied to
that person.　If *some* were replaced by *any*, then ES 2 would
cease to be vague; but it would also cease to be true.　A statement made in the words ' The author of *Paradise Lost* is a
younger son ' does not entail a statement made in the words
' John Milton has a brother '; for though the predicates are
applied to the same person, it is a matter of fact, and not of
logic, that the person who wrote *Paradise Lost* is John Milton.
We cannot eliminate the vagueness of ES 2 by replacing ' some '
by ' any '; so it seems that we shall have to eliminate it, if at
all, by specifying *which* statements applying the phrase ' has a
brother ' to a certain person, are entailed by a statement applying
the phrase ' is a younger son ' to that person.　It might seem
that a way of doing this would be to lay down the requirement
that in both the entailing and the entailed statement the person
to whom these predicates are applied should be referred to by the
use of one and the same expression : (that, e.g., in the above
case, he should be referred to as ' John Milton ' in both statements).　It might then seem that both the vagueness and the
cumbersomeness of ES 2 could be easily eliminated in the
following way.

Consider the expressions ' x is a younger son ', ' y has a
brother '.　Obviously all sentences used in applying the predicate ' is a younger son ' to anybody whatever, will resemble
one another in containing that phrase; and many of them will
differ from one another in containing different expressions to
refer to the different persons to whom the predicate is applied.
The expression ' x is a younger son ' may be regarded as pictur-
ing the resemblance, while allowing for the differences.　Such
an expression I shall call a formula.　Formulae are not sentences; but it is obvious that a sentence would be obtained if
one rewrote ' x is a younger son ', replacing ' x ' by such a word
or phrase as ' He ', ' Tom ', ' The Vicar of Wakefield '.　Those
expressions in formulae, the replacement of which by a word or
phrase would result in a sentence, are called free variables, or
simply, variables.　It might now seem that the non-vague
general entailment-statement of which we are in search could be
formulated as follows (ES 3) : any statement made by the use

of a sentence which could be obtained by substituting a certain word or phrase for the variable in the formula ' x is a younger son ' entails any statement made by the use of a sentence which could be obtained by making *the same substitution* for the variable in the formula ' y has a brother '. If we now abbreviate this to

' x is a younger son ' entails ' x has a brother '

using the repetition of ' x ' to indicate that the same substitution is required in each case, we seem to have got rid not only of the vagueness, but also of the cumbersomeness, of ES 2.

ES 3, however, is far from being an improvement on ES 2; for it is obviously false. The mere fact that the same name, pronoun, or phrase descriptive of an individual person is used in two different sentences is no guarantee that it is used in both to refer to the same person. It is not true that a statement made in the words ' Tom (the Vicar of Wakefield, &c.) is a younger son ' entails any statement made in the words ' Tom (the Vicar of Wakefield, &c.) has a brother '; for the statements may be about different people called Tom, or about different Vicars of Wakefield. Nor will an explicit provision against this possibility meet the case. Consider the two sentences : ' Tom is twenty-nine years old' and 'Tom is under thirty years old'. One is inclined to say that, assuming that the name is used to refer to the same person in each case, any statement made by the use of the first sentence would entail any statement made by the use of the second. But what if the statements are made at an interval of two years? Then the first might be true and the second false.

Logicians have commonly neglected such facts as that one and the same expression may be used on different occasions to refer to different individuals, that the time at which a sentence is uttered may make a difference to the truth or falsity of what is said. And one can see why there is a temptation to ignore these facts : they complicate matters a good deal. But it is possible to take account of them in a way which secures the simplification, while avoiding the error, which results from ignoring them. Suppose someone makes a statement by the use of the sentence ' Tom is twenty-nine years old '. Then it could not be the case both that in uttering this sentence he said something true, and that if the *same* speaker in exactly the *same* situation and context had instead pronounced the sentence ' Tom is under thirty years old ', he would have said something false.　Let us express this assumption of identity of speaker, time, and situation by the use of the phrase ' the same context '. Then we can frame our desired general entailments on the following model :　any statement made by the use of a sentence which could be obtained by substituting a certain word or phrase for the variable in the formula ' x is twenty-nine years old ' entails the statement made by the use *in the same context* of the sentence obtained by making the same substitution in the formula ' x is under thirty years old '.　And this we can abbreviate to

' x is twenty-nine years old ' entails ' x is under thirty years old '.

Some further, relatively unimportant, modifications are required.　For example, grammar permits ' Tom is twenty-nine years old ', ' Tom is a younger son ', but not ' I is a younger son ', ' They is twenty-nine years old '.　There is no reason to allow this fact to limit the generality of our entailment.　The statement (ES 4) by which we may finally replace ES 2 should accordingly be formulated somewhat as follows :　any statement made by the use of a sentence which could be obtained by substituting a certain word or phrase for the variable in the formula ' x is a younger son ' (and by making such other changes as may be grammatically necessary) entails the statement made by the use in the same context of the sentence obtained by making the same substitution in the formula ' x has a brother ' (and by making such other changes as may be grammatically necessary).　The form of words

' x is a younger son ' entails ' x has a brother '

is to be taken as an abbreviation of ES 4.[1]

---

[1] It will be convenient later to use the following abbreviations as well : the words ' statement made by the use of a sentence which could be obtained by substituting word(s) or phrase(s) for the variable(s) in the formula . . . and by making such other changes as may be grammatically necessary ' to be abbreviated to ' statement of the form . . .'; and the words ' the statement made by the use in the same context of the sentence obtained by making the same substitution(s) in the formula . . . and by making such other changes as may be grammatically necessary ' to be abbreviated to ' the corresponding statement of the form . . .'.

Using these abbreviations, we should express ES 4 as follows : any

Each general entailment-statement of this kind authorizes us to obtain from it a less general entailment-statement by making a substitution for the variable. Thus from ES 4 we obtain the following (ES 5) : any statement made by the use of the sentence ' Tom is a younger son ' entails the statement made by the use, in the same context, of the sentence ' Tom has a brother '. And this still general, but less general, entailment can similarly be written in the abbreviated form :

' Tom is a younger son ' entails ' Tom has a brother '

4. We have so far regarded the forms of words

(1) ' x is a younger son ' entails ' x has a brother '
(2) ' Tom is a younger son ' entails ' Tom has a brother '

as shorthand ways of making statements about *statements*; viz., about statements made by the use of the quoted sentences of (2), or by the use of sentences which could be obtained by substitution in the quoted formulae of (1). It is, as we saw, statements or groups of statements, not sentences or formulae, to which words of logical appraisal are correctly applied; we have given no meaning to talk of *sentences*, or *formulae*, entailing one another. There is, however, no reason why we should not use the word ' entails ' *in a new, though related, sense,* for (i) that relation which one *formula* has to another when statements

---

statement of the form ' x is a younger son ' entails the corresponding statement of the form ' x has a brother '.

It should be noted that when we frame our general entailments in this way (with this use of the phrase ' in the same context '), we do not thereby succeed in specifying which statements applying (e.g.) the phrase ' has a brother ' to someone referred to as ' Tom ' are entailed by a statement applying the phrase ' is a younger son ' to someone referred to as ' Tom '. We supply a sufficient, but not a necessary, condition of the entailment's holding. Given any two phrases related to each other as ' is a younger son ' is related to ' has a brother ', certain variations in the situation in which the phrases are applied to something (referred to by means of the same expression, e.g. ' Tom ', in each case) will count against the statement made by the use of the first entailing the statement made by the use of the second; others will not. For example, a change in the identity of the speaker and a short lapse of time will often not constitute relevant altera-tions in the ' context '. But I doubt whether it is possible to give an account which is both general and non-circular of the conditions which are both necessary and sufficient for such an entailment to hold. The formula-tion chosen, therefore, describes the ideal, limiting case in which all such possibly relevant variations are eliminated.

made by the use of sentences obtainable by substitutions in the first formula each entail the statements made by the use, in the same context, of sentences obtained by corresponding substitutions in the second; and (ii) that relation which one sentence has to another when a statement made by the use of the first entails the statement made by the use, in the same context, of the second. In this new sense of entailment, we *shall* be able to talk of entailments between formulae or between sentences; and (1) and (2) need no longer be regarded as abbreviations. In the same way, we can give analogous senses to the other words of logical appraisal (e.g., 'logically necessary', 'inconsistent', &c.) so that these, too, can be applied directly to expressions, such as sentences and formulae. We shall also permit the use of linking expressions like 'therefore' and 'so' between formulae; so that words like 'valid' can be applied to combinations of formulae. And by taking these final steps, we achieve the technical simplifications to be gained by carrying on the discussion solely in terms of rules for representative expressions.

5. We introduced and explained formulae as expressions such that, by substituting words or phrases for the variables, we could obtain from them sentences which could be used to make statements. This places an implicit restriction on the range of admissible substitutions for variables. One can assemble words in such a way that the resulting expression satisfies the grammatical requirements for a sentence, but has no meaning, and is therefore useless for making statements. We shall speak of the range of admissible or possible *values* of the variable in a formula, meaning thereby the range of expressions the substitution of any one of which for the variable yields a significant sentence. Thus we might say that, whereas 'Tom' is a possible value of the variable in the formula 'x is a younger son' the expression '$\sqrt{2}$' is not. But we must be careful here to avoid an easy dogmatism which ignores the flexibility of language. There are no precise rules determining, *for ordinary language*, what is nonsense and what is not. We saw, in discussing inconsistency, how meaning can be not unnaturally given to sentences which we should at first be inclined to regard as inconsistent. (Note that here I use 'inconsistent' of sen-

tences, in accordance with the procedure just discussed.) Similarly with the different kind of first-blush absurdity we are now considering.. A man might say, e.g., ' Multilateralism is a younger son '; and if he were prepared to pursue the analogy in a suitable way, we should say that this was not nonsense, but a metaphor. We shall see that one of the things which distinguish the activity of the formal logician from that of logical appraisal of ordinary discourse is just the fact that his systems are characterized by a rigidity and precision of rule, which have no counterpart in ordinary speech. Within a logician's system of rules, the questions of whether a formula or sentence is inconsistent or not, and of whether an expression belongs to the range of possible values of the variable in a given formula, are definitely answerable by reference to the rules. No such fine simplicity characterizes the richly various logic of our daily language.

6. We saw in the last chapter that to every entailment-statement there corresponded (i) a statement to the effect that some conjunctive statement is inconsistent, and (ii) a statement to the effect that the contradictory of this conjunctive statement is logically necessary. We now have to transfer these correspondences to talk of sentences and formulae entailing one another; for this purpose we shall have to frame formulae which can be regarded as the contradictories, or conjunctions, of other formulae. The contradictory of a given formula, F, will obviously be the formula such that a statement of that form is the contradictory of the corresponding statement of the form of F. We shall simply adopt the convention that the expression obtained by writing ' not ' either at some suitable place in F or, with a hyphen, before F, with F enclosed in brackets, is to be the contradictory formula of F. Similarly, we shall adopt the convention that the expression produced by writing ' and ' between two formulae is the conjunctive formula of those two formulae.[1] Thus, corresponding to

---

[1] These conventions are parallel to those used in the previous chapter. (See pp. 20 and 23.) But, though parallel, the conventions are not the same. In Chapter 1 the convention was that ' not ', ' and ', and ' ⊃ ' were to be used as abbreviations for items in the logician's higher-order vocabulary (e.g., ' contradictory of ', &c.), whereas here the convention is that ' not ' and ' and ' are to occur as words in first-order formulae, but as words with

(1) ' x is a younger son ' entails ' x has a brother '

we have

(3) ' x is a younger son and x has not a brother ' is inconsistent

and

(4) ' not-(x is a younger son and x has not a brother) ' is logically necessary.

Like (1), (3) and (4) can be regarded in either of two ways. E.g., we can regard (3) either as an abbreviated form of words for making the statement that any statement made by the use of a sentence obtainable by substituting a possible value of the variable for ' x ' in the formula ' x is a younger son and x has not a brother ' is inconsistent; or, with the appropriate shift in the meaning of ' inconsistent ', we can regard this adjective as being applied directly to the formula itself. Finally, we introduce the symbol ' ⊃ ', abbreviating (4) to :

(5) ' x is a younger son ⊃ x has a brother ' is logically necessary.

The forms of words (1), (3), (4), (5) are themselves not formulae, but *sentences* used for making statements *about formulae*. And just as we obtained (2) from (1), so we can derive from any of (3), (4), and (5) further *sentences* used for making statements about *sentences*. (Notice I here apply the word ' derive ' to sentences, on analogy with the application of the words ' entails ', ' inconsistent ', &c., to sentences and formulae.) Thus from (5), we derive :

(6) ' He is a younger son ⊃ he has a brother ' is logically necessary.

Whenever, from a rule about a formula, we derive, by substitution on the variables, a rule about a sentence or about another formula, we must observe the general rule (implicit in these

---

a definite logical force. Similarly, the symbol ' ⊃ ', introduced below, will now be used as a symbol capable of occurring in first-order formulae and sentences, and not (as in Chapter 1) as an abbreviation for the higher-order phrase ' the contradictory of the conjunction of, &c '.

explanations) that the same substitution must be made for every occurrence of a given variable (say, 'x'). The point of using the same letter as a variable in different places in a formula is just this. Where different substitutions are permissible, different letters are used.

7. Something must now be said about this symbol '$\supset$'; about the point of using it in logic, and about its possible mis-interpretations.[1] Earlier we discussed necessary statements and the way in which they were to be interpreted, the point of making them. As an example of a sentence which might be used for making such a statement, we gave ' He is not both over six foot tall and under six foot tall '. The corresponding formulation for our present example would be perhaps : ' It is not the case both that he is a younger son and that he does not have a brother '. This is an intolerably clumsy sentence which we are extremely unlikely to use for the purpose of making a necessary statement. Alternative sentences that we *might* use are such as the following : ' If he's a younger son, then he has a brother '; ' Either he's not a younger son or he has a brother '; ' He can't be a younger son without having a brother '. We saw that such sentences could not be interpreted as saying anything at all, as serving any purpose, unless we took them to be used in the same way as second-order logical sentences, to remind or inform our audiences of logical facts, and of the linguistic rules which lie behind such facts. That is to say, we must regard such sentences as equivalent, not simply to the sentence quoted in (6), but rather to (6) taken as a whole. The groups of conjunctions, or quasi-conjunctions ' If . . . then . . .', ' not . . . without . . .', ' either not . . . or . . .', which provide, in these sentences, the settings for the expressions ' he is a younger son ', ' he has a brother ', cannot therefore be safely identified in meaning with the symbol ' $\supset$ ', which provides the setting for these expressions in the sentence quoted in (6). The ordinary conjunctions incorporate, in their present contexts, the notion of logical necessity which is explicitly formulated, in (6), outside the quoted sentence, and which accordingly cannot be assumed to be incorporated in ' $\supset$ '. If this is overlooked, there is a strong temptation to identify '. . . $\supset$ . . .' with ' if . . .

---

[1] Cf. also Chapters 3 and 8 for fuller discussions of this subject.

then . . .', which, of the phrases in question, is the only unitary
conjunction, the only one which does not include ' not '.   There
are other factors which increase this temptation and aggravate
the consequences of yielding to it.   The sentence (6) is an un-
disguised   second-order   sentence.   The   equivalent   ordinary
English sentences are disguised second-order sentences.   But
there are other ordinary English sentences employing the
expressions 'if . . . then . . .', 'either . . . or . . .', ' not
. . . without . . .' which are first-order sentences, i.e., are used
to make assertions of a certain kind about things other than
sentences or statements; e.g., ' If it rains, then the party will
be a failure '.   These sentences suggest connexions other than
logical or linguistic; they suggest connexions between different
things in the world, discovered by experience of these things.
The existence of these sentences may encourage us to think of
sentences like ' If he is a younger son, then he has a brother '
as also genuine first-order sentences.   And this in its turn may
tempt us in one of two very different, but equally wrong,
directions.   It may tempt us in the direction I have already
commented on; the direction of thinking of analytic sentences
as suggesting or reporting connexions of a special kind between
different things in the world, or as giving very reliable non-
linguistic information.   Or it may tempt us again to think of
' If he is a younger son, then he has a brother ' as identical in
meaning with the first-order sentence quoted in (6), i.e., with
' He is a younger son $\supset$ he has a brother ', and hence may again
tempt us to think of '. . . $\supset$ . . .' as identical in meaning with
' if . . . then . . .'.   This is utterly wrong.   Although the
expressions ' if . . . then . . .', ' either not . . . or . . .',
' not . . . without . . .' have genuine first-order uses, there is
a certain analogy between the more common of their first-order
uses and their disguised second-order uses.   It is precisely this
analogy which makes this double employment natural, and
which makes it misleading to identify them, even in their
genuinely first-order uses, with ' $\supset$ '.   We may make this
analogy clear as follows.   When one statement entails another
and we know or believe the first statement to be true, we may
say something of the form ' p, so q '.   (The variables ' p ' and
' q ' in this formula have, as their range of possible values,
clauses, i.e., expressions which could, either as they stand or

with some modification of the mood of the verb, be used to make statements. We may call them 'statement-variables'.) The word ' so ' is one of the linking words we discussed earlier. And, in this context, it claims that the step in reasoning is a valid step. But not all reasoning is deductive reasoning. We often make transitions from one statement to another, in argument or inference, where the first statement does not entail the second and yet the transition is perfectly correct and reasonable, the use of the linking words perfectly justified : e.g., ' He's been travelling for seven hours, so he'll be tired '; ' The kettle has been on the fire for the last ten minutes, so it must be boiling by now '. The word ' so ' claims that a correct step in reasoning is being made; but it does not always claim that a deductively valid step is being made. The steps in these examples are justified, not by linguistic rules, but by the way things habitually happen in the world. The connexions involved are not logical, but causal, connexions. Let us say, when the step from one statement to another would, if made, be a correct step in reasoning *of either of these kinds*, that the first statement is a *ground* for the second. There is a likeness, and a difference, between typical circumstances in which we say something of the form ' p, so q ', and typical circumstances in which we say something of the form ' if p, then q '. If one statement is a ground for another and we believe the first statement to be true, we are justified in saying something of the form ' p, so q '; if one statement is a ground for another, and we are uncertain whether the first statement is true or not, or believe it to be false, we are justified in saying something of the form ' if p, then q ' Of course, these are not the only uses of ' so ' and ' if '. In saying ' You have disobeyed me, so I shall punish you ', I am not reasoning; though I am *giving a reason* for my announced intention. And the corresponding warning ' If you disobey me, I shall punish you ' indicates that disobedience will be held to be a ground of (reason for) punishment. So this use is broadly analogous to the others. There are further uses of ' if ', in which this analogy weakens or vanishes. But in general its employment in linking two clauses indicates that a statement made by the use of the first would be a ground or reason for a statement made by the use of the second. This is why, in its disguised second-order use, where the ground is a logical one, it does not simply the job done by ' ⊃ ', but the job done by ' ⊃ ' in combination with the phrase ' is analytic ' (or ' is logically necessary ').

In a sentence such as (6), the explicitly second-order phrases are essential in order to convey that there is a ground of connexion. The only use we could make of ' ⊃ ' by itself, in linking two sentences, would be simply to deny the statement resulting from the conjunction of the first sentence with the contradictory of the second. Thus, if somebody said ' John was there, and Peter was not there ', we might deny this simply because John was *not* there or simply because Peter *was* there; without for a moment thinking that John's being there would be a reason for expecting Peter to be there. Of course, if we were convinced that there *was* this connexion, then we should be inclined to deny the statement that John was there and Peter was not, even without information, from any other source, of John's absence or Peter's presence. We might deny the conjunctive statement for any of these reasons. The sentence ' John was there ⊃ Peter was there ', if it were used, would simply have the force of a bare denial of the conjunctive statement without any indication of the reason for the denial, and certainly without any suggestion that the reason for it was that John's being there would be a ground for expecting Peter to be there. Now there is as a matter of fact no single conjunction in English, and it seems doubtful whether there is any commonly used *combination* of expressions which consistently does just this job and no more. That is why the best course is to paraphrase the formula '$p \supset q$' by the unnatural-looking formula ' it is not the case both that p and that not-q ' or ' not-(p and not-q) '; and to forswear its more appealing identifications with ' if p, then q ', ' either not-p or q ', ' not-(p without q) ' and so on. Even when we use the form ' not both . . . and not . . . ' in ordinary speech, we usually intend more than ' ⊃ ' conveys; but the further intention is usually indicated by the use of an expression like ' can't both . . .' or ' surely '. We may summarize the whole point by saying : the first-order symbol ' ⊃ ' has in practice almost no use at all without the addition of the second-order expressions ' is analytic ' or ' is logically necessary '; though the latter may not be actually voiced (or written), but merely understood.

8. One might be inclined to ask : since the symbol ' ⊃ ' is so apt to receive misleading interpretations, and since the purpose of joining two formulae by it, and declaring the resulting formula analytic, is equally well served by stating that the first formula entails the second, what is the point of introducing it into logic ? Well, there are several points, the more important of which may not appear till later. But I can now indicate some convenient features of ' ⊃ '. Suppose the logician regards it as his task to write down all the general rules to which we appeal in making logical appraisals. There are several ways in which he might do this. He might write down all the general entailment-statements he could think of; or all the necessary (or analytic) formulae, with the general observation that he was writing down only analytic formulae; or all the inconsistent formulae, with a general remark that he was writing down only what was self-contradictory. There is a psychological resistance to the third way of doing it; and this is connected with our habit of calling analytic statements true, and self-contradictory statements false. We feel the logician ought to tell us what is right and not what is wrong; though, in this field, he could not do one without doing the other. There is a certain convenience in choosing the second way rather than the first. It enables us to drop an order, to write down only first-order formulae. Instead of a series of sentences like

' x is a younger son ' entails ' x has a brother '

we should have a series of sentences like

x is a younger son ⊃ x has a brother.

The place of the inverted commas and the second-order expression ' entails ' is taken by the general observation that we are writing down only analytic formulae. And there is another convenience about this method. When logicians were more exclusively interested than they are now in the validity of certain familiar types of inference or argument, they often used the method of writing down valid argument-formulae, or inference-patterns, with the general observation that this was what they were doing. That is to say, they wrote down first-order formulae incorporating such linking words as ' so ' and ' therefore '. Now we have sufficiently noticed that not every case in which we could correctly declare the result of linking two formulae by ' ⊃ ' analytic, is a case in which we should speak of a transition from a sentence exemplifying the first formula to a sentence exemplifying the second, as an inference. We might often call it a re-phrasing, or a repetition with something left out; or think that there was no point in making it at all. But if we think the transition sufficiently mind-exercising to be called an inference, we can always obtain a first-order valid inference pattern from the first-order analytic formula simply by replacing the ' ⊃ ' by ' therefore '. Thus corresponding to the first-order expression

$$x \text{ is a younger son} \supset x \text{ has a brother}$$

as analytic formula, we have the first-order expression

$$x \text{ is a younger son, therefore } x \text{ has a brother}$$

as valid inference-pattern.

II. FORM

9. It is time to discuss the second factor limiting the formal logician's task. To make the factor clear is to elucidate the qualifying adjective ' formal '. We supposed just now that the logician regarded his task as that of writing down all the general rules implicit in all logical appraisals. But there are so many ways of being inconsistent, so many ways of making valid and invalid steps in argument, so many correct and incorrect claims to be putting something into other words. We have seen that every definition leads to general equivalences and entail-ments, that for almost every predicate there are predicates incompatible with it. Is the statement, that the formula ' x is a younger son $\supset x$ has a brother ' is analytic, to count as a principle of logic ? Or the statement, that ' x is married ' is incon-sistent with ' x is a bachelor ' ? If so, the book which gives the principles of logic will be longer than any dictionary.

But the logician is not a lexicographer. He is not called upon to include in his books the general entailments created by every introduction of a new technical term into the language. This is a job for the specialist : the job of making clear the meanings of the words peculiar to his special subject-matter. The logic-ian's interest is wider. He is concerned with types of inconsistency, types of validity and invalidity, which are not confined to discussion of any one particular kind of subject, but may be found to occur in discussion of utterly heterogeneous topics. So the entailments of words like ' married ' and ' bachelor ', which carry on their face the limitation of their employment to discussion of a particular kind of subject-matter, will not, as such, figure in his lists. The sort of rules you may expect to find there are rules such that the knowledge that any one of them has been observed or broken in a certain piece of discourse gives no clue as to what that piece of discourse is about. We may put this, perhaps a little more precisely, in terms of entailments, as follows : whenever an entailment can be regarded as belonging to a class of entailments, such that the description of that class gives no indication of the subject-matter of the entailing or entailed statements, then the formulation of a general rule for entailments of that class, or (where this formulation is for any reason difficult) the general description of the class, may be regarded as an exercise in formal logic. But, of course, even within the sphere of activity thus circumscribed, the formal logician may be (and is) selective, and may (and does) impose further obligations upon himself.

Examples of principles of this perfectly general kind are not difficult to discover. We can state quite generally the principle that any assertion whatever about anything whatever is inconsistent with the denial of that same assertion. And we can state quite generally that any statement to the effect that all the members of a certain class are members of a second class, in conjunction with the statement, with regard to a particular thing, that that thing is a member of the first class, entails the statement that that thing is a member of the second class. There are several points to notice about such general statements as these. The first is that they fulfil the prescribed condition of indifference to subject-matter. The second is that they are themselves analytic second-order statements, behind which, as thus formulated, stand linguistic rules for such expressions (in the case of the first) as, ' assertion ', ' inconsistent ', ' denial '. The third is that they have the characteristics which we have already noted in logical, as opposed to overtly linguistic, statements ; i.e., they are not directly about the expressions of any particular language, but apply indifferently to all assertions of the kinds described, whether these assertions are made in Greek, French, English, or Hindi. They also have, very markedly in the case of the second, that unwieldiness which we are to expect of any attempt to do logic in terms of statements about statements, instead of in terms of rules for representative expressions. Accordingly, logicians seek to embody such principles in rules of this kind. We might offer, as a rule representing the first principle :

'p and not-p' is inconsistent

and as a rule representing the second principle :

' all fs are g and x is an f' entails 'x is g'

or

' all fs are g and x is an f ∴ x is g' is a valid inference-formula.

Here we encounter difficulties for which our previous discussions have prepared us. They might be summarized as follows : even for a single language, it is neither a necessary nor a sufficient condition of a statement or inference being of the kind referred to in a general logical principle, that the sentences used in making the statement or inference should exemplify the verbal pattern quoted in the rule representing that principle. To illustrate this point. The condition is not sufficient; for the words ' It is and it is not ' may be held to exemplify the verbal pattern 'p and not-p' and yet may be used to give a perfectly consistent answer to a question (e.g., ' Is it raining ? '). The condition is not necessary; for many (if not most) inferences answering to the general description given in the second of the above logical principles do not exemplify the verbal pattern ' all fs are g and x is an f ∴ x is g'.

We may put the point differently as follows. Different expressions may have, in some contexts, the same logical use, i.e., may play the same logical role in the types of entailment, &c., which interest the logician. Thus, the generalizing role of ' all ' may be played by ' a ' or by 'the'; any of these expressions may serve to introduce a statement to the effect that all the members of a certain class have a certain characteristic or are members of a certain other class. And the same expression may have different logical uses; i.e., may, in different contexts, play different logical roles, possess different entailments, &c. Thus,

a statement made in words involving a repetition of ' not ' may
sometimes be logically equivalent to the corresponding affirmative statement (' It's not true that he cannot come '); it may
sometimes be merely a more emphatic negation (' I'm not, *not*
coming with you '); and it may sometimes have a force different
from either of these (e.g., ' He cannot not come ' is equivalent
neither to ' He can come ' nor to ' He cannot come ' but to ' He
must come ').   In this situation it would be reasonable to expect
the logician's selection of verbal patterns for his representative
rules to be governed by two principles : first, that the verbal
pattern should be one *commonly* exemplified by, e.g., entailments of the class he is concerned with ; second, that the
expressions occurring in that pattern should *commonly* have the
logical use they have in those entailments.   In *selecting* a standard verbal pattern to illustrate a given logical principle, a
logician may be regarded as at the same time *adopting* a standard
logical use for the expressions occurring in that verbal pattern.
For reasons which will become clear when we discuss the logician's ideal of system, he cannot tolerate the occurrence, within
his set of rules, of expressions which are logically ambiguous
(have different logical uses), as the expressions of ordinary
language are apt to be.   So, in selecting a certain verbal pattern
for his rules, the logician imposes upon the expressions occurring
in that pattern a logical rigidity they do not ordinarily possess.
Within his system, the words occurring in his formulae have only
the logical uses that his rules prescribe.   Accordingly, we cannot be sure of the meaning of expressions occurring in a logician's
formulae until we have examined those rules.

10. One might now ask : how does it come about that there
are these general types of validity, or inconsistency, these
general classes of logically similar inferences, which interest the
logician, and which can be discussed independently of the subject-matter of the statements occurring in such inferences?
And how does it come about that there exist representative
verbal patterns for such a type or class, suitable for quotation
in logicians' rules? These are not easy questions; but the
earlier discussion of negation shows the way to a partial answer
to them. We saw then how natural it was that a language
should include a device for denial. Whatever subject we may

be discussing, we shall want some way of denying as well as asserting; so that a word which simply serves the purpose of denial will have that indifference to subject-matter which qualifies it for a place in a logician's representative verbal pattern. In general, whatever we may be talking about, there are certain functions we shall expect our language to be able to perform for us, if it is at all a developed language. In so far as these are logically related, or overlapping, functions, we have already the possibility of types of inconsistency and validity which transcend particular subject-matters. In so far as there are separately identifiable linguistic devices [1] which serve to perform these functions (e.g., ' not ' for denial), we have already the possibility of representative verbal patterns to figure in a logician's rules illustrative of these types of inconsistency and validity. Thus, an even more fundamental linguistic requirement than that of negation is the existence of some way of applying the expressions we use in describing things to the particular cases we are describing. We often do this by using, along with a descriptive predicate, an expression (e.g., demonstrative or personal pronoun or proper name) to refer to the particular case we wish to describe, and by linking the two by some form of the verb ' to be ' (e.g., ' x is a g '); though we often use other devices instead. But we use this device sufficiently generally to confer upon the word ' is ' the necessary indifference to subject-matter. Or again, whatever we are discussing, we may want some way of generalizing, of making conditional assertions, or of stating alternatives; and we may use the words ' all', ' if ', and ' or ', respectively, for these purposes, though again we may use other devices. Wherever we find ourselves able to describe a general linguistic function of this sort (e.g., negation or generalization), we may also expect to find separate expressions (e.g., ' not ' or ' all '), or other devices, to which, with due allowance for the flexibility of language, the performance of that function can be plausibly assigned. And the existence of such devices is almost a *sine*

---

[1] ' Separately identifiable linguistic devices ' need not, of course, be separate *words*. They might be suffixes; or other types of modification of individual words in a sentence; or ways of arranging words in a sentence; or some combination of these. In a purely spoken language they might be tones of voice. It has been suggested that a sentence might be negated by writing it upside down.

qua non of our noticing those analogies between inferences, &c., which lead us to classify them together as being of the same general type or form. For in noticing such formal analogies, what do we notice? We notice *resemblances* between valid inferences. And these are not resemblances in style or theme, but verbal resemblances; resemblances between groups of words with a recurring verbal pattern. It is not a convenient accident that inferences of the same form can be exhibited as exemplifying the same verbal pattern. The fact that they can be so exhibited is precisely the respect of analogy which leads us to classify them together as inferences of the same form. Now quite the most obvious way in which different inferences can share the same pattern is for that pattern to consist of a framework of identical words occupying the same relative positions in the different inferences. It is just such a framework as this, when the inferences sharing it are in general valid, that we choose as a representative pattern to be quoted and declared ' valid ' in a logician's rule. As I have already pointed out, inferences which do not possess the selected framework may nevertheless be classified with those that do. The selected framework is only *representative* of the class. And valid inferences which, with only minor verbal alterations and without change of sense, could be forced into the selected framework, are properly said to be formally analogous to those that already exhibit it.

When these points are understood, the two questions with which this section opened begin to look different : they begin to look like one question.

11. The existence of a framework of separate words (or other devices) suitable for quotation in a logician's rules is not quite, however, though it is almost, a *sine qua non* of our noticing a formal analogy. For sometimes the resemblances in the verbal patterns of valid inferences may be sufficiently striking for us to speak of their sharing a common form, even when there is no detachable framework of words for which we can lay down a logician's rule. Inferences of the following patterns, for example, belong to such a class :

x is congruent with y and y is congruent with z ∴ x is congruent with z

x is an ancestor of y and y is an ancestor of z $\therefore$ x is an ancestor of z

x is faster than y and y is faster than z $\therefore$ x is faster than z

x entails y and y entails z $\therefore$ x entails z.

It is easy enough to frame a single pattern which all such inferences exhibit. All we have to do is to introduce a new variable, say ' R ', to indicate the characteristic way in which a phrase is repeated in each of these inferences. Then we have, as the common pattern :

$$xRy \text{ and } yRz \therefore xRz.$$

But obviously, though this pattern successfully hits off the respect of resemblance between such inferences, it is quite unsuitable for quotation in a logician's rule of the form ' F is a valid inference pattern '. There are far too many possible inferences which would exemplify the pattern and be invalid for us to pass off, as a principle of inference, the declaration that this pattern is a valid inference-formula. Consider, for example, any which result from making, together with suitable substitutions for ' x ', ' y ' and ' z ', the following substitutions for ' R ' : ' loves ', ' hates ', ' amuses ', ' is the square root of ', ' is touching ', &c., &c. Some logicians have felt that all those words which, substituted for ' R ', would yield valid inference-patterns *ought* to have some common verbal feature which would make it possible to frame a principle of inference incorporating a quoted formula. Perhaps this reflects a certain uneasiness at extending the notion of a formal analogy to cases where no formula suitable for this purpose can be found. The absence of such a formula is less to be deplored than to be explained. That is to say, one should look for further differences between this case and the cases where such formulae can be found.[1]

In the absence of such a verbal framework, what can we do to record our sense of the formal similarity between inferences which exemplify the above pattern and are valid ? Well, we can give a common name to all the words or phrases which, when substituted for ' R ' in that pattern, yield a valid inference-formula. This is what is done. All such expressions are called

[1] See Chapter 7, Section 8.

' transitively relational '. We can then, if we wish, go on to formulate a general analytic principle, as follows: any statement to the effect that one thing is transitively related in a certain way to another thing, together with a statement to the effect that the second thing is related in the same way to a third, entails the statement that the first thing is related in that way to the third. But we must not think of ourselves as having discovered the general principle of this class of entailments. What we have done is to notice a logical resemblance transcending differences of subject-matter, and to invent a name for it. Not that it was a trivial matter to notice the resemblance. In the absence of a representative verbal framework suitable for quotation in a logician's rule, it has often taken a long time to notice such resemblances.

12. Formulae generally contain, besides variables, expressions (words or symbols) which are not variables. We shall sometimes refer to expressions which occur in formulae, but are not variables, as constants. Thus any ordinary word or phrase, since it may occur in a formula, may be referred to as a constant. Expressions dignified by selection by formal logicians to figure as constants in their representative verbal patterns or formulae are sometimes called ' logical (or formal) constants '; and formulae containing none but logical constants may correspondingly be called ' logical (or formal) formulae '. Thus, the word ' bachelor ' is a constant, but not a logical constant; for, e.g., the principle that ' x is a bachelor ' entails ' x is not married ' is a lexicographer's principle, not a formal logician's. But the word ' not ' is a logical constant; for we selected the word to figure in a representative formula quoted in a formal logician's rule, viz., the rule that ' p and not-p ' is inconsistent. Similarly, ' not-p ' is a logical formula, for it contains none but logical constants; but ' x is a younger son ' is not a logical formula, for it contains non-logical constants.

It is evident that there is nothing logically holy about logical constants. Inferences involving them do not, if valid, have a superior degree or kind of validity to inferences not involving them. We shall, of course, expect, and find, that logical constants will be expressions capable of figuring in discussion of a wide range of subjects; so that merely knowing what logical constants occurred in someone's speech would not tell us what the speech was about.   But we shall not find that *all* expressions which have this characteristic of indifference to subject-matter are logical constants, i.e., figure in the formulae quoted in logicians' rules.   We have already noticed that, from the resources of ordinary speech, the logician has a certain range of choice; indeed, an embarrassment of choice.   It is easy to see at least a part of the reason why ' provided that ' or ' under the condition that ' or ' given that ' should be neglected, when ' if ' is noticed; and why the logician need not supplement the entailments of the formula ' p and q ' with ¬ules for ' also' and ' in addition '.   The desire to avoid reduplication, however, is not the only reason for the logician's selectiveness.   The words ' but ', ' although ', ' nevertheless ', for example, are not mere stylistic variants on ' and '.   Their use implies at least that there is some element of contrast between the conjoined statements or attributes; and, sometimes, that the conjunction is unusual or surprising.   But this kind of implication, though it must not be neglected when we are discussing the meanings of words, is not readily expressible in an entailment- or inconsistency-rule.   If a man said ' Although she is kind, she is gentle ', we should be surprised and think that he had made some kind of mistake of language (perhaps that he didn't know what ' kind ' meant); but we should not say that he was being inconsistent or had contradicted himself.   The logician's neglect of these conjunctions, in spite of their distinctive meaning, is intelligible.   So, though for different reasons in each case, is his neglect of such prepositions as ' of ', ' for ', ' to ', ' with ', ' at ', ' in '; and of the group of kindred conjunctions, ' so ', ' consequently ', ' since ', ' because ', ' for '.   The role of the latter we have already discussed : it is not (in general) to assert, but to signalize a claim, that one thing is a ground or a reason for another.   The prepositions have the necessary indifference to subject-matter, and certainly help to determine the entailments of sentences in which they figure.   But their role in entailment-determinations is wholly dependent on their verbal setting.   We can discuss the entailments of ' father of ' but not the entailments of ' of '.   When we specify the context sufficiently to make entailment-determination possible, we forfeit the subject-matter-indifference which the logician prizes.   The

logician's selectiveness, however, is still not fully explained.
There are, for instance, words expressive of difference in degree
or quantity, for which definite entailment-rules can be given,
but which are not distinguished by inclusion among logical
constants. Why should ' all ' and ' at least one ', which secure
a place, in logicians' formulae, be preferred to 'many ', 'a few ',
' several ', ' most ', which do not ? The inference-pattern 'Most
fs are g. Most fs are h. ∴ At least one f is both g and h ' is a
valid pattern of the requisite generality, but does not appear in
the logical text-books. Is it just that logicians have failed to
notice the possibility of extending their rules in this direction ?
This may be part of the answer. A more important factor is
the logical ideal of system, which I shall soon discuss. Logicians
like to present a tidy system of interconnected rules. The
neatness of the system might suffer if it had too many constants
in it.

What this discussion of logical constants shows is that it is
partly a matter of choice what expressions are to count as
logical constants. We can give general criteria of eligibility;
but these leave open a certain field within which selection is
possible. One can still discuss the logician's reasons for the
selection he makes.

13. The existence of logical formulae encourages us to talk
of the *logical form* of sentences and statements ; and perhaps we
are inclined to think of the logical form of a statement as a sort
of verbal skeleton which is left when all expressions, except
those selected as logical constants, are eliminated from a sentence which might be used to make the statement, and replaced
by appropriate variables. But there are all sorts of difficulties
about this. A perfectly idiomatic sentence may contain none
of the narrow range of selected constants, and yet we may want
to say that a statement it is used to make is of a certain logical
form (e.g., hypothetical). Again, as we have seen, expressions
selected as constants enjoy in ordinary speech a logical licence
of which they are deprived when imprisoned in a logician's
rule ; so the fact that two sentences verbally exemplify the
same logical formula does not guarantee our willingness to say
that statements made by their use are of the same form. Indeed,
one and the same sentence (e.g., ' The cat is a hunter ') might be

used to make statements of different logical forms, viz., a statement about an individual cat and a generalization about cats.
Moreover, what of statements which we are disposed to say
are of the transitively relational form? There is no chance of
their being made in sentences exemplifying the right pattern of
logical constants and variables, for there is no such pattern.

To be clear about this notion of logical form, we shall have to
ask ourselves what use we want to make of it. Just now, we
talked of statements being *of the same form*; we have often
applied to statements words like ' hypothetical ', ' general ',
' conjunctive ', ' negative ', which are held to be the names of
logical forms; and we may sometimes want to talk of the
verbal form in which a statement is made being *misleading* as
to its logical form. We saw earlier that the formal logician was
concerned with analogies of a certain kind between inferences
on widely differing topics; analogies either close enough to
permit the framing of a genuinely representative pattern suitable for quoting in a logician's rule for inferences of that class,
or at least close enough to admit of a more or less precise description of the common features of such a class. The notion
of logical form can best be understood as the result of transferring this idea of logical analogy from the inferences belonging
to such a class to the statements making up these inferences.
Let us speak of the *logical powers* of a statement, meaning by
this the whole range of its possible logical relations (e.g., the
whole range of parts it could play in valid inferences, &c.).
Then let us restrict our attention to the general classes of inference (&c.) which interest the formal logician. We may then
speak of the *formal powers* of a statement, meaning by this the
range of parts it could play in inferences (&c.) belonging to such
general classes. In so far as two different statements may play
similar parts in inferences (&c.) *of the same general class*, we may
speak of an analogy between their formal powers. In so far as
their formal powers are not analogous (i.e., one statement can
play a certain part in an inference of some general kind, while
there is no other inference of that general kind in which the other
statement can play a similar part), we may speak of a difference
in their formal powers. We say that two statements are of the
same logical form when we are interested in an analogy between
their formal powers; we say that two statements are of different

logical forms when we are interested in a difference between
their formal powers. Thus any two denials are of the same
logical form; but may also be of different logical forms. As
denials, they exhibit formal analogies; but they may also
exhibit formal differences (e.g., ' Tom is not mad ', ' Not all
bulls are dangerous '). It is easy to see how we can name
logical forms when it is remembered that we can either formulate general principles for inferences (&c.) of a certain general
class, or can describe their common logical features. Such
principles or descriptions will refer to general classes of statements; and all we have to do is to give such a class of statements a name (e.g., ' denial ', as used above), using, perhaps,
for this purpose, a word or phrase extracted from the general
principle, or description, of the class of inferences (&c.) concerned. Thus, quoting from such principles as I have already
given, we can refer to ' any statement to the effect that all the
members of a certain class are members of another class ' as a
general statement; and to ' any statement to the effect that one
thing is transitively related in some way to another thing ' as
a statement of the transitively relational form. Finally, we
might reasonably say that the verbal form of a statement was
(at least potentially) misleading as to its logical form in the
following circumstances : (1) the sentence used to make it has
a certain verbal pattern in common with a great many other
sentences; (2) most, or a great number, of the statements made
by the use of sentences having that verbal pattern in common,
are analogous to one another in a certain formal respect; (3)
the statement in question is not analogous to these statements
in that formal respect. In practice, the notion of ' verbal
form being misleading as to logical form ' has been very much
more widely and loosely used; and is associated with so many
mistakes and incoherences that the phrase might well be dis-
carded.

   This account of logical form attaches the notion firmly to
those classes of inferences, &c., for which formal logicians frame
general principles or of which they give general descriptions.
The classification of statements with respect to their logical
form is made to depend upon the formal logicians' classification
of inconsistencies and validities. This restriction of the meaning of ' logical form ' is historically correct. There are many

other kinds of general logical resemblance and difference between statements which are of philosophical importance. But there is no point in blurring the distinction between different kinds of logical classification.

14. There is another way of explaining the notion of logical form, which (with one limitation) comes to the same thing as the account just given, but which links the notion more directly with logical formulae. We have seen that, in selecting an expression as a logical constant, the logician gives to that expression a standard logical use to which it is not necessarily limited in ordinary speech, but to which it *is* limited within the logician's system. (An example of this is the rule that ' p and not-p ' is inconsistent.) This fact enables us to explain logical form *by reference to a given system of rules* as follows. We may say that two statements are of the same logical form when they could correctly be made by the use of sentences (i) which exemplify the same logical formula [1] and (ii) *in which the logical constants have the logical use which is the standard use for the given system of rules*. As before, this allows of two statements having both the same, and different, logical forms. E.g., the sentences ' Tom is not mad ' and ' Not all bulls are dangerous ' both exemplify the formula ' not-p '; but the latter also exemplifies the formula ' not all fs are g ', while the former does not. The names of logical forms can now be attached directly to formulae : e.g., ' not-p ' may be the formula for the negative form, ' if p, then q ' for the hypothetical form, ' all fs are g ' for the general form, and so on. A statement will then be said to be of a certain form if it could correctly be made in a sentence which exemplifies the appropriate formula, so long as the logical constants in the sentence, as used to make that statement, have the logical use which is standard for that system of rules, i.e., obey the rules of that system. Finally, we could

---

[1] Here I use the phrase ' exemplify the same logical formula ' in an extended sense, to which an analogy can be found in the explanations of entailments between formulae given earlier in this chapter. E.g., sentences containing ' not ' in various positions (though not in all) may be held to exemplify the formula ' not-p '; sentences may be held to exemplify the formula ' x is a f ' whether or not they contain the indefinite article; and so on. ' Rules of exemplification ' could be framed for any set of logical formulae.

speak (again with reference to a given system of rules) of a statement being made in a misleading verbal form, if the sentence in which the statement is made exemplifies a certain logical formula, but the constants occurring in the sentence, as used to make that statement, do not have the logical use which is standard for that system of rules.

There is even more historical justification for this alternative (not incompatible) account of logical form. In the earlier text-books of logic, we often read of ' putting a statement into logical form '. And by this was meant, expressing the statement in a sentence exemplifying one of the logical formulae employed in the traditional set of rules. The demerit of this account is that it imposes an unwanted limitation on our talk of logical form. It would not permit us to refer in these terms to those formal powers of statements which are manifested in types of inference (e.g., transitively relational inferences) for which there exists no representative verbal pattern suitable for quotation in a logician's rule. Admittedly, we can always frame a rule for such types of inference in terms of a *manufactured* constant; e.g., '-trans ' in

' x R-trans y and y R-trans z ' entails ' x R-trans z '.

But to talk of ordinary sentences exemplifying the formula ' x R-trans y ' has a different kind of artificiality from that of the stretched use of ' exemplify ' which allows us to say, e.g., that ' Tom is not mad ' exemplifies ' not-p '.

15. It remains to mention some of the ways in which people have spoken misleadingly of logical form. One of the commonest of these is to talk of ' *the* logical form ' of a statement; as if a statement could never have more than one kind of formal power; as if statements could, in respect of their formal powers, be grouped in mutually exclusive classes, like animals at a zoo in respect of their species. But to say that a statement is of some one logical form is simply to point to a certain general class of, e.g., valid inferences, in which the statement can play a certain role. It is not to exclude the possibility of there being other general classes of valid inferences in which the statement can play a certain role. Thus we may say of a statement made in the words ' John is older than Mary ' that it is of the tran-

sitively relational form, reminding ourselves of the logical powers it may exhibit in conjunction with a statement such as one made in the words ' Mary is older than Jane '. But we may also say that it is of the ' subject-predicate ' form,[1] reminding ourselves of the logical role it can play in conjunction with a statement such as one made in the words ' All those older than Mary are too old to play with Jane '. The mistaken view of logical form as a segregating concept is encouraged by misleading analogies; e.g., with the form of a sonnet (a sonnet cannot be both Shakespearean and Petrarchan in form), or with the shape of a vase.

Sometimes it is said that inferences are valid in virtue of their form, or that all inferences depend on form alone; or that all inference is formal. Such remarks can mislead in two related ways. First, they suggest that all entailment-rules, or rules of inference, are formal logicians' rules; and this is false. The rule that ' x is a younger son ' entails ' x has a brother ' is not a logician's rule. The existence of logicians' rules does not render lexicographers' rules superfluous. These remarks also suggest something that may, or may not, be true. They suggest that any entailment whatever may be regarded as belonging to a general class of entailments, the common logical features of whose members can be described without indicating the type of subject-matter involved; or, in other words, that, for any entailment whatever, there exist other entailments concerned with widely different subject-matters, such that between it and them, formal analogies can be described.[2] Whether this is true or not is a question of how far we are prepared to push the notion of a formal analogy. But, whatever decision we may make on this point, there remains an important difference between those cases in which the resources of language allow of the framing of genuinely representative verbal patterns suitable for quota-

---

[1] Cf. Chapter 6.

[2] E.g., it might be maintained : (i) that the moves from ' This is a cat ' to ' This is an animal ', from ' This is green ' to ' This is coloured ', from ' He has influenza ' to ' He has a disease ' were formally analogous in that they were all moves from the ascription of a specific, to the ascription of a generic, character to something; and (ii) that the moves from ' It is green ' to ' It is not white ', from ' It is triangular ' to ' It is not square ', from ' He is irritable ' to ' He is not sweet-tempered ' were formally analogous in that they were all moves from the application of one predicate to the explicit withholding of an incompatible predicate.

tion in entailment-rules and those cases for which no such representative formula can be framed for a general class of entailments. This distinction is in danger of being blurred by the dictum that all inference is formal. And the distinction is important; for knowledge of logicians' principles is sufficient to determine whether an inference of a certain type is valid or not only if (though not always if) there exist in ordinary language representative constants for that type of inference. If we equipped ourselves with knowledge of a system of logicians' rules, incorporating quoted formulae, and then set ourselves to examine specimen inferences, then, with some general classes of inferences, we should get on fairly well, though we might make some mistakes because of the logical vagaries of words like ' not '. But when we came to specimens like ' Tom is the descendant of Harry, and Harry is the descendant of Richard, so Tom is the descendant of Richard ' or ' Tom hates Harry, and Harry hates Richard, so Tom hates Richard ', the logician's rule that ' x R-trans y and y R-trans z ' entails ' x R-trans z ' would give us no help at all. We should have no clue as to whether ' descendant of ' and ' hates ' were transitive-relation expressions or not. Now, one might be inclined to think it a trivial matter, an accident of language, that we had no constant, like ' trans- ', to identify transitively relational words for us. But it is not. It is not a trivial matter that one has to think of what sort of thing is being talked about by the use of certain relational words (that one has to think of the descriptive meaning of these words), in order to see the point of the rule that they are, or are not, transitive. The dictum that all inference is formal may be valuable in so far as it encourages us to look for formal analogies that we might not otherwise have noticed. It is dangerous and misleading in so far as it encourages us to overlook the distinction between the implicit, though general, logical features of descriptive words and the explicit performance of general logical functions such as denial or generalization.

There is another misleading feature about the statement that inferences are valid *in virtue of* their form, or the statement that inference *depends on* form. It emerges more clearly in the assertion, sometimes made, that the task of the logician is twofold : viz., first, to discover what logical forms statements may have; second, to discover the logical relations between statements possessing these forms. This suggests that there is some way of discovering the logical form of a statement independently of discovering what parts it can play in what general kinds of inference, and that the making of the first discovery is a condition of going on to make the second. And this is the precise reverse of the truth. To call a statement transitively relational in form is not to give a reason why it can play a certain role in a certain type of inference. On the contrary, we call it transitively relational just because it can play such a role; to call it transitively relational *is* to say that it can play such a role. Logical form is not a property which statements have *on account of which* (or in virtue of which) they have certain formal powers. Their possession of a certain form *is* their possession of those powers.

III. SYSTEM

16. It is time to speak of the third factor which further limits the logician's task and, perhaps, conditions his procedure more radically than anything I have so far mentioned. From what I have said so far, one might think that the formal logician envisaged his task as that of compiling lists of highly general rules of inference or types of entailment; embodying these, where possible, in rules for representative formulae. We have seen that this step—the adoption of rules for representative formulae—represents the beginning of a rift between the logic of certain expressions, figuring as constants in the formulae, and the logic of these same expressions as they figure in ordinary speech; where they may idiomatically be used in ways which conflict with the logician's rules. This does not mean that the logician's rules are incorrect, nor does it mean that ordinary language is inconsistent. It means simply that a word which has different logical uses in ordinary speech may be assigned a single standard logical use in logicians' rules.

What widens into a chasm the rift between expressions occurring in logicians' rules and expressions of ordinary speech, is something which might be called the logical ideal of system. The logician is not content to write down, haphazardly, a set of rules which satisfy the bare requirement of consistency—the requirement which forces him to deprive his constants of the logical licence they customarily enjoy. He aims at presenting, not a disconnected list, but a connected system, of principles. This ideal of system has been present in formal logic from the start.   The earliest logicians had seen that with the help of just a few logical principles, they could, taking a small number of patterns of valid inference as basic, *prove* the validity of a larger number of other patterns;   that is, they could apply logic within logic, use it to systematize itself.[1]   And it is this ideal of systematization which has most profoundly influenced the modern development of logic; so profoundly that the original conception of simply codifying the most general principles we appeal to in making our logical appraisals has pretty well been lost sight of.   For the expressions of ordinary speech, such as ' if ', ' and ', ' not ', ' all ', ' some ', ' or ', which figured so prominently as logical constants in the inference-patterns of early logicians, lack, as they are ordinarily used, not only the stability, but also the simplicity, of meaning which would make them the ideal candidates for the roles of constants in logical systems of the now desired kind.   So their place tends to be taken by fabricated expressions to which are assigned just the kinds of meaning needed to meet the requirements of system. The logical uses of these fabricated expressions correspond in part with, and diverge in part from, some uses of some expressions in ordinary speech;   the correspondence and the divergence being revealed in a partial parallelism and a partial discrepancy between the rules to which we appeal in our logical appraisals of ordinary talk, and the rules governing the new expressions.   The latter are written as symbols, not as words. And the change is itself symbolic; for there are few, if any, words which have just, and only, the meaning assigned to the symbols.

To put this another way.   The formal logician now aims at an exact and highly systematic logic, comparable in these respects with mathematics.   But he cannot give the exact and systematic logic of expressions of everyday speech;   for these expressions have no exact and systematic logic.   What he can, and does, do is to devise a set of rules which satisfies his requirements, and, at the same time, while not doing full justice to the complexities of ordinary usage, and diverging from it in many ways, does touch ordinary usage at some vital points.   The formal logician, in relation to ordinary language, might be

---

[1] Cf. Chapter 6, Section 3.

compared with a man ostensibly mapping a piece of country of which the main contours are highly irregular and shifting. But the man is passionately addicted to geometry, and insists on using in his drawings only geometrical figures for which rules of construction can be given; and on using as few of such rules as he can. Naturally his maps will never quite fit. But a good many landmarks are identifiable on his drawing, and there is a rough correspondence between some of the main features of the country and some of the main lines of the map. The logician, we may say, manufactures the elements of a language of his own, which, unlike ordinary language, is subject to rigid and systematically connected rules, and some of the symbols of which exhibit logical analogies to familiar expressions of ordinary speech, as these expressions are commonly, though not always, used. And in the process of system-construction he may, and does—if only by contrast—teach us a good deal about the logic of ordinary discourse.

17. Methods of systematization which have actually been used we shall see exemplified in the sequel. The one which has attracted logicians the most strongly, which has seemed to satisfy the ideal of system in the highest degree, is the deductive method, where the analogy with mathematics is the clearest. A small number of logicians' statements or rules (e.g., to the effect that certain formulae are analytic) are taken as premises, and further rules derived from them by the use of one or two higher-order rules of inference. This at least is the form which one might most naturally expect such a deductive system to take. In practice it is convenient to regard the process of deduction as applied to the analytic formulae themselves; i.e., to view it as a process of deriving analytic formulae from analytic formulae, rather than as a process of deriving rules about formulae from rules about formulae. This requires some explanation. In a deductive system regarded as a system in which rules about formulae are derived from rules about formulae, we might expect the principle, that any general logical rule entails any less general rule obtained by substitutions on the variables occurring in the formula quoted in the first rule, to be used as one of the higher-order rules of inference. Suppose we have a system which contains, as constants, the words ' or '

and ' not ' and the symbol ' $\supset$ ', and, as premises, the rules (1)
that ' $p \supset q$ ' entails ' not-$q \supset$ not-p ' and (2) that ' p or q ' entails ' q or p '; or, as they may be alternatively expressed, the
rules (1) that ' $(p \supset q) \supset$ (not-$q \supset$ not-p) ' is analytic and (2)
that ' $(p$ or $q) \supset (q$ or $p)$ ' is analytic. Then, by application of
the higher-order rule of inference, we could derive from (1) the
rule (3) that '$[(p$ or $q) \supset r] \supset$ [not-$r \supset$ not-$(p$ or $q)]$ ' is analytic.
Regarding the process of deduction as applied directly to for-
mulae consists in calling the formulae, quoted in the second formulation of rules (1) and (2), themselves premises; and in replacing the higher-order rule of inference *about rules* by a rule
sanctioning the derivation of *formulae* from *formulae* by means
of certain kinds of substitutions on the variables. This permits
us to speak of the formula ' $[(p$ or $q) \supset r] \supset$ [not-$r \supset$ not-$(p$ or
$q)]$ ' as entailed by, and deduced from, the formula ' $(p \supset q) \supset$
(not-$q \supset$ not-p) '. Now suppose, in the course of deriving formulae by means of the rule of substitution, we obtain a formula
of which the part on the left-hand side of the main ' $\supset$ ' sign is
itself an analytic formula of the system; as we might do by
deriving from the formula ' $(p \supset q) \supset$ (not-$q \supset$ not-p) ' the
formula ' $[(p$ or $q) \supset (q$ or $p)] \supset$ [not-$(q$ or $p) \supset$ not-$(p$ or $q)]$ '.
The rule of substitution alone allows us to write down this long
formula as an analytic formula of the system. But writing it
down as such a formula is equivalent to declaring that '$(p$ or
$q) \supset (q$ or $p)$ ' entails ' not-$(q$ or $p) \supset$ not-$(p$ or $q)$ '. If we now
explicitly introduce the further higher-order principle of in-
ference that any formula shown to be entailed by another
which is analytic in the system, is itself analytic in the system,
we thereby authorize ourselves, since '$(p$ or $q) \supset (q$ or $p)$ ' is
analytic in the system, to write down ' not-$(q$ or $p) \supset$ not-$(p$ or
$q)$ ' as an analytic formula of the system. That is to say, we can
regard

$$\text{not-}(q \text{ or } p) \supset \text{not-}(p \text{ or } q)$$

as itself derived from

$$(p \text{ or } q) \supset (q \text{ or } p)$$

together with

$$[(p \text{ or } q) \supset (q \text{ or } p)] \supset [\text{not-}(q \text{ or } p) \supset \text{not-}(p \text{ or } q)].$$

This second principle we can express as a rule for application to
formulae as follows : any formula F' can be derived as an analy-

tic formula of the system whenever there already exist as analytic formulae of the system both a formula F and the formula obtained by writing F followed by ' ⊃ ' followed by F'.

The convenience of applying the process of deduction directly to first-order formulae may be regarded as a further reason for the prevalence of the symbol ' ⊃ ' in logic. What this process of deduction amounts to is showing that it would be inconsistent to accept the fundamental rules of the system and to refuse to accept the derived rules. The criteria of inconsistency are here given by the higher-order principles of inference corresponding to the rules for obtaining formulae from formulae. There is nothing mysterious about these higher-order principles of inference. The character of the two I chose for the above example can be shown more obviously by illustrating their operation for cases which would not in fact occur in any logician's system. We should, for example, find no difficulty in agreeing that it would be inconsistent to accept the rule that ' x is a younger son ⊃ x has a brother ' is analytic and to refuse to accept the rule that ' Tom is a younger son ⊃ Tom has a brother ' is analytic. This illustrates the first of the higher-order principles of inference, and the corresponding rule of substitution in formulae. Now suppose we accept the rule that ' if p, then q ⊃ if not-q, then not-p ' is analytic, and derive from it, in accordance with the first principle, the rule that ' if x is a father, then x is male ⊃ if x is not male, then x is not a father ' is analytic. We should have no difficulty in agreeing that it would be inconsistent to accept *both* this derived rule *and* the rule that ' if x is a father, then x is male ' is analytic, and to refuse to accept the rule that ' if x is not male, then x is not a father ' is analytic. This illustrates the second of the higher-order principles of inference, and the corresponding rule for the derivation of formulae.

The intellectual charm of the deductive method of systematizing logic is the charm of any deductive system. It lies, partly, in the exhibition of the set of formulae in an ordered arrangement, each derived formula (or theorem) following from the ones before it; partly in a feeling of increased control and comprehension, a sense of having reduced a great mass of principles to a handful of premises and a couple of rules such that, by the application of these to those, the great mass can be re-erected as an orderly structure. A price is paid, however, for this intoxicating success, as I have suggested already and as we shall see more clearly hereafter.

A deductive method has one, at least apparent, disadvantage. It does not, at any rate obviously, provide any mechanical method of checking any formula, framed in terms of the constants of the system, to determine whether or not it would be inconsistent to refuse to accept it as an analytic formula of the system. To establish it as an analytic formula, a way of deriving it must be found; and this may seem a matter of some difficulty. This suggests the possibility of another way of systematizing logic : a way which consists simply in laying down a general method of *testing* any given formula, framed in terms of the constants of the system, to see whether it is logically necessary in the system or not. A method of this kind we shall also see exemplified. Where a testing-method is, from the point of view of system, inferior to a deductive method, is that it does not provide for the arrangement of the necessary formulae of the system in any particular order. Whether or not it generally gives an equally satisfying sense of mastery of logical complexities I do not know.

18. Before we consider any actual logical systems, I want to indicate a way of looking at the activity of system-construction which has its dangers but can be very illuminating; a way for which this discussion should have prepared us. I have said, roughly speaking, that whereas the older logicians tried to reveal some of the general types of inconsistency, validity, and invalidity which occurred in our ordinary use of ordinary language, the new formal logicians create instead the elements of a new kind of language which, although its elements have something in common with some pervasive words of ordinary speech, would not be particularly suitable for the purposes of ordinary speech, but is supremely well adapted for the purpose of building a comprehensive and elegant system of logical rules. Of course, in giving a meaning (or, as is sometimes said, an interpretation) to the constants of such a system, the logician must use words of which the meaning is already known. Sometimes the correspondence between one of his symbols and some word already in use may be sufficiently close for him to say merely that such and such a symbol means roughly the same as such and such a

word. Sometimes more complicated explanations must be
given. At best, such approximate identifications or more
complicated explanations can serve only as a guide to the
meaning of his symbols; we shall have to check, and perhaps
correct, the impressions we get from them, by an examination
of the rules of the system. And we may find that an examination of the rules reveals serious deficiencies in the explanation.
We shall then have to look for a more satisfactory explanation;
we shall have to find our own interpretation of the symbols.

This may encourage us to look at the formal logician's activity
from a slightly different angle. We may think of him as a man
whose task has two parts. The first part is the construction of
a *purely abstract* system of symbols. The system consists of:
(1) the introduction and classification of a number of symbols
(constants and variables); (2) rules laying down which combinations of symbols are permissible (the formation-rules of the
system); (3) rules laying down which permissible combinations
are the initial laws (or necessary formulae) [1] of the system, and
further rules (transformation-rules or rules of derivation) for
transforming these combinations into other combinations which
are also to count as laws; or, as an alternative to (3), (3a) rules
for testing permissible combinations to determine whether or
not they are to count as laws (or necessary formulae); [1] and (4)
a series of applications of the rules of (3) or (3a), i.e., a series of
' proofs '. Such a system is called ' abstract ' because no
meaning is attached to the symbols over and above the rules of
combination and transformation. The second part of the task
will then be that of giving the symbols a meaning or interpretation; and for this it will be necessary to use expressions of which
the meaning is regarded as already known.

The reason why this way of looking at the matter is apt to be
misleading is that it suggests that the two parts of the logician's
activity are quite distinct; whereas, in practice, the logician
always approaches the task of system-construction with some
particular kind of interpretation in mind. The reasons why it
is illuminating are at least two : (i) it suggests, what we shall see

---

[1] This is one possible choice among others. The combinations of
symbols thus given a special status need not, when the system is interpreted, count as analytic formulae. See Chapter 4, and Section 8 of this
chapter.

to be the case, that a system constructed with one interpretation in mind may turn out to be susceptible of more than one interpretation (i.e., we may be put on the track of further formal analogies); (ii) it reminds us that we cannot be quite sure how the symbols of a system are to be interpreted until we have supplemented the explanations given with a study of the rules of the system. If a certain interpretation of a system is inconsistent, it does not follow that there are no consistent interpretations of it. (This fact is important in view of certain current criticisms, founded on misinterpretations, of traditional logic.) All that is shown is that the interpretation we are considering is not a possible interpretation of the system as it stands. Of course, a system for which we were unable to find any consistent interpretation would be of no interest. Any system is a logical (as opposed to, say, a mathematical) system, if it can be, and is, so interpreted that the interpreted rules are of the general character discussed in the second part of this chapter, or diverge from that character only in the way discussed in its third part.

CHAPTER 3

TRUTH-FUNCTIONS

I. TRUTH TABLES

1. THE first logical system we shall consider is the system of truth-functions. This can be developed either by a deductive or by a testing method. We shall first consider the latter.

The system contains, as variables, the letters ' p ', ' q ', ' r ', ' s ', &c.; and as constants, the symbols ' $\sim$ ', ' $.$ ', ' $\vee$ ', ' $\supset$ ', and ' $\equiv$ '. Permissible combinations of the constants and variables of the system we shall call ' truth-functional formulae '. Any expression obtained either by writing ' $\sim$ ', followed by any variable, or by writing any other of the constants of the system with a variable on each side of it, is a truth-functional formula. Formulae obtained in this way we shall call simple formulae, and formulae obtained in any other way, complex formulae. Thus ' $\sim q$ ' and ' $p \supset q$ ' are both simple truth-functional formulae. Any expression obtained by writing ' $\sim$ ' followed by any truth-functional formula, the latter being enclosed in brackets, is a truth-functional formula; e.g. ' $\sim (p \supset q)$ '. Any expression obtained by writing any of the other constants of the system with *either* a variable *or* a bracketed truth-functional formula on either side of it is a truth-functional formula. The last rule obviously permits the framing of truth-functional formulae of any degree of complexity. E.g., ' $p \vee (q \supset r)$ ' is a truth-functional formula; so is ' $[p \vee (q \supset r)] \supset [\sim (p \supset q)]$ '; so is ' $\{[p \vee (q \supset r)] \supset [\sim (p \supset q)]\} \vee \{[p \vee (q \supset r)] . [\sim (q \supset p)]\}$ '.

Brackets are a clumsy device, and we can economize in them as follows. It is clear from the formation-rules given that the symbol ' $\sim$ ', whenever it occurs, will be *immediately* followed by a single variable or by a bracketed formula. We shall say that the formula consisting of the expression [1] immedi-

---

[1] In this paragraph I use the word ' expression ' to refer only to variables or truth-functional formulae.

ately following the occurrence of ' $\sim$ ', together with that occurrence of ' $\sim$ ' itself, constitutes *the scope* of that occurrence of ' $\sim$ '. Similarly, each occurrence of any of the other constants will have, immediately following, and immediately preceding it, either two variables or two bracketed formulae, or one variable and one bracketed formula. We shall say that the formula consisting of the pair of expressions immediately following and preceding the occurrence of the constant, together with that occurrence of the constant, constitutes *the scope* of that occurrence of the constant. We can now largely eliminate brackets by laying down a kind of rule of precedence among the constants of the system. We lay it down that, *in the absence of guiding brackets,* the symbol ' $\equiv$ ' is to be taken as having the most extensive scope, and the symbol ' $\sim$ ' the least extensive scope in any formula. Between these two extremes we range the other constants, so that the order of ' scope-precedence ' is as follows : ' $\equiv$ ' ' $\supset$ ' ' $\lor$ ' ' . ' ' $\sim$ '. On the strength of this rule for supplying brackets, we shall now often, but not always, be able to omit them. For instance, we shall be able to write the formula ' $p \supset (q \lor r)$ ' as ' $p \supset q \lor r$ ', which leaves the scope of the constants unchanged. But the formula ' $p \lor (q \supset r)$ ' we must still write with brackets; for if we omitted them we should obtain ' $p \lor q \supset r$ ', which by our new rule is the same as ' $(p \lor q) \supset r$ '. So, by omitting brackets, we should, in this case, have altered the scope of the constants. Brackets actually present in a formula are to be taken always as overriding the precedence-rule.

2. So far the approach to the system has been abstract. But I shall not continue to expound it as a purely abstract system. It was in fact constructed with a certain kind of interpretation in mind, and I shall now say what that interpretation is, and shall continually refer to the interpretation in further developing the system. Later, we shall look at it once more as an abstract system, when we seek a second interpretation for it. But the name ' truth-functional ' is applicable to the system only when we interpret it in the way we are now to discuss. The *truth-functional system* is an interpreted, not an abstract, system.

The variables of this system have as their possible values groups of words which could occur as separate sentences of the kind which could be used for making statements. If all the variables in a truth-functional formula are replaced by such groups of words, the resulting expression is a truth-functional sentence (e.g., ' ∼ Tom is mad '). The groups of words replacing the variables in a truth-functional formula to form a truth-functional sentence will be called *the constituent sentences* of the truth-functional sentence. Any statement made by the use of a truth-functional sentence would be a truth-functional statement; and any statements made by the use, in the same context, of the constituent sentences of that truth-functional sentence will be called, analogously, the constituent statements of the truth-functional statement. Thus ' Tom is mad ' is the constituent sentence of the truth-functional sentence ' ∼ Tom is mad '; and a statement made by the use of the sentence ' Tom is mad ' would be the constituent statement of the truth-functional statement made by the use, in the same context, of the sentence ' ∼ Tom is mad '. *Truth-functional statements are so called because their truth or falsity is determined entirely, and only, by the truth or falsity of their constituent statements.* The rules which govern the determination of the truth or falsity of a truth-functional statement by the truth or falsity of its constituent statements are the rules which give the meaning (the interpretation) of the constants of the system. These rules exhaust their meaning. That is why they are called truth-functional constants.

The term ' truth-function ' is sometimes used to mean ' truth-functional formula ' and sometimes used to mean ' truth-functional statement '.

We have now seen, in general, the kind of meaning that truth-functional constants have, and that it is a very simple kind of meaning. Let us see in detail what is the meaning of each. From our account of their general kind of meaning, it is clear that this can be done simply by indicating how the truth or falsity of a truth-functional statement of each of the forms ' $\sim p$ ', ' $p \cdot q$ ', ' $p \vee q$ ', ' $p \supset q$ ', ' $p \equiv q$ ' is determined by the truth or falsity of its constituent statements. This we do, first in words, as follows :

(1) Any statement of the form [1] ' $\sim p$ ' is true if and only if its constituent statement is false, and false if and only if its constituent statement is true.

(2) Any statement of the form ' $p \cdot q$ ' is true if and only if both its constituent statements are true, and false if and only if at least one of its constituent statements is false.

(3) Any statement of the form ' $p \vee q$ ' is true if and only if at least one of its constituent statements is true, and false if and only if both its constituent statements are false.

(4) Any statement of the form ' $p \supset q$ ' is true if and only if it is not the case both that the first of its constituent statements is true and the second false, and false if and only if the first of its constituent statements is true and the second false.

(5) Any statement of the form ' $p \equiv q$ ' is true if and only if its constituent statements are either both true or both false, and false if and only if one of them is true and the other false.

There is a clear and simple way of giving these meanings which enables us to dispense with the verbal explanations. All we have to do is to *picture* the effects of the truth or falsity of the constituent statements on a truth-functional statement of any one of the forms. We can write down in one column a list of the various possible ways in which truth or falsity can be combined in the constituent statements; and against each of these possible combinations we indicate the truth-value (truth or falsity) which the truth-functional statement of a given form will have for that combination of truth-values of the constituent statements. Where there is only one constituent statement, it is inappropriate to speak of possible *combinations* of truth-values; we have merely to indicate the effect of (1) the truth and (2) the falsity of the constituent statement on the

---

[1] Cf. Chapter 2, p. 30 n., for the explanation of this phrase. It can here be expanded into ' any statement made by the use of a sentence obtainable by substituting a group of words which could occur separately as a sentence in the formula. . . .'

truth-functional statement. This we do, schematically, as follows :

$$(1) \qquad \begin{array}{c|c} p & \sim p \\ \hline T & F \\ F & T \end{array}$$

where the left-hand column represents (1) the case in which the constituent statement is true, and (2) the case in which the constituent statement is false; and where the right-hand column represents the way in which the truth-value of a truth-functional statement of the form ' $\sim p$ ' is determined for each of these cases. For truth-functional statements which have two constituent statements, truth and falsity may clearly be combined in four different ways in the constituent statements; and the determination of the truth-values of the truth-functional statements will have to be given for each of these four different ways. Thus we have

$$(2) \qquad \begin{array}{c|c|c|c|c} & (a) & (b) & (c) & (d) \\ p\ q & p \cdot q & p \lor q & p \supset q & p \equiv q \\ \hline T\ T & T & T & T & T \\ T\ F & F & T & F & F \\ F\ T & F & T & T & F \\ F\ F & F & F & T & T \end{array}$$

as definitions of the remaining constants of the system. The first column of letters represents possible truth-values of the first constituent statement, the second column of letters possible truth-values of the second constituent statement, and the two columns taken together as one column represent the possible *combinations* of truth-values of the two constituent statements. The column of possible combinations will have eight rows instead of four in the case of a form of truth-functional statement with three constituent statements; and, in general, 2^n rows for a form of truth-functional statement with n constituent statements.

Someone might say : But what guarantees that there is just this number of possibilities in each case? Do we not speak of half-truths, and are we not inclined, sometimes, with all the facts before us, to hesitate to call a statement either true or false; or perhaps, inclined to call it both? Moreover, when a man tells a story or writes a novel, it seems inappropriate to call the things he says, or writes, either true or false. He uses the sort of sentences which *could* be used to make true or false statements, but he uses them in a different way, with a different purpose. He uses them neither to inform nor to misinform; but to entertain. Fiction is not the same thing as falsehood, though we sometimes politely disguise the nature of falsehood by calling it fiction. The question of the truth or falsity (in the ordinary sense) of what the story-teller says is one that does not arise. And we have already seen [1] that there are other ways than that of story-telling in which the question of truth or falsity can fail to arise. To assume, then, that there is just this number of possibilities in each case, is to ignore such facts as these. There are different ways of answering this. One could answer it by saying: Very well, we make it a rule that for the purposes of this system nothing is to count as a statement unless it is either true or false and not both. But I shall not choose this answer; it encumbers the system with a superfluous rule. Instead, I shall say: The purpose of these tables (truth-tables) is to give a certain kind of meaning to certain constants; a meaning which is exhaustively given when it is shown how the truth or falsity of statements of certain forms is completely, and solely, determined by the question of which one of two truth-values each of their constituent statements has. So we are concerned only with the cases in which the constituent statements each have one, and only one, of these two truth-values. We do not exclude, by any rule or assumption, the possibility of other cases. Only they are irrelevant for our purpose; which is just to give this kind of meaning to these constants. We do not insist that every truth-functional state-ment or every constituent statement must have just one of these two truth-values; we only lay it down that if, and only if, each of the constituent statements of a truth-functional statement has just one of these two truth-values, then the truth-functional statement has just one of these two truth-values. The rules show how this truth-value is determined for every case in which each of the constituent statements *does* have just one of these two truth-values.

[1] See Chapter 1, Section 12, p. 18.

3. We shall say that the definitions we have so far given lay down the *truth-conditions* of the formulae considered in the last section. That is to say, the truth-conditions of a truth-functional formula are the ways in which the truth-value of any statement of the form of that formula is determined by the truth-values of its constituent statements. We shall now describe a procedure for determining the truth-conditions of more complex formulae. This procedure is extremely simple; it consists simply in repeated applications of the rules already given as definitions. Let us take, as an example, the complex formula ' $\sim(p \cdot q)$ '; and compare it with the formulae ' $\sim p$ ' and ' $p \cdot q$ ' for which we have already given the truth-conditions. When we gave the truth-conditions of ' $\sim p$ ', we gave them for *any statement whatever* of that form. Therefore we gave them for the cases where the constituent statement of the statement of that form is itself a truth-functional statement; e.g., for the case where the constituent statement is of the form ' $p \cdot q$ '. Thus, by table (1) any statement of the form ' $\sim(p \cdot q)$ ' is true if and only if the corresponding statement [1] of the form ' $p \cdot q$ ' is false, and false if and only if the corresponding statement of the form ' $p \cdot q$ ' is true. The truth-value of any statement of the form ' $p \cdot q$ ' for each possible combination of truth-values of its constituents is given in column (*a*) of table (2). So the truth-value of any statement of the form ' $\sim(p \cdot q)$ ' is given by applying the rule of table (1) to column (*a*) in table (2), i.e., by writing ' F ' wherever ' T ' occurs in that column and ' T ' wherever ' F ' occurs in that column. By applying (1) to (2*a*) we obtain (2*e*):

(1)			(2)		(*a*)	(*e*)
	p	$\sim p$		$p \ q$	$p \cdot q$	$\sim(p \cdot q)$
	T	F		T T	T	F
	F	T		T F	F	T
				F T	F	T
				F F	F	T

This procedure can be generalized as follows. Any formula contains one main constant of which the scope is the formula

---

[1] The phrase 'corresponding statement' here acquires the simple meaning 'statement with the same constituents'.

as a whole; and one or more other subordinate constants, of each of which the scope is some formula less than the formula as a whole. Let us say that each such formula is subordinate to the next largest formula which includes it as a part. Then the general procedure for obtaining the truth-conditions of any complex function is as follows : (1) write down the truth-conditions for the smallest subordinate formulae involved, i.e., the formulae with the constants of smallest scope (which will be simple formulae); then (2) apply to the results the rules for the constants of next widest scope, thus obtaining the truth-conditions for the formulae to which the simple formulae are subordinate; and (3) continue this procedure until the main constant of the whole formula is reached. To illustrate this procedure for another simple example : the truth-conditions of the formula ' $\sim p \cdot \sim q$ ' are given by the heavily printed column of the table :

p q	$\sim p$	$.$	$\sim q$
T T	F	**F**	F
T F	F	**F**	T
F T	T	**F**	F
F F	T	**T**	T

which is obtained by first applying to ' $\sim p$ ' and ' $\sim q$ ' the rule of table (1) and then applying to the resulting columns the rule given in table (2a).

4. The final step in the development of the system is the use of this tabular method of writing down the truth-conditions of any truth-functional formula, for the purposes : (i) of establishing logical relations between such formulae, and (ii) of establishing whether or not any such formula is analytic in the system. This is once more an extremely simple matter. Suppose we write down in a single table the truth-conditions of several different formulae, and compare the truth-conditions of any pair of them, say F_1 and F_2. There are various possibilities. We might find :

   (1) That among the various possible combinations of truth or falsity in the constituents, there was no combination which conferred truth on any statement of the

form of F_1 while conferring falsity on any statement of the form of F_2. Since the tables give the only possible ways in which either truth or falsity may be conferred on statements of either form, the absence of such a combination would mean that it was logically impossible for a statement of the form of F_1 to be true while the corresponding statement (i.e., the statement with the same constituents) of the form of F_2 was false. But to say this is to say that F_1 entails F_2. As an example, we may take the case where F_1 is '$p \cdot q$' and F_2 is '$p \vee q$'.

$p\ q$	$p \cdot q$	$p \vee q$
T T	T	T
T F	F	T
F T	F	T
F F	F	F

Of the possible combinations listed in the left-hand column, there is none for which any statement of the form '$p \cdot q$' has the truth-value, truth, and for which any statement of the form '$p \vee q$' has the truth-value, falsity. That is to say, '$p \cdot q$' entails '$p \vee q$'.

We can state further possibilities summarily as follows :

(2) We may find that for every possible combination, statements of the forms F_1 and F_2 have the same truth value. But this is to say that it is logically impossible for corresponding statements of the forms of F_1 and F_2 to have different truth-values; i.e., that F_1 is *logically equivalent* to F_2. Example : '$p \vee q$' and '$\sim(\sim p \cdot \sim q)$'.

(3) Two formulae are contradictories if, for every possible combination, statements of these forms have opposite truth-values. (Example : '$p \vee q$' and '$\sim p \cdot \sim q$'.)

(4) Two formulae are contraries if there is no combination for which statements of both forms are true. (Example : '$p \cdot q$' and '$\sim p \cdot \sim q$'.)

(5) Two formulae are subcontraries if there is no combination for which statements of both forms are false. (Example : '$p \vee q$' and '$\sim p \vee \sim q$'.)

In this way we can obtain from the tables logical rules, i.e., rules to the effect that one formula entails another, is logically equivalent to another, is the contradictory of another, &c. But there is an alternative way of expressing any such rule. For example, to say that two formulae are logically equivalent is to say that corresponding statements of these forms, if they have either truth-value, have, *as a matter of logical necessity*, the same truth-value. That is to say, the statement, with regard to corresponding statements of these forms, that, if they have either truth-value, they have the same truth-value, is an analytic statement. But we have already defined a symbol, ' $\equiv$ ', in such a way that a statement of the form ' $p \equiv q$ ' is true if and only if its two constituent statements have the same truth-value, and false if and only if its two constituent statements have different truth-values. So where the two constituent statements of a statement of this form are logically equivalent (i.e., it is logically impossible for them to have opposite truth-values), the statement of the form ' $p \equiv q$ ' of which they are constituents is itself analytic (i.e., cannot be denied without self-contradiction) ; and, correspondingly, the formula which results from joining two logically equivalent formulae by ' $\equiv$ ' is an analytic formula. Conversely, when a formula of which the main constant is ' $\equiv$ ' is analytic, the two formulae subordinate to the whole formula are logically equivalent. This will show itself in the tables as follows : the application of the procedures for determining truth-conditions, to any formula which results from joining the two logically equivalent formulae by ' $\equiv$ ', will always yield a column consisting entirely of T's ; and, conversely, whenever such a column is obtained for a formula of which the main constant is ' $\equiv$ ', the formulae subordinate to the whole formula will be logically equivalent. Thus, corresponding to the rule that ' $p \vee q$ ' is logically equivalent to ' $\sim(\sim p . \sim q)$ ' we have the rule that ' $p \vee q \equiv \sim(\sim p . \sim q)$ ' is analytic.

Analogous correspondences exist for the other cases. Thus :

(1) For every entailment there is an analytic formula of the form [1] ' $p \supset q$ '. E.g., the rule that ' $p . q$ ' entails ' $p \vee q$ ' corresponds to the rule that ' $p . q \supset p \vee q$ ' is analytic.

---

[1] We shall speak of any formula of which the main constant is ' $\supset$ ' as a formula *of the form* ' $p \supset q$ '; of any formula of which the main constant is ' $\equiv$ ' as a formula of the form ' $p \equiv q$ '; and so on.

(2) For every logical equivalence, there is an analytic formula of the form ' $p \equiv q$ '. (Example above.)

(3) For every case of contradictory formulae, there is an analytic formula of the form ' $(p \lor q) \cdot \sim(p \cdot q)$ '. E.g., the rule that ' $p \lor q$ ' is the contradictory of ' $\sim p \cdot \sim q$ ' corresponds to the rule that ' $[(p \lor q) \lor \sim p \cdot \sim q] \cdot \sim [(p \lor q) \cdot (\sim p \cdot \sim q)]$ ' is analytic.

(4) For every case of contraries, there is an analytic formula of the form ' $\sim(p \cdot q)$ '. E.g., the rule that ' $p \cdot q$ ' and ' $\sim p \cdot \sim q$ ' are contraries corresponds to the rule that ' $\sim[(p \cdot q) \cdot (\sim p \cdot \sim q)]$ ' is analytic.

(5) For every case of subcontraries, there is an analytic formula of the form ' $p \lor q$ '. E.g., the rule that ' $p \lor q$ ' and ' $\sim p \lor \sim q$ ' are subcontraries corresponds to the rule that ' $(p \lor q) \lor (\sim p \lor \sim q)$ ' is analytic.

Establishing that two truth-functional formulae are logically related in some way is thus essentially the same as establishing that some one formula which includes these two is analytic.

Analytic truth-functional formulae (i.e., formulae such that the application to them of the procedure for determining truth-conditions yields a column consisting entirely of T's) are sometimes called tautologous formulae. Formulae for which the application of this procedure yields a column consisting entirely of F's are called self-contradictory formulae. (The simplest example is ' $p \cdot \sim p$ '.) Formulae for which the application of this procedure yields a mixed column (e.g., any of the simple formulae) are called contingent (or synthetic) formulae.

5. We have now at our disposal a general method for testing any truth-functional formula to determine whether or not it is analytic. Analytic formulae we may call *laws* of the system. We shall consider a number of examples of such laws.

(a) First we may note a set which establish the interdefinability of the constants of the system.

$$(1) \quad p \supset q \ \equiv \ \sim(p \cdot \sim q)$$
$$(2) \quad p \lor q \ \equiv \ \sim(\sim p \cdot \sim q)$$
$$(3) \quad (p \equiv q) \ \equiv \ \sim(p \cdot \sim q) \cdot \sim(q \cdot \sim p)$$

Each of the formulae (1)–(3), if checked by the truth-tables, will be found to be analytic. Since they are all analytic

formulae of the form ' $p \equiv q$ ', the formulae on either side of
the main constant in each case are logically equivalent. Instead, therefore, of giving separate verbal or schematic definitions of ' $\equiv$ ', ' $\supset$ ', and ' v ', we could have defined each of
these in terms of the two remaining constants (e.g., ' $p \supset q$ ' =
$_{Df}$ ' $\sim(p . \sim q)$ '). It is not difficult to find further equivalences
permitting alternative definitions of some of the constants in
terms of others : e.g., ' $\equiv$ ' can be defined in terms of ' $\supset$ ' and
' . '; ' $\supset$ ' and ' . ' in terms of ' v ' and ' $\sim$ '; ' v ' and ' . ' in
terms of ' $\supset$ ' and ' $\sim$ '.

(b) From the formation-rules given in the first section of this
chapter, it appears that every truth-functional formula must
have one and only one main constant, identifiable by the position
of brackets and the rule of precedence among constants. And
this we have so far assumed to be the case in our exposition.
Indeed, in the absence of a method of identifying the main constant, it would be impossible to apply the rules we have given
for establishing the truth-conditions of a given formula, and
hence impossible to use the tables for the purpose of establishing laws and rules of the system. Suppose, for example, we
were asked to determine the truth-conditions of the formula
' $p \supset q \supset p$ '. We might try guessing which ' $\supset$ ' sign was intended to be the main constant. But in this case different guesses
would yield different sets of truth-conditions; in fact,
' $(p \supset q) \supset p$ ' is a contingent formula, whereas ' $p \supset (q \supset p)$ ' is
analytic. We might say that if ' $p \supset q \supset p$ ' were admissible as
a truth-functional formula, it would be ambiguous; statements
of that form would mean one thing if we took the first ' $\supset$ '
sign as the main constant, and quite another if we took the
second sign as the main constant. In fact, ' $p \supset q \supset p$ ', by the
formation-rules, does not qualify as a truth-functional formula
at all. For the formation-rules are designed to ensure that a
combination of symbols shall count as a truth-functional
formula if and only if the procedure for determining truth-
conditions can be mechanically applied to that formula in such
a way as to yield just one set of truth-conditions. Now suppose
we came across expressions which were like ' $p \supset q \supset p$ ' or
' $p \supset q \supset r$ ' in that there were no brackets to identify the main
constant for us, but were unlike ' $p \supset q \supset r$ ' in that, whatever
guess we made, we always got the same set of truth-conditions.

Then we might amend the formation-rules to sanction the omission of the brackets in these cases, i.e., to admit such expressions as truth-functional formulae. And in fact there are such expressions; of which the most commonly encountered are expressions in which we seem at liberty to choose any one of a series of ' . ' signs or any one of a series of ' v ' signs as the main constant. We may put the point simply as follows :

and
$$(4)\ (p \, . \, q) \, . \, r \, \equiv \, p \, . \, (q \, . \, r)$$
$$(5)\ (p \, \lor \, q) \, \lor \, r \, \equiv \, p \, \lor \, (q \, \lor \, r)$$

are analytic formulae, or laws, of the system, whereas '$p \supset (q \supset r) \equiv (p \supset q) \supset r$' is not an analytic, but a contingent, formula. The formulae on either side of the ' $\equiv$ ' sign in (4) and (5) have the same truth-conditions, whereas the formulae on either side of the ' $\equiv$ ' sign in the last expression have different truth-conditions. Consequently, where we have expressions like '$p \, . \, q \, . \, r$' or '$p \lor q \lor r$' (or say, '$p \, . \, q \lor q \, . \, r \lor (q \supset s)$') where a number of ' . ' signs or a number of ' v ' signs seem to compete for the role of main constant, it makes no difference which we choose for that role; whereas, if the competitors are a number of '$\supset$' signs, it does make a difference which we choose. So expressions of the former kind are allowed, and expressions of the latter kind, disallowed, as truth-functional formulae; and we are authorized to write ' $(p \lor q) \lor r$ ' and ' $p \lor (q \lor r)$ ' alike as ' $p \lor q \lor r$ '. We modify the formation-rules, sanction some bracket-omission, in the light of some results of applying the testing-rules. Laws (4) and (5) are called ' Associative Laws '.

(c) I now list a number of other laws which are, for various reasons, of logical interest. To many of these I shall refer in succeeding sections.

$$(6)\ \sim(p \, . \, \sim p)$$
$$(7)\ p \lor \sim p$$
$$(8)\ p \supset p$$
$$(9)\ \sim \sim p \, \equiv \, p \ [1]$$
$$(10)\ p \, . \, q \supset p$$
$$(11)\ p \, . \, q \, \equiv \, q \, . \, p$$
$$(12)\ q \supset p \lor q$$

[1] We adopt the convention of writing ' $\sim(\sim p)$ ' as ' $\sim\sim p$ '.

(13) $(p \lor q) \cdot \sim p \supset q$

(14) $\sim (p \cdot q) \cdot p \supset \sim q$

(15) $(p \supset q) \cdot p \supset q$

(16) $(p \supset q) \cdot \sim q \supset \sim p$

(17) $p \supset q \equiv \sim q \supset \sim p$

(18) $(p \supset q) \cdot (q \supset r) \supset (p \supset r)$

(19) $\sim p \supset (p \supset q)$

(20) $\sim p \supset (p \supset \sim q)$

(21) $q \supset (p \supset q)$

(22) $q \supset (\sim p \supset q)$

(23) $\sim p \equiv (p \supset q) \cdot (p \supset \sim q)$

(24) $\sim (p \cdot q) \equiv \sim p \lor \sim q$

(25) $\sim (p \lor q) \equiv \sim p \cdot \sim q$

(26) $p \cdot (q \lor r) \equiv p \cdot q \lor p \cdot r$

(27) $p \cdot q \lor r \equiv (p \lor r) \cdot (q \lor r)$

(28) $p \cdot q \lor p \cdot \sim q \lor \sim p \cdot q \lor \sim p \cdot \sim q$

(29) $p \lor p \supset p$

(30) $p \lor q \supset q \lor p$

(31) $(q \supset r) \supset (p \lor q \supset p \lor r)$

(32) $p \lor (q \lor r) \supset q \lor (p \lor r)$

(*d*) Finally, I illustrate once more the use of the truth-tables for establishing formulae as analytic, by reproducing the table for formula (18). It will be seen that establishing the analyticity of the formula is establishing the transitivity of the ' $\supset$ ' sign.

$p\ q\ r$	$(p \supset q)$	.	$(q \supset r)$	$\supset$	$(p \supset r)$
T T T	T	T	T	T	T
T T F	T	F	F	T	F
T F T	F	F	T	T	T
T F F	F	F	T	T	F
F T T	T	T	T	T	T
F T F	T	F	F	T	T
F F T	T	T	T	T	T
F F F	T	T	T	T	T

It is evident that as truth-functional formulae increase in complexity, contain more and more variables, the use, without any modification, of the tabular method of determining their status (as analytic, synthetic, or self-contradictory) becomes increasingly cumbersome. Great ingenuity has been devoted to framing sets of rules for swifter and more elegant methods of testing complex formulae.[1] These I shall not describe. For my main concern is not with the craftsmanship of logic, pleasing as this can be, but with the fundamental character of logical systems and their relations to ordinary discourse.

II. TRUTH-FUNCTIONAL CONSTANTS AND ORDINARY WORDS

6. What of the relations between the truth-functional constants and expressions of ordinary speech? The meaning, or interpretation, of those constants was given, in words, on p. 67, and this explanation was to be understood in the light of the subsequently developed procedures for determining truth-conditions and establishing logical rules. We have to ask, with regard to each of those constants, whether there is any expression of ordinary speech which has at least a standard use identifiable with the meaning of that constant. It is quite common to suggest, with certain reservations, the following identifications : ' $\sim$ ' with ' not ', or ' it is not the case that '; ' . ' with ' and '; ' . . . $\vee$ . . .' with ' either . . . or . . .'; ' . . . $\supset$ . . ' with ' if . . . then . . .'; ' . . . $\equiv$ . . .' with ' . . . if and only if . . .' Of these identifications the first two are the least misleading. We shall find that the remainder are not only misleading, but definitely wrong. We shall be entitled to say that such an identification is definitely wrong, wherever we find that the ordinary conjunction, in its standard or primary use, does not conform to a logical rule which holds for the truth-functional constant with which it is identified, and whenever we find, conversely, that the truth-functional constant does not conform to a logical rule which holds for the ordinary conjunction in its standard or primary use. But we shall also find that even the most mistaken of these identifications has a point : we shall find not only some degree of formal parallelism (which could be noted independently of interpretation) but some degree of interpenetration of meanings of the interpreted expressions of the system and of ordinary speech respectively. We could not, of course, find the latter without the former.

---

[1] See, for example, Quine, *Methods of Logic*.

7. Laws (6) and (7), taken together, show that any truth-functional sentence or formula in which the main constant is a ' ∼ ' sign is the contradictory of the sentence or formula which results from omitting that sign. We have seen that a standard and primary use of ' not ' in a sentence is to assert the contradictory of the statement which would be made by the use, in the same context, of the same sentence without the word ' not '.[1] This identification, then, involves only those minimum departures from the logic of ordinary language which must always result from the formal logician's activity of codifying rules with the help of verbal patterns : viz., (i) the adoption of a rigid rule when ordinary language permits variations and deviations from the standard use (cf. rules (6) and (9) and the discussions in Chapter 1, Section 3, and Chapter 2, Section 9); (ii) that stretching of the sense of ' exemplify ' which allows us, e.g., to regard ' Tom is not mad ' as well as ' Not all bulls are dangerous ' as ' exemplifications ' of ' not-p '. So we shall *call* ' ∼ ' the negation sign, and *read* ' ∼ ' as ' not '.

One might be tempted to suppose that declaring formulae (6) and (7) *laws* of the system was the same as saying that, as regards this system, a statement cannot be both true and false and must be either true or false. But it is not. The rules that (6) and (7) are analytic are not rules about ' true ' and ' false '; they are rules about ' ∼ '. They say that, given that a statement has one of the two truth-values, then it is logically impossible for both that statement and the corresponding statement of the form ' ∼p ' to be true, and for both that statement and the corresponding statement of the form ' ∼p ' to be false.

8. In the identification of ' and ' with ' . ' there is already a considerable distortion of the facts. ' And ' can perform many jobs which ' . ' cannot perform. It can, for instance, be used to couple nouns (' Tom and William arrived '), or adjectives (' He was hungry and thirsty '), or adverbs (' He walked slowly and painfully '); while ' . ' can be used only to couple expressions which could appear as separate sentences. One might be

---

[1] Of course we must not suppose that the insertion of ' not ' *anywhere* in *any* sentence *always* has this effect. ' Some bulls are not dangerous ' is not the contradictory of ' some bulls are dangerous '. This is why the identification of ' ∼ ' with ' it is not the case that ' is to be preferred to its identification with ' not ' *simpliciter.*

tempted to say that sentences in which ' and ' coupled words or phrases, were *short for* sentences in which ' and ' couples clauses; e.g., that ' He was hungry and thirsty ' was short for ' He was hungry and he was thirsty '. But this is simply false. We do not say, of anyone who uses sentences like ' Tom and William arrived ', that he is speaking elliptically, or using ab- breviations. On the contrary, it is one of the functions of ' and ', to which there is no counterpart in the case of ' . ', to form plural subjects or compound predicates. Of course it is true of many statements of the forms ' x and y are f ' or ' x is f and g ', that they are logically equivalent to corresponding statements of the form ' x is f and y is f ' or ' x is f and x is g '. But, first, this is a fact about the use, in certain contexts, of the word ' and ', to which there corresponds no rule for the use of ' . '. And, second, there are countless contexts for which such an equivalence does not hold. For example, ' Tom and Mary made friends ' is not equivalent to ' Tom made friends and Mary made friends '. They mean, usually, quite different things.[1] Nor does such an equivalence hold if we replace ' made friends ' by ' met yesterday ', ' were conversing ', ' got married ' or ' were playing chess '. Even ' Tom and William arrived ' does not mean the same as ' Tom arrived and William arrived '; for the first suggests ' together ' and the second an order of arrival. It might be conceded that ' and ' has functions which ' . ' has not (e.g., may carry in certain contexts an implication of mutuality which ' . ' does not), and yet claimed that the rules which hold for ' and ', *where it is used to couple clauses*, are the same as the rules which hold for ' . '. Even this is not true. By law (11), ' $p . q$ ' is logically equivalent to ' $q . p$ '; but ' They got married and had a child ' or ' He set to work and found a job ' are by no means logically equivalent to ' They had a child and got married ' or ' He found a job and set to work'.

One might try to avoid these difficulties by regarding ' . ' as having the function, not of ' and ', but of what it looks like, namely a full stop. We should then have to desist from talking of statements of the forms ' $p . q$ ', ' $p . q . r$ ' &c., and talk of

[1] But notice that one could say ' Tom and Mary made friends; but not with one another '. The implication of mutuality in the first phrase is not so strong but that it can be rejected without self-contradiction; but it is strong enough to make the rejection a slight shock, a literary effect.

sets-of-statements of these forms instead. But this would not avoid all, though it would avoid some, of the difficulties. Even in a passage of prose consisting of several indicative sentences, the *order* of the sentences may be in general vital to the sense, and in particular, relevant (in a way ruled out by law (11)) to the truth-conditions of a set-of-statements made by such a passage. The fact is that, in general, in ordinary speech and writing, clauses and sentences do not contribute to the truth-conditions of things said by the use of sentences and paragraphs in which they occur, in any such simple way as that pictured by the truth-tables for the binary connectives ('$\supset$', '$.$', '$\vee$', '$\equiv$') of the system, but in far more subtle, various, and complex ways. But it is precisely the simplicity of the way in which, by the definition of a truth-function, clauses joined by these connectives contribute to the truth-conditions of sentences resulting from the junctions, which makes possible the stylized, mechanical neatness of the logical system. It will not do to reproach the logician for his divorce from linguistic realities, any more than it will do to reproach the abstract painter for not being a representational artist; but one may justly reproach him if he *claims* to be a representational artist.

An abstract painting may be, recognizably, a painting *of* something. And the identification of '$.$' with 'and', or with a full stop, is not a simple mistake. There is a great deal of point in comparing them. The interpretation of, and rules for, '$.$' define a minimal linguistic operation, which we might call 'simple conjunction' and roughly describe as the joining together of two (or more) statements in the process of asserting them both (or all). And this is a part of what we often do with 'and', and with the full stop. But we do not string together at random any assertions we consider true; we bring them together, in spoken or written sentences or paragraphs, only when there is some further reason for the *rapprochement*, e.g., when they record successive episodes in a single narrative. And that for the sake of which we conjoin may confer upon the sentences embodying the conjunction logical features at variance with the rules for '$.$'. Thus we have seen that a statement of the form 'p and q' may carry an implication of temporal order incompatible with that carried by the corresponding statement of the form 'q and p'. This is not to deny that statements corresponding to these, but of the forms ' $p \cdot q$ ' and ' $q \cdot p$ ' would be, if made, logically equivalent; for such statements would carry no implications, and therefore no incompatible implications, of temporal order. Nor is it to deny the point, and merit, of the comparison; the statement of the form ' $p \cdot q$ ' means at least a part of what is meant by the corresponding statement of the form ' p and q '. We might say : the form ' $p \cdot q$ ' is an abstraction from the different uses of the form ' p and q '. Simple conjunction is a minimal element in colloquial conjunction. We may speak of ' . ' as the conjunctive sign; and read it, for simplicity's sake, as ' and ' or ' both . . . and . . .'.

I have already remarked that the divergence between the meanings given to the truth-functional constants and the meanings of the ordinary conjunctions with which they are commonly identified is at a minimum in the cases of ' $\sim$ ' and ' . '. We have seen, as well, that the remaining constants of the system can be defined in terms of these two. Other interdefinitions are equally possible. But since ' $\sim$ ' and ' . ' are more nearly identifiable with ' not ' and ' and ' than any other constant with any other English word, I prefer to emphasize the definability of the remaining constants in terms of ' . ' and ' $\sim$ '. It is useful to remember that every rule or law of the system can be expressed in terms of negation and simple conjunction. The system might, indeed, be called the System of Negation and Conjunction.

9. The relations between ' if ' and ' $\supset$ ' have already, but only in part, been discussed.[1] The sign ' $\supset$ ' is called the Material Implication sign—a name I shall consider later. Its meaning is given by the rule that any statement of the form ' $p \supset q$ ' is false in the case in which the first of its constituent statements is true and the second false, and is true in every other case considered in the system. That is to say, the falsity of the first constituent statement or the truth of the second are, equally, sufficient conditions of the truth of a statement of material implication; the combination of truth in the first with falsity in the second is the single, necessary and sufficient, condition

---

[1] Chapter 2, Section 7.

of its falsity. The standard or primary [1] use of an 'if . . . then . . .' sentence, on the other hand, we saw to be in circumstances where, not knowing whether some statement which could be made by the use of a sentence corresponding in a certain way to the first clause of the hypothetical is true or not, or believing it to be false, we nevertheless consider that a step in reasoning from that statement to a statement related in a similar way to the second clause would be a sound or reasonable step; the second statement also being one of whose truth we are in doubt, or which we believe to be false. Even in such circumstances as these we may sometimes hesitate to apply the word 'true' to hypothetical statements (i.e., statements which could be made by the use of 'if . . . then . . .' in its standard significance), preferring to call them reasonable or well-founded; but if we apply the word 'true' to them at all, it will be in such circumstances as these. Now one of the sufficient conditions of the truth of a statement of material implication may very well be fulfilled without the conditions for the truth (or reasonableness) of the corresponding hypothetical statement being fulfilled; i.e., a statement of the form '$p \supset q$' does not entail the corresponding statement of the form 'if p, then q'. But if we are prepared to accept the hypothetical statement, we must in consistency be prepared to deny the conjunction of the statement corresponding to the first clause of the sentence used to make the hypothetical statement with the negation of the statement corresponding to its second clause; i.e., a statement of the form 'if p then q' does entail the corresponding statement of the form '$p \supset q$'.

The force of the word 'corresponding' in the above paragraph needs elucidation. Consider the three following very ordinary specimens of hypothetical sentences :

(1) If the Germans had invaded England in 1940, they would have won the war.

(2) If Jones were in charge, half the staff would have been dismissed.

(3) If it rains, the match will be cancelled.

---

[1] The importance of this qualifying phrase can scarcely be over-emphasized. There are uses of 'if . . . then . . .' which do not answer to the description given here, or to any other descriptions given in this chapter.

The sentences which could be used to make statements *corresponding* in the required sense to the subordinate clauses can be ascertained by considering what it is that the speaker of each hypothetical sentence must (in general) be assumed either to be in doubt about or to believe to be not the case. Thus, for (1) to (3), the corresponding pairs of sentences are :

> (1*a*) The Germans invaded England in 1940; they won the war.
> (2*a*) Jones is in charge; half the staff has been dismissed.
> (3*a*) It will rain; the match will be cancelled.

Sentences which could be used to make the statements of material implication *corresponding* to the hypothetical statements made by sentences (1) to (3) can now be framed from these pairs of sentences as follows :

> (M1) The Germans invaded England in 1940 ⊃ they won the war.
> (M2) Jones is in charge ⊃ half the staff has been dismissed.
> (M3) It will rain ⊃ the match will be cancelled.

The very fact that these verbal modifications are necessary, in order to obtain from the clauses of the hypothetical sentence the clauses of the corresponding material implication sentence is itself a symptom of the radical difference between hypothetical statements and truth-functional statements. Some detailed differences are also evident from these examples. The falsity of a statement made by the use of ' The Germans invaded England in 1940 ' or ' Jones is in charge ' is a sufficient condition of the truth of the corresponding statements made by the use of (M1) and (M2); but not, of course, of the corresponding statements made by the use of (1) and (2). Otherwise, there would normally be no point in using sentences like (1) and (2) at all; for these sentences would normally [1] carry, in the tense or mood of the verb, an implication of the speaker's belief in the falsity of the statements corresponding to the clauses of the hypothetical. Its not raining is sufficient to verify a statement

---

[1] But not necessarily. One may use the pluperfect or the imperfect subjunctive when one is simply working out the consequences of an hypothesis which one may be prepared eventually to accept.

made by the use of (M3), but not a statement made by the use of (3). Its not raining is also sufficient to verify a statement made by the use of (M4) ' It will rain $\supset$ the match will *not* be cancelled '. The formulae ' $p \supset q$ ' and ' $p \supset \sim q$ ' are consistent with one another, and the joint assertion of corresponding statements of these forms is equivalent to the assertion of the corresponding statement of the form ' $\sim p$ '. But ' If it rains, the match will be cancelled ' is inconsistent with ' If it rains, the match will not be cancelled ', and their joint assertion in the same context is self-contradictory.

Suppose we call the statement corresponding to the first clause of a sentence used to make a hypothetical statement the antecedent of the hypothetical statement; and the statement corresponding to the second clause, its consequent. It is sometimes fancied that whereas the futility of identifying conditional statements with material implications is obvious in those cases where the implication of the falsity of the antecedent is normally carried by the mood or tense of the verb (e.g., (1) or (2)), there is something to be said for at least a partial identification in cases where no such implication is involved, i.e., where the possibility of the truth of both antecedent and consequent is left open (e.g., (3)). In cases of the first kind (' unfulfilled ' or ' subjunctive ' conditionals) our attention is directed only to the last two lines of the truth-tables for ' $p \supset q$ ', where the antecedent has the truth-value, falsity; and the suggestion that ' $\sim p$ ' entails ' if p, then q ' is felt to be obviously wrong. But in cases of the second kind we may inspect also the first two lines, for the possibility of the antecedent's being fulfilled is left open; and the suggestion that ' $p \cdot q$ ' entails ' if p, then q ' is not felt to be obviously wrong. This is an illusion, though engendered by a reality. The fulfilment of both antecedent and consequent of a hypothetical statement does not show that the man who made the hypothetical statement was right; for the consequent might be fulfilled as a result of factors unconnected with, or in spite of, rather than because of, the fulfilment of the antecedent. We should be prepared to say that the man who made the hypothetical statement was right only if we were also prepared to say that the fulfilment of the antecedent was, at least in part, the explanation of the fulfilment of the consequent. The reality behind the illusion is complex :

it is, partly, the fact that, in many cases, the fulfilment of both antecedent and consequent may provide confirmation for the view that the existence of states of affairs like those described by the antecedent is a good reason for expecting states of affairs like those described by the consequent; and it is, partly, the fact that a man who says, for example, ' If it rains, the match will be cancelled ' makes a prediction (viz., that the match will be cancelled) under a proviso (viz., that it rains), and that the cancellation of the match because of the rain therefore leads us to say, not only that the reasonableness of the prediction was confirmed, but also that the prediction itself was confirmed.

Because a statement of the form ' $p \supset q$ ' does not entail the corresponding statement of the form ' if p, then q ' (in its standard employment), we shall expect to find, and have found, a divergence between the rules for ' $\supset$ ' and the rules for ' if ' (in its standard employment). Because ' if p, then q ' *does* entail ' $p \supset q$ ', we shall also expect to find some degree of parallelism between the rules; for whatever is entailed by ' $p \supset q$ ' will be entailed by ' if p, then q ', though not everything which entails ' $p \supset q$ ' will entail ' if p, then q '. Indeed, we find further parallels than those which follow simply from the facts that ' if p, then q ' entails ' $p \supset q$ ' and that entailment is transitive. To laws (19)–(23) inclusive we find no parallels for ' if '. But for

(15) $(p \supset q) . p \supset q$

(16) $(p \supset q) . \sim q \supset \sim p$

(17) $p \supset q \equiv \sim q \supset \sim p$

(18) $(p \supset q) . (q \supset r) \supset (p \supset r)$

we find that, with certain reservations,[1] the following parallel laws hold good :

---

[1] The reservations are important. For example, it is often impossible to apply entailment-rule (iii) directly without obtaining incorrect or absurd results. Some modification of the structure of the clauses of the hypothetical is commonly necessary. But formal logic gives us no guide as to which modifications are required. If we apply rule (iii) to our specimen hypothetical sentences, without modifying at all the tenses or moods of the individual clauses, we obtain expressions which are scarcely English. If we preserve as nearly as possible the tense-mood *structure*, in the simplest way consistent with grammatical requirements, we obtain the sentences :

If the Germans had not won the war, they would not have invaded England in 1940.

(i) (if p, then q; and p) $\supset q$
(ii) (if p, then q; and not-q) $\supset$ not-p
(iii) (if p, then q) $\supset$ (if not-q, then not-p)
(iv) (if p, then q; and if q, then r) $\supset$ (if p, then r)

(One must remember that calling the formulae (i)–(iv) *laws* is the same as saying that, e.g., in the case of (iii), ' if p, then q ' entails ' if not-q, then not-p '.)   And similarly we find that, for some steps which would be *invalid* for ' if ', there are corresponding steps that would be *invalid* for ' $\supset$ '.   For example:

$$(p \supset q) \cdot q \therefore p$$
$$(p \supset q) \cdot \sim p \therefore \sim q$$

are invalid inference-patterns, and so are

if p, then q; and $q \therefore p$
if p, then q; and not-$p \therefore$ not-q.

The formal analogy here may be described by saying that neither ' $p \supset q$ ' nor ' if p, then q ' is a simply convertible formula.

We have found many laws (e.g., (19)–(23)) which hold for ' $\supset$ ' and not for ' if '.   As an example of a law which holds for ' if ', but not for ' $\supset$ ', we may give the analytic formula ' $\sim[($if p, then $q) \cdot ($if p, then not-$q)]$ '.   The corresponding formula

---

If half the staff had not been dismissed, Jones would not be in charge.
If the match is not cancelled, it will not rain.

But these sentences, so far from being logically equivalent to the originals, have in each case a quite different sense.   It is possible, at least in some such cases, to frame sentences of more or less the appropriate pattern for which one can imagine a use and which do stand in the required logical relationship to the original sentences (e.g., ' If it is *not* the case that half the staff *has* been dismissed, then Jones *can't be* in charge '; or ' If the Germans *did not win* the war, *it's only because they did not invade* England in 1940 '; or even (should historical evidence become improbably scanty) ' If the Germans did not win the war, it can't be true that they invaded England in 1940 ').   These changes reflect differences in the circumstances in which one might use these, as opposed to the original, sentences.   Thus the sentence beginning ' If Jones were in charge . . . ' would normally (though not necessarily) be used by a man who antecedently knows that Jones is not in charge: the sentence beginning ' If it's not the case that half the staff has been dismissed . . . ' by a man who is working towards the conclusion that Jones is not in charge.   To say that the sentences are nevertheless logically equivalent is to point to the fact that the grounds for accepting either, would, in different circumstances, have been grounds for accepting the soundness of the move from ' Jones is in charge ' to ' Half the staff has been dismissed '.

' $\sim[(p \supset q) \cdot (p \supset \sim q)]$ ' is not analytic, but (cf. (23)) is equivalent to the contingent formula ' $\sim\sim p$ '.

The rules to the effect that formulae such as (19)–(23) are analytic are sometimes referred to as ' paradoxes of implication '. This is a misnomer. If ' $\supset$ ' is taken as identical either with ' entails ' or, more widely, with ' if . . . then . . .' in its standard use, the rules are not paradoxical, but simply incorrect. If ' $\supset$ ' is given the meaning it has in the system of truth-functions, the rules are not paradoxical, but simple and platitudinous consequences of the meaning given to the symbol.

Throughout this section, I have spoken of a ' primary or standard ' use of ' if . . . then . . .', or ' if ', of which the main characteristics were : that for each hypothetical statement made by this use of ' if ', there could be made just *one* statement which would be the antecedent of the hypothetical and just *one* statement which would be its consequent; that the hypothetical statement is acceptable (true, reasonable) if the antecedent statement, if made or accepted, would, in the circumstances, be a good ground or reason for accepting the consequent statement; and that the making of the hypothetical statement carries the implication either of uncertainty about, or of disbelief in, the fulfilment of both antecedent and consequent.[1] Not all uses of ' if ', however, exhibit all these characteristics. In particular, there is a use which has an equal claim to rank as standard and which is closely connected with the use described, but which does not exhibit the first characteristic and for which the description of the remainder must consequently be modified. I have in mind what are sometimes called ' variable ' or ' general ' hypotheticals : e.g., ' If ice is left in the sun, it melts '; ' If the side of a triangle is produced, the exterior angle is equal to the sum of the two interior and opposite angles '; ' If a child is very strictly disciplined in the nursery, it will develop aggressive tendencies in adult life '; and so on. To a statement made by the use of a sentence such as these there corresponds no single pair of statements which are, respectively, its antecedent and consequent. On the other

---

[1] There is much more than this to be said about this way of using ' if '; in particular, about the meaning of the question ' whether the antecedent would be a good ground or reason for accepting the consequent ' and about the exact way in which this question is related to the question of whether the hypothetical is true (acceptable, reasonable) or not.

hand, for every such statement there is an indefinite number of non-general hypothetical statements which might be called exemplifications, applications, of the variable hypothetical; e.g., a statement made by the use of the sentence 'If this piece of ice is left in the sun, it will melt'. To the subject of variable hypotheticals I shall return later.[1]

Two relatively uncommon uses of 'if' may be illustrated respectively by the sentences 'If he felt embarrassed, he showed no signs of it' and 'If he has passed his exam, I'm a Dutchman (I'll eat my hat, &c.)'. The sufficient and necessary condition of the truth of a statement made by the first is that the man referred to showed no sign of embarrassment. Consequently, such a statement cannot be treated either as a standard hypothetical or as a material implication. Examples of the second kind are sometimes erroneously treated as evidence that 'if' does, after all, behave somewhat as '⊃' behaves. The evidence for this is, presumably, the facts (i) that there is no connexion between antecedent and consequent; (ii) that the consequent is obviously not (or not to be) fulfilled; (iii) that the intention of the speaker is plainly to give emphatic expression to the conviction that the antecedent is not fulfilled either; and (iv) the fact that '$(p \supset q) \cdot \sim q$' entails '$\sim p$'. But this is a strange piece of logic. For, on any possible interpretation, 'if p then q' has, in respect of (iv), the same logical powers as '$p \supset q$'; and it is just these logical powers that we are jokingly (or fantastically) exploiting. It is the absence of connexion referred to in (i) that makes it a quirk, a verbal flourish, an odd use of 'if'. If hypothetical statements were material implications, the statements would be not a quirkish oddity, but a linguistic sobriety and a simple truth.

Finally, we may note that 'if' can be employed not simply in making statements, but in, e.g., making provisional announcements of intention (e.g., 'If it rains, I shall stay at home') which, like unconditional announcements of intention, we do not call true or false but describe in some other way. If the man who utters the quoted sentence leaves home in spite of the rain, we do not say that what he said was false, though we *might* say that he lied (never really intended to stay in); or that he changed his mind. There are further uses of 'if' which I shall not discuss.

[1] See Chapter 7, Part I.

The safest way to *read* the material implication sign is, perhaps, ' not both . . . and not . . .'.

10. The material equivalence sign ' ≡ ' has the meaning given by the following definition :

$$ 'p \equiv q' =_{Df} '(p \supset q) \cdot (q \supset p)' $$

and the phrase with which it is sometimes identified, viz., ' if and only if ', has the meaning given by the following definition :

' p if and only if q ' $=_{Df}$ ' if p then q, and if q then p '.

Consequently, the objections which hold against the identification of ' $p \supset q$ ' with ' if p then q ' hold with double force against the identification of ' $p \equiv q$ ' with ' p if and only if q '.

11. The relations between ' v ' and ' or ' (or ' either . . . or . . .') are, on the whole, less intimate than those between ' . ' and ' and ', but less distant than those between ' ⊃ ' and ' if '. Let us speak of a statement made by coupling two clauses by ' or ' as an *alternative* statement; and let us speak of the first and second *alternates* of such a statement, on analogy with our talk of the antecedent and consequent of a hypothetical statement. At a bus-stop, someone might say : ' Either we catch this bus or we shall have to walk all the way home '. He might equally well have said ' If we don't catch this bus, we shall have to walk all the way home '. It will be seen that the antecedent of the hypothetical statement he might have made is the negation of the first alternate of the alternative statement he did make. Obviously, we should not regard our catching the bus as a sufficient condition of the ' truth ' of either statement; if it turns out that the bus we caught was not the last one, we should say that the man who had made the statement had been wrong. The truth of one of the alternates is no more a sufficient condition of the truth of the alternative statement than the falsity of the antecedent is a sufficient condition of the truth of the hypothetical statement. And since ' $p \supset p$ v q ' (and, equally, ' $q \supset p$ v q ') is a law of the truth-functional system, this fact sufficiently shows a difference between at least one standard use of ' or ' and the meaning given to ' v '. Now in all, or almost all, the cases where we are prepared to say something of the form ' p or q ', we are also prepared to say something

of the form ' if not-p, then q '.　And this fact may tempt us to exaggerate the difference between ' v ' and ' or ', to think that, since in some cases, the fulfilment of one alternate is not a sufficient condition of the truth of the alternative statement of which it is an alternate, the fulfilment of one alternate is *never* a sufficient condition of the truth of an alternative statement. And this is certainly an exaggeration.　If someone says : ' Either it was John or it was Robert—but I couldn't tell which ', we are satisfied of the truth of the alternative statement if either of the alternates turns out to be true;　and we say that the speaker was wrong only if neither turns out to be true.　Here we seem to have a puzzle ; for we seem to be saying that ' Either it was John or it was Robert ' entails ' If it wasn't John, it was Robert ' and, at the same time, that ' It was John ' entails the former, but not the latter.　What we are suffering from here is perhaps a crudity in our notion of entailment, a difficulty in applying this too undifferentiated concept to the facts of speech ; or, if we prefer it, an ambiguity in the notion of a sufficient condition. The statement that it was John entails the statement that it was either John or Robert *in the sense that it confirms it*;　when it turns out to have been John, the man who said that either it was John or it was Robert is shown to have been right.　But the first statement does not entail the second in the sense that the step ' It was John, so it was either John or Robert ' is a logically proper step (unless the person saying this means by it simply that the alternative statement made previously was correct, i.e., ' it *was* one of the two ').　For the alternative statement carries the implication of the speaker's uncertainty as to which of the two it was, and this implication is inconsistent with the assertion that it was John.　So in this sense of ' sufficient condition ', the statement that it was John is no more a sufficient condition of (no more entails) the statement that it was either John or Robert than it is a sufficient condition of (entails) the statement that if it wasn't John, it was Robert.　The further resemblance, which we have already noticed, between the alternative statement and the hypothetical statement, is that whatever knowledge or experience renders it reasonable to assert the alternative statement, also renders it reasonable to make the statement that (under the condition that it wasn't John) it was Robert.　But we are less happy about saying that the hypothetical statement is *confirmed* by the discovery that it was John, than we are about saying that the alternative statement is confirmed by this discovery. For we are inclined to say that the question of confirmation of the hypothetical statement (as opposed to the question of its reasonableness or acceptability) arises only if the condition (that it wasn't John) turns out to be fulfilled. This shows an asymmetry, as regards *confirmation*, though not as regards acceptability, between ' if not p, then q ' and ' if not q, then p ' which is not mirrored in the forms ' either p or q ' and ' either q or p '. This asymmetry is ignored in the rule that ' if not p, then q ' and ' if not q, then p ', are logically equivalent,[1] for this rule regards acceptability rather than confirmation. And rightly. For we may often discuss the ' truth ' of a *subjunctive* conditional, where the possibility of confirmation is suggested by the form of words employed to be not envisaged.

It is a not unrelated difference between ' if ' sentences and ' or ' sentences that whereas, whenever we use one of the latter, we should also be prepared to use one of the former, the converse does not hold. The cases in which it does not generally hold are those of subjunctive conditionals. There is no ' or ' sentence which would serve as a paraphrase of ' If the Germans had invaded England in 1940, they would have won the war ', as this sentence would most commonly be used. And this is connected with the fact that ' either . . . or . . .' is associated with situations involving choice or decision. ' Either of these roads leads to Oxford ' does not mean the same as ' Either this road leads to Oxford or that road does '; but both confront us with the necessity of making a choice.

This brings us to a feature of ' or ' which, unlike those so far discussed, *is* commonly mentioned in discussion of its relation to ' v '; the fact, namely, that in certain verbal contexts, ' either . . . or . . .' plainly carries the implication ' and not both . . . and . . .', whereas in other contexts, it does not. These are sometimes spoken of as, respectively, the exclusive and inclusive senses of ' or '; and, plainly, if we are to identify ' v ' with either, it must be the latter. The reason why, unlike others, this feature of the ordinary use of ' or ' is commonly mentioned, is that the difference can readily be accommodated

[1] Cf. footnote to p. 86.

in the symbolism of the truth-functional system : it is the difference between ' $(p \vee q) . \sim(p . q)$ ' (exclusive sense) and ' $p \vee q$ ' (inclusive sense).

' Or ', like ' and ', is commonly used to join words and phrases as well as clauses. The ' mutuality difficulties' attending the general expansion of ' x and y are f ' into ' x is f and y is f ' do not attend the expansion of ' x or y is f ' into ' x is f or y is f '. (This is not to say that the expansion can always correctly be made.)

We may call ' $\vee$ ' the disjunctive sign and, being warned against taking the reading too seriously, may read it as ' or '.

III. TRUTH-FUNCTIONAL CONSTANTS AND LOGICAL RELATIONS. THE DEDUCTIVE SYSTEM OF TRUTH-FUNCTIONS

12. Certain things should now be clear about the system of truth-functions. It should be clear that the constants of the system cannot be simply identified in meaning with those expressions of ordinary speech with which they are sometimes equated by writers on logic. It should be clear, too, that the decision on the meanings of the constants of the system, the selection of a set definable in terms of simple conjunction and simple negation (of ' . ' and ' $\sim$ ') is not just an odd caprice of the formal logician, but is dictated by the desire for systematic simplicity. For this characteristic, while admirably exemplified by the truth-functional system, is exemplified not at all by a veridical account of the maze of logical uses through which we unhesitatingly thread our way in our daily employment of the customarily related conjunctions. Finally, it should be clear that, though it is a mistake to *identify*, it is illuminating to *compare*, the customary conjunctions with the truth-functional constants. The comparison compels us to a better understanding of some of the most general logical features of our speech.

It should also be clear that an error which overlaps with (but is not the same as) that of identifying the constants and the conjunctions is that of identifying material implication with logical implication or entailment (' $\supset$ ' with ' entails '); material equivalence with logical equivalence (' $\equiv$ ' with ' is logically equivalent to '); the negation of a conjunction with inconsistency ('$\sim(p \cdot q)$' with 'the statement that p is inconsistent with the statement that q'), &c. This range of identifications embodies a mistake which is both peculiarly obvious and yet peculiarly attractive. The very names are evidence of this. One might say that the function of the adjective 'material' was to cancel the misleading suggestions of the nouns 'implication' and 'equivalence'. The names incorporate both the error and its correction.

The reason for the attractiveness of this mistake is, no doubt, the fact that we can and do use truth-functional constants as the main constants in writing down logical laws (or analytic formulae) both of the truth-functional system and of other systems, and even of ordinary speech. For instance, if we write down *as a law* the expression

$$(p \supset q) \supset (\sim q \supset \sim p)$$

we can, correctly, read this as ' "$p \supset q$" entails "$\sim q \supset \sim p$" '. But in so reading it we are tacitly supplying the quotation marks, and the second-order phrase 'is analytic', whose understood accompaniment of the formula '$(p \supset q) \supset (\sim q \supset \sim p)$' alone justifies us in adopting this reading. This accounts also in part for the temptation to identify '$\supset$' with 'if'. For we can also indicate that we understand '$(p \supset q) \supset (\sim q \supset \sim p)$' as a law by reading it 'if $p \supset q$, then $\sim q \supset \sim p$'. But the fact that '$\supset$', where it is the main constant of a formula understood as escorted by quotation marks and the words 'is analytic', can be replaced by 'entails' (with other appropriate amendments), or be read as 'if . . . then . . .', does not, of course, justify this replacement or this reading where the formula is not (even invisibly) so escorted, or where '$\supset$' occurs in any other position than that of the main constant in a formula so escorted. Failure to observe this simple rule leads straight to the alleged 'paradoxes of implication'. Saying, for example, that '$\sim p \supset (p \supset q)$' is a law of the system is the same as saying that '$\sim p$' entails '$p \supset q$'; but it is not at all the same as saying that '$\sim p$' entails 'the statement that p entails the statement that q'. To say that '$\sim p \supset (p \supset q)$' is a law or analytic formula is to give a rule about the symbol '$\supset$' (in its second occurrence) and is to make use of the symbol '$\supset$' (in its first occurrence) in giving the rule; it is not to give a rule about, or say anything about, the word 'entails'. Alternatively, we can indicate that we understand '$\sim p \supset (p \supset q)$' as a law, by reading it 'if $\sim p$, then $p \supset q$.' But if we try to indicate this by reading it 'if $\sim p$, then if p then q' we misread it; for to call '$\sim p \supset (p \supset q)$' analytic is to give a rule about '$\sim$' and '$\supset$', not a rule about 'if . . . then . . .', though in indicating that it *is* a rule, we may replace the first '$\supset$', by 'if . . . then . . .'.

The fact that the constants of the truth-functional system can be thus used (as main constants) in giving logical rules is a direct consequence of their being definable solely in terms of simple negation and simple conjunction. We saw, for example, in Chapter 1 that 'S_1 entails S_2' could be defined as 'the *conjunction* of S_1 with the *contradictory* of S_2 is self-contradictory', or, alternatively as 'the *contradictory* of the *conjunction* of S_1 with the *contradictory* of S_2 is analytic'. And to '$\sim$' and '.' (in terms of which the remaining constants can be defined) we respectively accorded (i) the function of contradicting whatever statement was made by the rest of the sentence of which it was the main constant, and (ii) the function of simple conjunction.[1] It is an equally simple consequence of the meanings initially given to the constants of the system and elaborated in the instructions for the use of the truth tables, that the analyticity of any formula framed in terms of those constants should show itself by means of a column of T's in the tables, and that the self-contradictoriness of any such formulae should show itself in a column of F's. The logical rules governing the constants of the system are, *of course*, different from the rules governing logical-appraisal words, though the constants of the systems defined can be used *in co-operation with* logical-appraisal words (e.g., 'analytic') to do the jobs of other logical-appraisal words (e.g., 'entails'). What causes confusion are the facts : first, that the constants seem to live a double life, according as they are or are not in harness with 'is analytic' and 'is self-contradictory', and, second, that, within the truth-functional system, they are used *in harness* to give rules for their own employment out of harness.[2]

[1] See p. 81.
[2] For a fuller discussion of the use of '$\supset$' in the construction of logical systems, see Chapter 8, Part I, Section 3.

13. We observed earlier that each of the constants of the system could be defined in terms of ' $\sim$ ' together with one other constant; so that it would be possible to express all the laws of the system in terms of, e.g., simple negation and simple conjunction. But the quest for symbolic economy can be carried a stage further. There is no reason why we should not introduce a single symbol, giving it such a meaning that all the remaining constants can be defined in terms of it alone. Thus the symbol ' | ' is introduced, for which the formation rules are similar to those for ' $\supset$ ' or ' v ' and of which the interpretation is given, verbally, by :

Any statement of the form ' $p \mid q$ ' is true if and only if one at least of its constituent statements is false, and false if and only if both its constituent statements are true

and, schematically, by :

$p \; q$	$p \mid q$
T T	F
T F	T
F T	T
F F	T

If we now frame the formula ' $(p \mid q) \mid (p \mid q)$ ', the determination of its truth-conditions is given by the central column of the following table

$p \; q$	$(p \mid q) \mid (p \mid q)$		
T T	F	T	F
T F	T	F	T
F T	T	F	T
F F	T	F	T

From this it is apparent that ' . ' can be defined in terms of ' | ' as follows :

$$ \text{`} p \cdot q \text{'} =_{Df} \text{`} (p \mid q) \mid (p \mid q) \text{'} $$

Moreover, a comparison of the two tables shows that ' $(p \mid q) \mid (p \mid q)$ ' is the contradictory of ' $p \mid q$ '. That is to say ' $(p \mid q) \mid (p \mid q)$ ' has the same interpretation as ' $\sim(p \mid q)$ '.

But ' $(p \mid q) \mid (p \mid q)$ ' exemplifies the formula ' $p \mid p$ '. So we can also define ' $\sim$ ' in terms of ' $\mid$ ' as follows :

$$ `\sim p \text{'} = _{\text{Df}} `p \mid p \text{'} $$

Hence all the constants of the system are definable in terms of the stroke-formula. And this result could equally, though differently, have been achieved by giving ' $p \mid q$ ' the meaning ' both not-p and not-q ' instead of, as above, the meaning ' not both p and q '.

All the laws of the system could thus be written as formulae of which the main constant was the stroke-sign; and the declaration that any such formula was analytic would be equivalent to the declaration that the formula preceding the main constant was inconsistent (or incompatible) with the formula following the main constant. Thus the declaration that ' $(p \cdot q) \mid \sim (p \vee q)$ ' was analytic would be equivalent to the declaration that ' $p \cdot q$ ' was inconsistent with ' $\sim (p \vee q)$ ', and both would be equivalent to the declaration that ' $p \cdot q$ ' entailed ' $p \vee q$ '. A further symptom of the fatal ease with which truth-functional constants are misinterpreted as logical relation words because of their use as main constants in formulae declared analytic, is the fact that the stroke sign, on its first introduction, was said to express the notion of incompatibility. In fact, it is given the meaning of the negation of a conjunction. Only where the contradictory of the conjunction is itself analytic are the conjuncts mutually incompatible. The stroke-formula has an especial charm in that it illustrates with peculiar clarity the remoteness of the conception of definition within a formal system from the ordinary conception of verbal elucidation of meaning. For one is inclined to say that it can be *explained* only in terms of the notions (negation and conjunction) which it is used, within the system, to define.

14. The possibility of defining all the constants of the truth-functional system in terms of the single constant ' $\mid$ ' is in fact of more interest in connexion with the deductive method of developing the system than in connexion with the testing method, involving the use of truth-tables, which I have so far described. In the testing method, as I introduced it, the truth-conditions of the simple formulae and, hence, the definitions of the individual constants, were each given separately by means

of the truth-tables. The interdefinability of the constants was seen as a fact which resulted from these initial definitions separately given. But in the deductive method the procedure is different. Here we start from an initial set of laws taken as premises and derive further laws from them, employing in the process certain higher-order rules of derivation such as those I described in the last part of Chapter 2.[1] At least some of the constants occurring in the initial set of laws are taken as undefined, or *primitive, within the system,*[2] though, of course, they may all be given a verbal interpretation as a preliminary to the construction of the system. The remainder of the constants occurring in the system are then defined, directly or indirectly, in terms of the primitive constants, and the higher-order rules of derivation are supplemented by a rule permitting the substitution of any expression for its defined equivalent. To illustrate this from the deductive system of truth-functions (sometimes referred to as the propositional calculus) as it was first developed by Whitehead and Russell in *Principia Mathematica*.[3] The signs ' $\sim$ ' and ' $\vee$ ' were taken as the primitive, or undefined, constants of the system. The following definitions were then introduced :

Def. I   ' $p \supset q$ ' $=_{Df}$ ' $\sim p \vee q$ '
Def. II   ' $p \cdot q$ ' $=_{Df}$ ' $\sim(\sim p \vee \sim q)$ '
Def. III ' $p \equiv q$ ' $=_{Df}$ ' $(p \supset q) \cdot (q \supset p)$ '

The following five primitive propositions, or initial laws or postulates, were formulated as the premises from which the remaining laws of the system were to be deduced :

$p \vee p \supset p$ (Taut.) [4]
$q \supset p \vee q$ (Add.)
$p \vee q \supset q \vee p$ (Perm.)
$(q \supset r) \supset (p \vee q \supset p \vee r)$ (Summ.)
$p \vee (q \vee r) \supset q \vee (p \vee r)$ (Ass.)

[1] See Chapter 2, Section 17.
[2] Analogously, the T's and F's which constitute the apparatus of the tabular definitions of the testing method cannot be regarded as defined *within the system*, though their use is explained in the interpretational remarks which precede the construction of the system.
[3] The formation-rules for the deductive method will, of course, be identical with those given for the tabular method.
[4] These abbreviated titles of the laws mean respectively ' Tautology ', ' Addition ', ' Permutation ', ' Summation ', ' Association '.

The selection of a set of initial laws is not governed by their intrinsic interest or importance, which may be small.   Nor is it governed by any such consideration as that the interpretation given to the undefined constants of the system, together with the definition of the remainder in terms of these, renders their logical necessity particularly obvious.   One prime consideration is that they should be consistent (i.e., for this system, that they should not include, or be so framed as to permit of having deduced from them, any formula of the form '$p . \sim p$').   A second is that they should be adequate to allow of the development of the system to the full extent desired by its authors.   In the present case we may regard this as the requirement that any formula which can be shown to be analytic by the truth-table method should be derivable, by the employment of the higher-order principles of inference, from these five postulates. Finally, it is regarded as an aesthetic desideratum in such a system that the number of primitive propositions and the number of undefined constants should be the minimum which is consistent with the satisfaction of the requirement of adequacy.   This entails at least that the postulates should be independent, i.e., that no one of them should be derivable from the others—a condition not satisfied by the above set, of which the fifth postulate is superfluous.   And the introduction of the stroke-formula, which, as we have seen, permits the reduction of the primitive constants to one, in fact allows of a further reduction in the number of postulates.

I have already mentioned the rules of derivation employed by Whitehead and Russell.   They are :

(1) *The Rule of Substitution on Variables*, which may be phrased as follows : Any formula F may be derived as an analytic formula in the system provided the system already contains an analytic formula F' such that F is obtained from F' by substituting variables or formulae for variables of F', the same substitution being made for the same variable throughout.

(2) *The Rule of Inference*.   Any formula F may be derived as an analytic formula of the system provided the system already contains both some analytic formula, F',

and the formula resulting from writing F′ followed by ' ⊃ ' followed by F.

(3) *The Rule of Definitional Substitution.* Any formula F may be derived as an analytic formula of the system provided the system already contains an analytic formula F′ such that F is obtained from F′ by substituting some formula for a definitionally equivalent formula appearing in F′; and two formulae are definitionally equivalent if they occur on opposite sides of the ' $=_{Df}$ ' sign in Defs. I to III, or if one can be obtained by substitution on the variables of one of the formulae quoted on one side of any of the definitions I to III while the other can be obtained by making the same substitutions for the variables of the formula quoted on the other side of the same definition.

15. Formulae derived in the systems are called *theorems.* I shall illustrate the derivation of formulae in the system by two examples. We are to take it that the system already contains as a theorem the formula

$$(a) \quad p \lor \sim p.$$

From this we are to derive, as further theorems, the two formulae

$$(b) \quad \sim p \lor \sim q \supset \sim (p \cdot q)$$
$$(c) \quad \sim (p \cdot \sim p)$$

by the use of the three rules of derivation quoted above. To them I shall refer as Sub., Inf., and Def. respectively. The first derivation follows :

From (a) by Sub. (' $\sim p$ ' for ' p ')

$$\sim p \lor \sim \sim p \quad . \quad . \quad . \quad . \quad . \quad . \quad \text{(i)}$$

From (i) by Def. (I)

$$p \supset \sim \sim p \quad . \quad . \quad . \quad . \quad . \quad . \quad \text{(ii)}$$

From (ii) by Sub. (' $\sim p \lor \sim q$ ' for ' p ')

$$\sim p \lor \sim q \supset \sim \sim (\sim p \lor \sim q) \quad . \quad . \quad . \quad \text{(iii)}$$

From (iii) by Def. (II)

$$\sim p \lor \sim q \supset \sim (p \cdot q) \quad . \quad . \quad . \quad . \quad (b)$$

Now the second derivation follows :

From (a) by Sub. (' $\sim p$ ' for ' p ')

$$\sim p \lor \sim \sim p \quad . \quad . \quad . \quad . \quad . \quad . \quad \text{(i)}$$

From (b) by Sub. (' $\sim p$ ' for ' q ')

$$\sim p \lor \sim \sim p \supset \sim (p \, . \, \sim p) \quad . \quad . \quad . \quad \text{(ii)}$$

From (i) and (ii) by Inf.

$$\sim (p \, . \, \sim p) \quad . \quad . \quad . \quad . \quad . \quad . \quad \text{(c)}$$

CHAPTER 4

CLASSES: AN ALTERNATIVE INTERPRETA-
TION OF THE TABULAR SYSTEM

1. ONCE we had laid it down that the variables of the system considered in the last chapter were statement-variables, and had given the meaning we did give to the apparatus of columns and lines, T's and F's, then the only kind of logical rules we could use the tabular apparatus to establish were rules of the truth-functional system. But this is not to say that we could not find another interpretation altogether for the symbolic apparatus of the system. This possibility I wish now to illustrate. First, one must remember that the system could be regarded as purely abstract, and detached from any interpretation whatever. Its use could be taught as a kind of exercise, to be carried out with characters to which no meaning was attached. Before looking for an alternative interpretation, let us see how this could be done. We might draw up a set of rules, beginning as follows :

(1) The signs to be used in the exercise are : (i) the small letters ' p ', ' q ', ' r ', &c.; (ii) the capital letters ' T ' and ' F '; (iii) the signs ' $\sim$ ', ' $.$ ', ' $\vee$ ', ' $\supset$ ', ' $\equiv$ '; and (iv) brackets.

(2) Certain combinations of these signs are called ' expressions '. Any small letter preceded by ' $\sim$ ' is an expression. A combination consisting of any small letter followed by any other sign of group (iii) followed by another small letter is an expression. Further, any expression bracketed and preceded by ' $\sim$ ' forms an expression; and any combination consisting of a small letter or bracketed expression followed by any other sign of group (iii) followed by a small letter or bracketed expression is itself an expression.

(3) Every expression has a *T-or-F set*, determinable in accordance with certain rules, and is either an *all-T* expression or an *all-F* expression or a *mixed* expression. The

object of the exercise is to discover which of these classes any given expression belongs to; and the right answer is the one which results from the correct application of the following rules. . . .

And so, it is obvious, one could continue; introducing at this point tables involving the letters ' T ' and ' F ', and giving rules, all the while mentioning only letters and signs, for determining the ' T-or-F sets ' (i.e., what, in the truth-functional interpretation, we called 'truth-conditions') of any expression. Where the T-or-F set of an expression consisted of a column of T's, we could rule that it was to be called an ' all-T ' expression, and accorded a special place; and so on. We could then set exercises in determining to which class given expressions belonged, and could mark the answers ' right ' or ' wrong '. And we could do all this without giving any interpretation to the signs of the system whatever; just as one could, perhaps, teach someone how to do multiplication sums without teaching him the use of numerals in counting things.

2. In seeking an alternative interpretation for the system, then, we are seeking another way of giving meaning to its signs and operations such that we can use the tables to establish logical rules of another kind. In suggesting another interpretation, I shall in fact use different signs. But this is simply a convenience, designed partly to avoid confusion, partly to conform to standard practice. I could equally well use the signs with which we are already familiar; but they are customarily appropriated to the interpretation we have so far been considering. The important point is that there should be an exact correspondence, as far as the rules of combination and the rules governing the use of the tables are concerned, between the signs with which we are already familiar and those which I propose now to introduce.

The variables ' *p* ', ' *q* ', ' *r* ', &c., I shall replace by the Greek letters ' α ', ' β ', ' γ ', &c. They are to take as values, not clauses which could appear as complete sentences, but *class-expressions*. By a class-expression, I mean, roughly, a noun, or noun-phrase, in the plural. E.g., the expressions ' red things ', ' people who live in glass houses ', ' fathers ' are all to count as class-expressions. As an alternative explanation, we may say that any expression which could significantly replace the second variable in the formula ' x is a member of the class of α ' is a class-expression. An expression can significantly replace the second variable in this formula if the resulting formula, e.g., ' x is a member of the class of people who live in glass houses ', is one from which some significant sentence could be framed by making a substitution of a word or phrase for the variable ' x '. Such sentences we shall call class-membership sentences, and statements made by their use class-membership statements. These sentences would, of course, be unnecessarily cumbersome, and we should rarely use them in ordinary speech. But if we did come across such a sentence, we should normally have no difficulty in producing a standard English sentence which we should be inclined to say had the same meaning. And conversely there are many standard English sentences which we could paraphrase in this cumbersome way. E.g., ' John is a father ', ' John lives in a glass house ', ' It is red ' could all be rendered by the use of the phrase ' is a member of the class of ' together with one or another of the class-expressions I listed above. The phrase ' is a member of the class of ' (or, an occasional variant, ' belongs to the class of ') is sometimes represented by the letter ' ε ', which is, accordingly, a constant and not a variable. (But ' ε ' is not one of the constants which belongs to the tabular system in its alternative interpretation. We are to use it, not to replace any of the truth-functional constants within the system, but only in the explanatory and interpretational remarks about the system.) We can now write the class-membership sentences we have just been considering as

John ε fathers
John ε people who live in glass houses
It ε red things

and the formula they all exemplify as

$$x\varepsilon\alpha.$$

It will be evident that once a value has been given to one of the variables in this formula, the range of possible values of the other is likely to be restricted.[1]

As constants of the tabular system in its new interpretation, we shall replace ' $\sim$ ' by ' $-$ ', ' v ' by ' $+$ ', ' . ' by ' $\times$ ',

---

[1] See Chapter 2, Section 5.

'⊃' by '∗', and '≡' by '∗∗'. Allowing for these replacements, the formation-rules are, of course, unchanged; and we are thereby authorized to frame formulae like 'α + β', '— (α × β)', '— (α × — β)', 'α ∗∗ β', and so on. These formulae will differ from truth-functional formulae, however, from the interpretational point of view. The meaning now to be given to the constants is such that when the variables in these formulae are replaced by class-expressions, the resulting expressions are themselves to count as class-expressions and not, as in the truth-functional interpretation, as sentences. This widens our conception of a formula. We have so far considered formulae as expressions containing constants and variables of which it is true that when the variables are replaced by words or phrases, a sentence is obtained. We have now to consider formulae where the replacement of the variables by words or phrases of the appropriate kind yields class-expressions, which we may call *compound* class-expressions (e.g., 'fathers × people who live in glass houses') in contrast with unitary class-expressions like 'fathers'. The formulae which they exemplify we may call class formulae. The unitary class-expressions occurring in a compound class-expression we shall call its constituent class-expressions.

Expressions analogous to compound class-expressions often occur in ordinary speech. That is to say, we often combine plural nouns with other nouns or adjectives or relative clauses, to form noun-phrases which are themselves class-expressions. For this purpose we often simply juxtapose the combined expressions (e.g., 'women lunatics', 'red carpets', 'fathers who neglect their children'), and sometimes join them by the use of conjunctions like 'and' and 'or' (e.g., 'cabbages and kings', 'doctors or lawyers', 'fishermen and people who play games'). Although we never, of course, employ for this purpose the constants I have just introduced, the devices we do employ can be used to illustrate informally the meanings given to some of those constants. Thus, when we speak of *women lunatics*, we commonly mean those people each of whom is both a woman and a lunatic; when we speak of *women and lunatics* (as being, say at one time ineligible for the vote) we commonly mean those people each one of whom is either a woman or a lunatic or both. The first expression, so understood, has the same meaning as the class-expression ' women × lunatics '; the second expression, so understood, has the same meaning as the class-expression ' women + lunatics '. The formulae they respectively exemplify are called the logical product formula (' α × β ' or, as it is sometimes written, ' αβ ') and the logical sum formula (' α + β '). The logical sum of two classes is generally wider than, and includes, their logical product.

We also, in ordinary speech, commonly use class-expressions which incorporate the word ' not ' or some equivalent device. E.g., we may talk of ' people who do not play bridge '. This phrase has the same meaning as the compound class-expression ' — people who play bridge ', which exemplifies the formula ' — α '. The latter we shall call the complementary formula; and shall speak of the class of those things or persons which do not belong to a given class as the complement of the given class. We are now in a position to see, roughly, how class-expressions of greater complexity, which embody just these three constants, are to be interpreted. Thus, the class-expression ' (lawyers + doctors) × — those who play bridge ' will have the same meaning as the ordinary English phrase ' lawyers or doctors, who do not play bridge '. This example enables us to see, in a rough-and-ready way, how conventions of scope are no less essential for this interpretation than for the truth-functional. If we eliminate the brackets in the above class-expression, we obtain ' lawyers + doctors × — those who play bridge ', where, by the formation-rules, the constant of widest scope is now ' + ' instead of ' × '. In ordinary English, where the distinction is marked less unambiguously in writing than in speech, this becomes ' lawyers, or doctors who don't play bridge '; and the class of persons referred to is obviously not identical with that referred to by the previous expression, though they will have some members in common. The formulae exemplified by the two class-expressions are, respectively, ' (α + β) × — γ ' and ' α + β × — γ '.

A rather less informal interpretation (or explanation of the meaning) of these constants may be given by means of the following definitions[1] :

---

[1] Brackets as used in these definitions are, of course, not strictly necessary. Their removal would lead to no ambiguity. They are inserted only for convenience and ease of reading, and will be omitted when they seem unnecessary for this purpose.

$$' x\varepsilon(\alpha \times \beta) ' =_{Df} ' x\varepsilon\alpha \cdot x\varepsilon\beta '$$
$$' x\varepsilon(\alpha + \beta) ' =_{Df} ' x\varepsilon\alpha \vee x\varepsilon\beta '$$
$$' x\varepsilon - \alpha ' =_{Df} ' \sim(x\varepsilon\alpha) '.$$

The meaning of the remaining two constants can now be given, either in terms of those already defined :

$$' x\varepsilon(\alpha * \beta) ' =_{Df} ' x\varepsilon - (\alpha \times - \beta) '$$
$$' x\varepsilon(\alpha ** \beta) ' =_{Df} ' x\varepsilon[(\alpha * \beta) \times (\beta * \alpha)] ' \ ' [1]$$

or, alternatively, as follows :

$$' x\varepsilon(\alpha * \beta) ' =_{Df} ' x\varepsilon\alpha \supset x\varepsilon\beta '$$
$$' x\varepsilon(\alpha ** \beta) ' =_{Df} ' x\varepsilon\alpha \equiv x\varepsilon\beta '.$$

There are no simple expressions or types of combination in ordinary speech which correspond to the symbols ' * ' and ' ** ' in the interpretations we have just given. And the reason is obvious when we consider what these interpretations are. The expression ' women ** lunatics ' would mean, roughly, ' those who are either both women and lunatics or neither women nor lunatics '; and the expression ' women * lunatics ' would mean roughly ' those of whom it is not true to say that they are women but not lunatics '. To classes described in such a way we rarely have occasion to refer.

3. As a preliminary to seeing how the tabular method can be used to establish logical rules about class formulae, we must consider certain types of statement which might be made by the use of sentences incorporating class-expressions. That is to say, we must consider certain types of *statement*-formulae incorporating class-expression variables. Let us call these class-statement formulae.

(1) *The class-membership formula.* One type of class-statement formula has already been mentioned. This is the class-membership formula, ' $x\varepsilon\alpha$ ', exemplified by such more complex formulae as ' $x\varepsilon\alpha + \beta$ ', ' $x\varepsilon\alpha ** \beta$ ', &c., and by such sentences as ' John ε people who live in glass houses $\times$ people who throw stones '.

---

[1] An obvious and expected feature of these last two definitions is their analogy to : ' " $p \supset q$ " $=_{Df}$ " $\sim(p \cdot \sim q)$ " ' and ' " $p \equiv q$ " $=_{Df}$ " $(p \supset q) \cdot (q \supset p)$ " '.

(2) *Existential formulae.* Consider the class-expression 'red things × unicorns' or, in English, 'red unicorns'. There are no such things. We could say, in English : There is nothing to which the phrase 'red unicorn' applies; or we could say : There aren't any red unicorns. Let us bear in mind both these ways of saying this. In the language of class-expressions we invent ways of saying it, parallel to both these. First, we might say it, quoting the class-expression, in one of these ways : The class-expression 'red things × unicorns' has no application; or, The class-expression 'red things × unicorns' has zero extension; or, The class-expression 'red things × unicorns' is empty (or null). Alternatively, we might say it, not quoting, but employing, the class-expression, in one of these ways : *There is nothing which is a member of the class of* red things × unicorns; or, *The class of* red things × unicorns *is empty* (*is null, has no members*). Let us abbreviate this second set of ways of saying it to :

$$\text{red things} \times \text{unicorns} = 0$$

where the expression ' $= 0$ ' is a constant, and an abbreviation of any of the expressions italicized above. Then the sentence ' red things × unicorns $= 0$ ' exemplifies the *negatively existential* formula ' $\alpha\beta = 0$ ', and therefore, of course, the negatively existential formula ' $\alpha = 0$ '.

Suppose someone wishes to contradict the assertion that there are no red unicorns. He might say : ' There *are* some, you know.' But in saying this, he is committing himself to more than he need; for ' some ' implies ' more than one ', and it is enough, for the purpose of truthfully contradicting the negatively existential statement, that he should be able truthfully to say that there was one. He might say : ' There is in fact just one red unicorn.' But in saying this, he is again committing himself to more than he need; for what he says this time is false if there are several red unicorns, but he may truthfully contradict the negatively existential assertion if there are several. He incurs the minimum risk of falsity, consistently with fulfilling his purpose of contradicting the negatively existential statement, by saying, ' There is at least one red unicorn '. The contradictory of the negatively existential formula ' $\alpha = 0$ ' is the formula ' $\alpha \neq 0$ '; and this is, accordingly, to be interpreted :

' There is at least one member of the class of α ' or ' The class of α is not empty (not null) '.

Compare the formula ' $\alpha \neq 0$ ' with the formula ' $- \alpha = 0$ '. They are very different. The former is used for the assertion, the latter for the denial, of the existence of at least one thing of a certain class. The latter is to be read : ' There is nothing which is a member of the class of $- \alpha$ ', which, in accordance with earlier instructions, may be expanded into ' There is nothing which is a member of the class of things or persons which are not members of α ' and contracted again into ' There is nothing which is not a member of the class of α '. It is tempting to construe this as meaning the same as ' Everything is a member of the class of α '; and, in consequence, to give the meaning ' Everything is a member of the class of . . .' to a new constant, viz., ' $= 1$ ', which is introduced at this stage and may be defined as follows :

$$\text{' } \alpha = 1 \text{ ' } =_{Df} \text{ ' } - \alpha = 0 \text{ ' } \quad \text{and} \quad \text{' } - \alpha = 1 \text{ ' } =_{Df} \text{ ' } \alpha = 0 \text{ '}$$

This reading of ' $= 1$ ' as ' Everything is a member of the class of . . .' is harmless, and useful, if strictly adhered to. But, if carelessly handled, the use of ' every ' may lead, as we shall see, to mistakes in interpretation; and it is a safeguard against these to practise the negatively existential reading of which the right-hand side of the definitions reminds us. The contradictories of formulae exemplifying ' $\alpha = 1$ ' are framed, as are the contradictories of formulae exemplifying ' $\alpha = 0$ '; that is, by cancelling the equation-sign. As before, we shall obtain a formula, sentences exemplifying which are used to assert the existence of at least one member of a certain class.

(3) *Class-inclusion and class-identity formulae.* There is a certain negatively existential formula which is of special interest, since two further constants occurring in class-statement formulae can be defined in terms of it. This is the formula ' $\alpha \times - \beta = 0$ '. A useful convention to adopt in some cases is that of writing the ' $-.$ ' sign above the whole of the remainder of the expressions which make up its scope instead of before them; which yields, for the above formula, the conveniently abbreviated form ' $\alpha \bar{\beta} = 0$ '. In terms of this, the class-inclusion formula, ' $\alpha \subset \beta$ ', is defined as follows :

$$\text{' } \alpha \subset \beta \text{ ' } =_{Df} \text{ ' } \alpha \bar{\beta} = 0 \text{ '}$$

and then the class-identity formula, ' $\alpha = \beta$ ', as follows :

$$' \alpha = \beta ' =_{Df} ' \alpha \subset \beta . \beta \subset \alpha ' ^{1}$$

To be clear about the interpretation of the new class-statement formulae, and to be prepared to resist certain too readily canvassed identifications of these and other formulae with certain common forms of ordinary speech, we must refine a little on the interpretation given to ' $= 0$ ', especially when this appears after a logical product class formula. The interpretation we have already given is such as to induce us to read ' $\alpha\beta = 0$ ' as ' There is nothing which is a member of the class of $\alpha\beta$ '. The refinement on which we have to insist is that this is to be so understood that ' There is nothing which is a member of the class of α ' and ' There is nothing which is a member of the class of β ' are equally, and independently, sufficient, though not necessary, conditions of the truth of ' There is nothing which is a member of the class of $\alpha\beta$ '.[2]

It is particularly important to stress this fact, because ' $\alpha\beta = 0$ ' is sometimes said to have the same meaning as ' No α are β ' (or ' None of the α are β ') and ' $\alpha\bar\beta = 0$ ' (or ' $\alpha \subset \beta$ ') to have the same meaning as ' All α are β '. We should scarcely regard it as a sufficient condition of a statement made in the words ' All the men at the party wore tail-coats ', that there weren't any men there, only women ; nor should we be inclined to regard this as a sufficient condition of the truth of the statement that none of the men at the party wore tail-coats. We should be more inclined to regard it as incompatible with the truth of either statement. But ' men at the party $= 0$ ' is a sufficient condition of the truth both of ' men at the party $\times$ those wearing tail-coats $= 0$ ' and of ' men at the party $\times -$ those wearing tail-coats $= 0$ '. It is, on the other hand, obviously true that the statement that all the men at the party wore tail-coats logically implies the statement that the class of men at the party not wearing tail-coats was empty. ' All α are β '

---

[1] Alternative defining expressions would be :
    for ' $a \subset \beta$ ' either ' $a * \beta = 1$ ' or ' $- (a * \beta) = 0$ '
    for ' $a = \beta$ ' either ' $a ** \beta = 1$ ' or ' $- (a ** \beta) = 0$ '.

[2] That is to say, a statement of the form ' $a\beta = 0$ ' is entailed by the corresponding statement of the form ' $a = 0$ ', and also by the corresponding statement of the form ' $\beta = 0$ '; but does not entail either of these statements.

entails ' $\alpha \subset \beta$ ', but is not entailed by it. This situation is reminiscent of some of the claims to identity of meaning between truth-functional constants and ordinary words which we discussed in the last chapter. I shall say more about this question later. We may also note now, however, that there is the same unplausibility about the identification of ' $\alpha = \beta$ ' with ' All α are β and all β are α '.

4. In order to make good the claim that the tabular system for which we have already described the truth-functional interpretation can be given an alternative interpretation in terms of class formulae, we shall have to show that the tabular method can be used, in an exactly parallel way, to establish logical rules about class formulae. We might expect our results to take the form of showing that some class-statement formulae were analytic. But there seems to be an obvious difficulty about doing this; and that is that none of the constants we introduced in order to make possible the framing of class-*statement* formulae (as opposed to class formulae) figured in our original list of the constants which were to embody the re-interpretation of the truth-functional constants. That list included ' $-$ ', ' $\times$ ', ' $+$ ', ' $*$ ', and ' $**$ '; but not ' ε ', ' $=$ ', ' $\subset$ ', ' $\neq$ ', ' $= 0$ ', and ' $= 1$ '. We should obviously be abandoning the claim to use the same abstract system of rules, if we incorporated in the machinery of proof any symbols which were not the strict counterparts of those used for the propositional interpretation.

We may note, however, that all the class-statement formulae we have discussed, with the exception of class-membership formulae, can be expressed *either* as equations to ' 0 ' of some class formula (or, which comes to the same thing, as the equation to ' 1 ' of the complement of that class formula) *or* as the denials of such equations. Now to say that a statement-formula in which some class formula was equated to ' 0 ' was analytic would be to say that, as a matter of logical necessity, a class-expression exemplifying that formula would be empty or null; that it would be logically impossible for such a class-expression to apply to anything. We might express this by saying that the class formula in question was self-contradictory, or *logically null*. Similarly, to show that the statement-formula in which the complement of a given class formula was equated to ' 1 ' was analytic, would also be to show that the class formula was logically null. We might say that the complementary formula of that class formula would be thereby shown to be *logically comprehensive*. So our problem can be re-stated in the form : Is it possible to use the tabular method to determine whether class formulae are logically null, logically comprehensive, or neither ? If so, the rules for determining this must be exactly parallel to the rules for determining whether truth-functional formulae are self-contradictory, analytic, or contingent.

It is in fact perfectly possible to use the tabular method to determine the status of a class formula in a way exactly parallel to that in which it is used to determine the status of a truth-functional formula. This is a consequence of the parallelism between the meanings given to the constants of the two interpretations. The truth-value of a truth-functional statement is entirely determined by the truth-values of its constituent statements. One might say : the 'membership-value' of a compound class-expression is entirely determined by the membership-values of its constituent class-expressions.

Let me begin by giving a meaning to the phrase ' extension of a class-expression '. This I shall do informally by means of an illustration : the extension of the class-expression ' green things ' is the whole set of things of which it would be true to say that they are green. Then I shall explain the ' exclusion ' of this class-expression as the whole set of things of which it would be true to say that they are not green. (The exclusion of a class-expression is the extension of its complement; but we may not use this as a definition if we wish to avoid circularity in what follows.) Then I shall define the ' universe of discourse' of a class-expression as the whole set of things comprising both its extension and its exclusion. Let us first note what this definition excludes from the universe of discourse of a class-expression. First, and most obviously, it excludes all those things which do not belong to the range of possible values of the variable in the formula framed by writing ' x ' followed by ' ε ' followed by the class-expression. If the class-expression in question is ' green things ', all those things of which it does not make literal sense to say that they are or are not green are excluded from the universe of discourse of the class-expression. Second, it excludes (is to be taken as excluding) from the universe of discourse all the border-line cases.   In the case of our example, it excludes from the universe of discourse of the class-expression ' green things ' all those things of which, while it would make sense to say that they were green, it would not be definitely true to say that they were green and would not be definitely true to say that they were not green.   There belong to the universe of discourse only those things of which one of these assertions would be definitely true.   This restriction of our attention to these two classes is analogous to the restriction of our attention, in determining the meaning to be given to truth-functional constants, to the cases of statements which definitely have one of the two truth-values, truth or falsity.

Thus the universe of discourse of a single class-expression is divided into two mutually exclusive and jointly exhaustive classes or sets of things : the extension and the exclusion of the class-expression.   Let us now speak of the universe of discourse of a pair of class-expressions, and define it as the set of things which belong either to the extension or to the exclusion of each of the two class-expressions; i.e., as the set of things which belong to the universes of discourse of both class-expressions. Evidently, the universe of discourse of a pair of class-expressions is divided into four mutually exclusive and jointly exhaustive classes : namely, the set of things which belong to the extensions of both class-expressions; the set of things which belong to the extension of the first, but not to the extension of the second; the set of things which belong to the extension of the second, but not to that of the first; and the set of things which belong to the extensions of neither, i.e., which belong to the exclusions of both.   For a trio of class-expressions there will be eight subdivisions of the universe of discourse; and, in general, for n class-expressions, the universe of discourse will have 2^n subdivisions.

Now we give a certain kind of meaning to the constants belonging to the system.   We give them all a meaning such that the answer to the question of whether something which belongs to the universe of discourse of a compound class-expression is a member of its extension or its exclusion (and it must be one or the other) is entirely determined, once the thing's membership of the extensions or exclusions of the constituent class-expressions is given.   Suppose we have a compound class-expression, say of the form ' α × β '. Then each thing belonging to the universe of discourse of the compound class-expression must belong to one only, and may belong to any one, of the four subdivisions of that universe of discourse. The rules which show, for each of these four subdivisions, whether a thing's membership of that subdivision makes it a member of the extension or of the exclusion of the compound class-expression, entirely exhaust the meaning of the constant ' × '. And so for the other constants.

These rules can be given in a schematic form which is strictly parallel to the schematic form of the truth tables. Suppose once again we have a class-expression of the form ' α × β '. Let us represent its universe of discourse by a circular figure, and the four subdivisions of that universe by a quartering of

the circle. Let us indicate the subdivision consisting of those things, if any, which are members of the extensions of both constituent class-expressions by writing 'MM' in the top left-hand quarter; the subdivision consisting of those things, if any, which are members of the extension of the first constituent class-expression, but not of that of the second, by writing 'MN' in the top right-hand quarter; the subdivision consisting of those things, if any, which are members of the extension of the second, but not of that of the first, constituent class-expression, by writing 'NM' in the quarter underneath this; and the subdivision consisting of those things, if any, which are members of the extensions of neither constituent class-expression by writing 'NN' in the remaining quarter. Then we may give the meaning of the constant ' × ' by the rule that all those things, if any, which are members of the MM subdivision are members of the extension of the compound class-expression, and all the other members of its universe of discourse are not members of its extension, i.e., are members of its exclusion. Similarly, we can define the logical sum of two class-expressions as the class-expression whose extension comprises all the members of its universe of discourse except those, if any, which belong to the NN subdivision; the latter will belong to its exclusion. And so on. It is obvious that we may represent these rules in the familiar tabular form, with the difference that the columns, instead of exhibiting (i) possible combinations of truth-values of constituent statements of a given type of statement and (ii) the effect of each of these upon the truth-value of the statement as a whole, will exhibit (i) subdivisions of the universe of discourse of a given type of class-expression and (ii) the effect of membership of each of these upon membership of the extension of the class-expression in question.

Thus we shall have table (1) as below :

α	— α
M	N
N	M

and table (2) as below

α β	(a) α × β	(b) α + β	(c) α * β	(d) α ** β
M M	M	M	M	M
M N	N	M	N	N
N M	N	M	M	N
N N	N	N	M	M

How these patterns are to be read I have already indicated. They are just summary representations of the preceding remarks, of rules including those there given and others of the same sort. In the columns under the compound formulae, a letter ' M ' shows that the members of the corresponding [1] subdivision of the universe of discourse are members of the extension of the compound class-expression of that form; and an ' N ' shows that the members of the corresponding subdivision of the universe are members of the exclusion of the compound class-expression. We can, obviously, as in the case of the truth-tables, use the patterns as rules for obtaining columns of M's and N's for far more complicated formulae containing the same constants. For instance, the ' membership conditions ' for the formula ' — (α × β) ' are given, by the application of the rule of table (1) to column (2a), in the column

---

[1] I.e., the subdivision indicated by the pair of letters in the left-hand column in the same row.

(e) below; and the column for ' $-(\alpha \times -\beta)$ ' is given next to it. We may note, for later reference, that the column for this last formula is identical with that given above for ' $\alpha * \beta$ '. (Where more than one column appears beneath a complex class formula, the resultant column for the whole formula is, of course, that which appears beneath the constant of widest scope. The other columns represent intermediate stages in the application of the rules.)

α β	(e) $-(\alpha \times \beta)$	(f) $-(\alpha \times -\beta)$		
M M	N	M	MN	N
M N	M	N	MM	M
N M	M	M	NN	N
N N	M	M	NN	M

Now let us consider some cases where the application of these rules yields, for some complex formula, a column consisting entirely either of M's or of N's. We select the formulae ' $(\alpha\beta) \times -(\alpha + \beta)$ ', ' $-[(\alpha\beta) \times -(\alpha + \beta)]$ ', and ' $\alpha\beta * \alpha + \beta$ '. For these we obtain the following results :

α β	(g) $(\alpha\beta) \times -(\alpha + \beta)$				(h) $-[(\alpha\beta) \times -(\alpha + \beta)]$	(j) $\alpha\beta * \alpha + \beta$		
M M	M	N	N	M	M	M	M	M
M N	N	N	N	M	M	N	M	M
N M	N	N	N	M	M	N	M	M
N N	N	N	M	N	M	N	M	N

How are we to interpret these results? Consider, first, the result for the formula of column (g). Now the column on the extreme left of the tables depicts the entire universe of discourse of a class-expression exemplifying the formula in question, in its four mutually exclusive and jointly exhaustive subdivisions. But the resultant column of N's for (g) excludes the membership of each of these four subdivisions from membership of the extension of any class-expression exemplifying the formula of (g). That is, nothing belonging to the universe of discourse of such a class-expression can belong to its extension. That is, nothing at all can belong to its extension; and this is a consequence of the meaning given to the constants concerned. That is, the class formula ' $(\alpha\beta) \times - (\alpha + \beta)$ ' is logically null, or logically empty or self-contradictory. We have already at our disposal an alternative way of expressing this result; to say that the class formula is logically null is the same as to say that the class-statement formula framed by equating the class formula to 0 is logically necessary (or analytic). Thus we have :

$$\text{' } (\alpha\beta) \times - (\alpha + \beta) = 0 \text{ ' is analytic.}$$

The formula of column (h) is the complement of the formula of column (g). The application of the rule of table (1) yields for it a column consisting entirely of M's. The way to interpret the result is obvious. Every member of each of the jointly exhaustive subdivisions of the universe of discourse of a class-expression of this form belongs to the extension of that class-expression. That is, every member of its universe of discourse belongs to its extension. Thus we have :

$$\text{' } - [(\alpha\beta) \times - (\alpha + \beta)] \text{ ' is logically comprehensive}$$

which we may otherwise express in the form :

$$\text{' } - [(\alpha\beta) \times - (\alpha + \beta)] = 1 \text{ ' is analytic.}$$

Similarly for (j) we have the result that

$$\text{' } \alpha\beta * \alpha + \beta \text{ ' is logically comprehensive}$$

or

$$\text{' } \alpha\beta * \alpha + \beta = 1 \text{ ' is analytic.}$$

Next we may note that, as in the case of the truth-functional interpretation, we may obtain the same results in a superficially different way. Suppose we compare the columns $(2a)$ and $(2b)$, i.e., the columns for the formulae ' $\alpha\beta$ ' and ' $\alpha + \beta$ '. We note that there is no one of the four subdivisions of the universe of discourse of which any member belongs to the extension of a class-expression of the form ' $\alpha\beta$ ' but does not belong to the extension of the corresponding class-expression of the form ' $\alpha + \beta$ '. In other words, there is, as a matter of logical necessity, nothing which is a member of the extension of a class-expression of the first form and not a member of the extension of the corresponding class-expression of the second form. We have at our disposal different ways of expressing this. One is by declaring the class-inclusion formula '$\alpha\beta \subset \alpha + \beta$' to be analytic; another is, again, by declaring the negatively existential formula '$\alpha\beta \times - (\alpha + \beta) = 0$' to be analytic.

Now compare the columns for '$\alpha * \beta$' and '$-(\alpha \times - \beta)$'; i.e., column 2(c) and column (f). We observe that the arrangement of M's and N's is the same. This result we may interpret as follows. It is logically impossible for anything to be a member of the extension of a class-expression exemplifying the first formula and not a member of the extension of the corresponding class-expression exemplifying the second formula; and vice versa. That is to say, there is, as a matter of logical necessity, nothing which is a member of either one extension and not of the other. But that is to say: the formula '$\alpha * \beta = - (\alpha \times - \beta)$' is analytic.

In these ways, we can use the tabular mechanism to establish as analytic, class-statement formulae of the negatively existential kind and, in particular, those special cases of such formulae which are class-inclusion and class-identity formulae. Two things in particular are worth noticing. They are : (i) that wherever, by the application of the rules, we obtain a column of M's under a complex class formula of the form '$\alpha * \beta$', we thereby establish, as analytic, the corresponding class-statement formula of the form '$\alpha \subset \beta$'; and (ii) that wherever, by the application of the rules, we obtain a column of M's under a complex class formula of the form '$\alpha ** \beta$', we thereby establish as analytic the corresponding class-statement formula of the form '$\alpha = \beta$'. For to say that the column for a class-expression of the form '$\alpha * \beta$' consists entirely of M's is to say that there can be no member of its universe of discourse which is not a member of its extension, i.e., that there is, as a matter of logical necessity, nothing which is a member of the extension of the first of its constituent class-expressions and not a member of the extension of the second; and to say this is just to say that the corresponding class-sentence of the form '$\alpha \subset \beta$' is logically necessary. Similarly, to say that a class-expression of the form '$\alpha ** \beta$' is logically comprehensive is to say that every member of its universe of discourse must logically be either a member of the extensions of both its constituent class-expressions or a member of the extension of neither; and to say this is just to say that the corresponding class-sentence of the form ' α = β ' is logically necessary.

5. The tabular method, then, can be used for establishing logical rules about class formulae. And the symbol-for-symbol, rule-for-rule correspondence between this use of the tables and the truth-functional use is exact. That is to say, if we take any correctly worked-out table of the truth-functional system and substitute ' M ' for ' T ', ' N ' for ' F ', ' × ' for ' . ', ' — ' for ' ~ ', ' + ' for ' v ', ' * ' for ' ⊃ ', ' ** ' for ' ≡ ', and ' α ', ' β ', ' γ ' for ' p ', ' q ', ' r ' throughout, we shall obtain a correctly worked out table of the class system. The use of the two different sets of symbols is, from the point of view of the mechanism of the system, unnecessary. We could use the same set of symbols, apply the same *abstract* rules (i.e., rules mentioning only letters and signs), and read or interpret the results in two different ways. In the class-interpretation we shall express our results (in the first instance) by declaring formulae logically null or logically comprehensive where, in the truth-functional interpretation, we express our results by declaring formulae self-contradictory or logically necessary.

In many cases we may find parallels between the rules for class formulae established in this way, and the behaviour of class-expressions in ordinary speech. For instance, the class formulae ' αβ ** βα ' and ' α(β + γ) ** αβ + αγ ' are found, if checked by the tables, to be logically comprehensive. This result we can otherwise express by declaring analytic the class-statement formulae

$$\alpha\beta = \beta\alpha$$
$$\alpha(\beta + \gamma) = \alpha\beta + \alpha\gamma.$$

The first class-identity has its rough counterpart in ordinary speech in the identity of the extensions of such expressions as ' red-haired barristers ' and ' barristers with red hair ', ' card-playing women ' and ' women card-players '; i.e., in the frequent logical indifference of the order of plural nouns and their qualifying phrases. For the second we find such correspondences as the absence of logical distinction between, e.g., ' Scotsmen who are lawyers or scientists ' and ' Scottish lawyers and Scottish scientists '.

Every declaration that a class-inclusion or class-identity

5

formula is analytic can be re-expressed as an entailment or logical equivalence between class-membership formulae. For to say that two class formulae are analytically identical is to say that membership of the extension of a class-expression exemplifying either of the formulae logically necessitates membership of the extension of the corresponding class-expression exemplifying the other. For example,

$$\text{`} \alpha(\beta + \gamma) = \alpha\beta + \alpha\gamma \text{' is analytic}$$

can be re-expressed as

$$\text{`} x\varepsilon\alpha(\beta + \gamma) \text{' is logically equivalent to `} x\varepsilon(\alpha\beta + \alpha\gamma) \text{'.}$$

Similarly, the declaration that a class-inclusion formula is analytic is equivalent to the declaration that membership of the extension of a class-expression exemplifying the first subordinate formula necessitates membership of the extension of the corresponding class-expression exemplifying the second subordinate formula. Thus from

$$\text{`} \alpha\beta \subset \alpha + \beta \text{' is analytic}$$

we have

$$\text{`} x\varepsilon\alpha\beta \text{' entails `} x\varepsilon(\alpha + \beta) \text{'.}$$

Such entailments and equivalences can then be re-expressed as declarations that certain truth-functional formulae incorporating class-membership formulae are analytic. Thus we have

$$\text{`} x\varepsilon\alpha(\beta + \gamma) \equiv x\varepsilon(\alpha\beta + \alpha\gamma) \text{' is analytic}$$

and

$$\text{`} x\varepsilon\alpha\beta \supset x\varepsilon(\alpha + \beta) \text{' is analytic.}$$

6. This last way of expressing our results calls attention to a considerable limitation of this entire method of developing a logical system for class formulae and class-statement formulae. The constants we have been using in the exposition of the system are of two kinds. We may call them A-constants and B-constants. A-constants comprise all those which actually occur in the tables themselves, where they obey the same abstract rules as the truth-functional constants. That is, they consist of `$-$', `$+$', `$\times$', `$*$' and `$**$'. They are used to frame class formulae and, unless supplemented by other constants,

can be used to frame only class formulae. B-constants do not occur in the tables, but only in the expressing of the results obtained from the tables. They comprise those constants at least one of which must be used to frame a class-statement formula. That is, they consist of ' $\subset$ ', ' $=$ ', ' $= 0$ ', ' $= 1$ ' and ' ε '. So long as the only constants we make use of are class constants (i.e., A- and B-constants), all the interpretable formulae we can frame containing a B-constant must contain only one B-constant, and that as the main constant of the formula. We cannot, for example, attach a meaning to ' $(\alpha \subset \beta) \subset (\gamma \subset \delta)$ ', nor to ' $(\alpha \subset \beta) + \gamma$ '. The former, since its main constant is ' $\subset$ ', purports to be a class-statement formula; the latter, since its main constant is ' $+$ ', purports to be a class formula. The latter is ruled out as meaningless straight away by the formation rules for class formulae. For only class formulae or class variables can be joined by A-constants to form further class formulae; and ' $\alpha \subset \beta$ ' is not a class for-mula, but a class-statement formula. As for the former, if we try to interpret it, we have, first : ' There is nothing which is a member of the class of $\alpha \subset \beta$ and not a member of the class of $\gamma \subset \delta$ '; and then, if we try to expand this further : ' There is nothing which is a member of the class of there is nothing which is a member of the class . . .' &c., which is nonsense. Only a class-expression or a class formula can follow the words ' is a member of the class of '. So long as we confine our atten-tion, then, to formulae which can be framed by the use of no other constants than A- and B-constants, we can (with the exception of those whose one B-constant is ' ε ') always deter-mine their logical status by reference to the tables. For the question of their logical status can always, in the case of class-statement formulae, be transformed into the question of whether some class formula is logically null, logically comprehensive, or neither; and, in the case of class formulae, already is that question.

The way of expressing our results adopted at the end of the last section, however, suggests that we may allow ourselves to supplement our A- and B-constants with the constants of the truth-functional system. If we do this, we can frame formulae which are perfectly interpretable, though containing more than one B-constant, and the logical status of which will not (in general) be determinable by the use of the tabular method as we have so far described it. For example, the following formulae

(1) $\alpha \subset \beta \supset \bar{\beta} \subset \bar{\alpha}$

(2) $\alpha \subset \beta \, . \, \beta \subset \gamma \supset \alpha \subset \gamma$

(3) $\alpha = 0 \supset \alpha \subset \beta$

(4) $\alpha \subset \beta \, . \, \beta = 0 \supset \alpha = 0$

are interpretable; but the tabular method, as so far described, gives us no means of deciding what logical status to accord to them. To decide that they were analytic would be deciding that the formula on the left-hand side of the '$\supset$' sign entailed the formula on the right-hand side in each case. But at present the only entailments between statement-formulae incorporating class formulae which we have a method of establishing are entailments between class-membership formulae, such as those mentioned at the end of Section 5; which these are not.

Now let us compare these formulae with certain results which we can obtain by the tabular method. We can by this method establish as analytic the following class-inclusion formulae, in which all the constants are A- or B-constants:

(1.1) $\alpha * \beta \subset - \beta * - \alpha$

(2.1) $(\alpha * \beta) \times (\beta * \gamma) \subset \alpha * \gamma$

(3.1) $- \alpha \subset \alpha * \beta$

(4.1) $(\alpha * \beta) \times - \beta \subset - \alpha$

Transforming the declarations that these class-inclusion formulae are analytic into statements of entailments between class-membership formulae, we have:

(1.2) '$x\epsilon\alpha * \beta$' entails '$x\epsilon - \beta * - \alpha$'

(2.2) '$x\epsilon(\alpha * \beta) \times (\beta * \gamma)$' entails '$x\epsilon\alpha * \gamma$'

(3.2) '$x\epsilon - \alpha$' entails '$x\epsilon\alpha * \beta$'

(4.2) '$x\epsilon(\alpha * \beta) \times - \beta$' entails '$x\epsilon - \alpha$'

Making use of earlier definitions, we can express these as follows:

(1.3) 'not-$(x\epsilon\alpha\bar{\beta})$' entails 'not-$(x\epsilon\bar{\beta}\bar{\alpha})$'

(2.3) 'not-$(x\epsilon\alpha\bar{\beta})$ and not-$(x\epsilon\beta\bar{\gamma})$' entails 'not-$(x\epsilon\alpha\bar{\gamma})$'

(3.3) 'not-$(x\epsilon\alpha)$' entails 'not-$(x\epsilon\alpha\bar{\beta})$'

(4.3) 'not-$(x\epsilon\alpha\bar{\beta})$ and not-$(x\epsilon\beta)$' entails 'not-$(x\epsilon\alpha)$'

Now these are general entailments. They hold whatever values are given to the variables, provided the same substitutions are made for the same variables throughout. They hold, in particular, for all values of ' x '. Now suppose we give values to ' α ' and ' β ' in the first formula, i.e., in (1.3), which are such that whatever values we give to ' x ' in the resulting formula on the left-hand side of ' entails ', a true statement would be made by the use of the resulting sentence. Then for every case the corresponding statement made by the use of the corresponding sentence on the right-hand side of ' entails ' will be true; for it will be entailed by a true statement. But the supposition that for every value given to ' x ' in the left-hand formula a statement made by the resulting sentence is true, is the supposition that, for the selected values of ' α ' and ' β ', the statement made by the use of the sentence of the form ' $\alpha\bar{\beta} = 0$ ' or ' $\alpha \subset \beta$ ' is true. The consequence of this supposition was the truth of all statements made by the use of sentences exemplifying the right-hand formula (with the chosen values for ' α ' and ' β '). And to say that all these statements are true is to say that the statement made by the use of the corresponding sentence of the form ' $\bar{\beta}\bar{\alpha} = 0$ ' or ' $\bar{\beta} \subset \bar{\alpha}$ ' is true. These considerations apply whatever substitutions we make for ' α ' and ' β '. If those substitutions yield truths whatever substitutions we make for ' x ' in the left-hand side of the entailment (1.3), they must yield truths whatever substitutions we make for ' x ' in the right-hand side of that entailment. Hence it seems to be a logical consequence of (1.3) that

$$' \alpha \subset \beta ' \text{ entails } ' \bar{\beta} \subset \bar{\alpha} '$$

or that

$$' \alpha \subset \beta \supset \bar{\beta} \subset \bar{\alpha} ' \text{ is analytic.}$$

By similar reasoning, we can satisfy ourselves that the analyticity of each of

(2) $\alpha \subset \beta . \beta \subset \gamma \supset \alpha \subset \gamma$
(3) $\alpha = 0 \supset \alpha \subset \beta$
(4) $\alpha \subset \beta . \beta = 0 \supset \alpha = 0$

follows respectively from the entailments (2.3) to (4.3).

We may not unreasonably suppose that for all formulae of the type (1) to (4) whose logical status is not directly determinable by the tabular method, there can be framed some formula containing only A- and B-constants whose logical status can be determined by the tabular method, such that from the logical status of the latter the logical status of the former can be inferred by a process of reasoning such as that exemplified above. But this process is tortuous and complicated, far from the simplicity of the systematic ideal where the desired results are obtained by the quasi-mechanical application of just a few rules. A comparison of the analytic formulae (1) to (4) with the analytic formulae (1.1) to (4.1) does indeed show such a symbolic correspondence as to encourage the hope that it would be possible to devise a fairly simple set of rules for making the required derivations.[1] But these rules would be additional to the rules for the use of the tabular mechanism which enable us to establish that certain class formulae are null or comprehensive and hence that certain statement-formulae containing only one B-constant are analytic.

We must conclude, then, that whilst the claim to find an alternative interpretation of the tabular mechanism in class terms is vindicated, the full development of which the ' logic of classes ' seems capable cannot conveniently be directly achieved in this way. In the next chapter we shall consider an alternative method of achieving it.

---

[1] In fact, the correspondence is such as to suggest another and mechanically simpler possibility : viz., that we should adopt a set of rules which would enable us to test formulae like (1) to (4) for analyticity *directly* by means of the tables, instead of first establishing as analytic a formula containing only A- and B-constants and then deriving the desired formula from this by the use of further rules. And it is pretty clear what form such a set of rules for the direct testing of these formulae would take. First we should devise formation-rules for formulae of this kind. Then selecting *either* T's and F's *or* M's and N's, we should give identical rules for operating in the tables with ' ∼ ', ' = 0 ', and ' — '; identical rules for operating with ' ⊃ ', ' * ', and ' ⊂ '; identical rules for operating with ' + ' and ' v '; and so on. On the strength of a resultant column of T's (or M's) beneath a formula, we should declare that formula analytic. But notice that if we adopted this course, we should simply be following a hunch suggested by the symbolic parallelism we had noticed. On the purely truth-functional interpretation, or the purely class formula interpretation, the tabular rules were backed up with an explanation, were themselves, one might say, interpretable. The present suggestion would make them a mechanical expedient whose employment was justified simply by its success in yielding results held to be acceptable on independent grounds. No doubt it would be possible to represent them as ' interpretable ' rules; but the result would be likely to be clumsy.

CHAPTER 5

PREDICATIVE FORMULAE AND QUANTIFIERS

I. THE ELEMENTS OF THE PREDICATIVE SYSTEM

1. THAT it should be possible to use the same set of mechanical rules to establish the analyticity of two sets of formulae with different meanings, might at first seem surprising. One might think it mysterious that there should exist such a formal parallelism between the laws of the truth-functional system and a section of the laws of the system of classes. Or, again, one might wonder why, given that such a degree of parallelism existed, the parallel was not complete; why some of the laws of the class system can be directly established by the tabular mechanism, while others seem to require supplementary reasoning or additional rules.

I want now to show, first, that there is nothing surprising about either of these things, that both are quite natural. For those laws of the class system which can be directly established by the tabular method are, in a sense, simply special cases of the corresponding laws of the truth-functional system. And those laws of the class system which cannot be directly established in this way are not special cases of truth-functional laws, though they are closely connected with others which are. Supplementary rules are accordingly necessary to derive them from the latter. Second, I want to show how, by the adoption of a different notation for expressing what we have so far expressed in the symbolism of class-expression variables and class-constants, we can make more perspicuous the connexion between truth-functional laws and class-laws. Partly, the new notation does this by making more use of the truth-functional constants themselves and employing fewer new symbols. In the eyes of formal logicians, the new notation has other merits as well.

To illustrate the first of these points by an example. We have seen how one and the same application of the mechanism of the tables yields, for one of the two interpretations discussed, the result that the expression

$$p \cdot q \supset p \vee q$$

is an analytic formula or truth-functional law, and for the other interpretation, the result that

$$\alpha\beta * \alpha + \beta$$

is a logically comprehensive class formula. This second result can be otherwise expressed as the conclusion that the expression

$$\alpha\beta * \alpha + \beta = 1$$

is a law of the class system. An alternative formulation of the same law, as we have seen, is

$$\alpha\beta \subset \alpha + \beta.$$

If we can show that the class law is, in some sense, a special case of the truth-functional law, this will help to replace the general picture of two independent interpreted systems, miraculously having the same formal structure, by the picture of one of the systems (or, more exactly, a certain part of it) as simply a less general version of the other, having as a matter of course the same formal structure. To show this in the case of our example will be to show how the class law can be *derived* from the truth-functional law merely by the use of the principle of substitution and by reminding ourselves of the interpretation given to the symbols of the two systems. As a first step, we may substitute class-membership formulae for the statement-variables in

$$(1) \quad p \cdot q \supset p \vee q$$

obtaining, say, the expression

$$(2) \quad x\epsilon\alpha \cdot y\epsilon\beta \supset x\epsilon\alpha \vee y\epsilon\beta$$

Since (1) holds good whatever sentences are substituted for ' p ' and ' q ', so long as identical substitutions are made for identical variables throughout, it will hold for the restricted class of cases in which the substituted sentences exemplify simple class-membership formulae. Law (2) is therefore simply a special case of law (1). Since (2) holds good whatever values we give to the variables of the class-membership formulae, provided we give identical values to identical variables throughout, it will hold for the restricted class of cases in which the variables 'x' and 'y' have the *same* values in the two class-membership formulae. Therefore

(3) $x\varepsilon\alpha \,.\, x\varepsilon\beta \supset x\varepsilon\alpha \lor x\varepsilon\beta$

is simply a special case of (2) and hence of (1). Now, by the interpretational rules given for the logical product and logical sum symbols of the class system, (3) is equivalent to

(4) $x\varepsilon\alpha\beta \supset x\varepsilon(\alpha + \beta)$

And by the interpretational rules for the '$*$' symbol of the class system, (4) is equivalent to

(5) $x\varepsilon(\alpha\beta * \alpha + \beta)$

Now to assert (5) as a law or analytic formula, as we are here doing, is to assert that an analytic sentence results from it *whatever* significant word-substitutions we make for 'x', 'α', and 'β', provided we make the same substitutions for the same variables throughout. It is precisely the point of variables to ensure this generality. Now let us, as regards the variable 'x', write this permitted generality of substitution into the formula itself, by the use of the word 'everything'. Thus we obtain

(6) Everything is a member of the class of $\alpha\beta * \alpha + \beta$

which is the meaning given by the interpretational rules for '$= 1$' to

(7) $\alpha\beta * \alpha + \beta = 1$

which is equivalent to

(7a) $\alpha\beta \subset \alpha + \beta$

These steps show in what sense I wish to say that (7), or (7a), is a special case of (1). Although something more than the bare use of the principle of substitution is involved, it does not seem a very unnatural use of the words 'a special case'.

Each of those laws of the class system which can be directly established by the tabular method, as I described it in the previous chapter, has to some truth-functional law just the relation which (7) has to (1); that is, can be derived from some truth-functional law by an analogous series of steps. Now let us consider, as a consequence of (7), a law which cannot be directly established by the tabular method as I described it. To assert

(7) or (7a) is to assert that the logical product of two classes is included in their logical sum; i.e. that there is nothing which belongs to the logical product of two classes and does not belong to their logical sum. But suppose that in the universe of discourse of a certain two classes there is nothing at all which does not belong to their logical product, i.e. everything belongs to their logical product. Then, evidently, there is nothing at all which does not belong to their logical sum, i.e. everything belongs to their logical sum. For our law states that anything belonging to the former belongs to the latter. So from (7) or (7a) there follows, by this reasoning, the law

$$(8) \quad \alpha\beta = 1 \supset \alpha + \beta = 1$$

But in taking this further step, we use a principle of inference quite different from any exemplified in the quasi-specialization of (1) into (7). The new principle might be expressed as the rule that ' $\alpha \subset \beta$ ' entails ' $\alpha = 1 \supset \beta = 1$ '. And each of the laws of the class system which cannot be directly established by the tabular method, is related to some law which can be so established, as (8) is related to (7) or (7a); that is, can be derived from it by the use of principles such as the one just stated. The number of these additional principles required is small. Another example would be the rule that ' $\alpha\beta = 1$ ' is equivalent to ' $\alpha = 1 . \beta = 1$ '.

I will illustrate all these points with one further example, setting down analogous steps with the same numbering as in the previous illustration, but without repeating the explanation. We are to derive, from the law ' $(p \supset q) \supset (\sim q \supset \sim p)$ ', first the law ' $\alpha * \beta \subset \bar{\beta} * \bar{\alpha}$ ', which can be directly established by the tabular method, and, second, the law ' $\alpha \subset \beta \supset \bar{\beta} \subset \bar{\alpha}$ ', which cannot.

$$(1) \quad (p \supset q) \supset (\sim q \supset \sim p)$$
$$(2) \quad (x\varepsilon\alpha \supset y\varepsilon\beta) \supset (\sim y\varepsilon\beta \supset \sim x\varepsilon\alpha)$$
$$(3) \quad (x\varepsilon\alpha \supset x\varepsilon\beta) \supset (\sim x\varepsilon\beta \supset \sim x\varepsilon\alpha)$$
$$(4) \quad x\varepsilon\alpha * \beta \supset x\varepsilon\bar{\beta} * \bar{\alpha}$$
$$(5) \quad x\varepsilon(\alpha * \beta) * (\bar{\beta} * \bar{\alpha})$$

(6) Everything is a member of the class of $(\alpha * \beta) * (\bar{\beta} * \bar{\alpha})$

$$(7) \quad (\alpha * \beta) * (\bar{\beta} * \bar{\alpha}) = 1$$
$$(7a) \quad \alpha * \beta \subset \bar{\beta} * \bar{\alpha}$$
$$(8) \quad \alpha * \beta = 1 \supset \bar{\beta} * \bar{\alpha} = 1$$

Since ' $\alpha * \beta = 1$ ' is definitionally [1] equivalent to ' $\alpha \subset \beta$ ', (8) is equivalent to

$$(8a) \quad \alpha \subset \beta \supset \bar{\beta} \subset \bar{\alpha}$$

In its last formulation the law asserts that if one class is included in another, then the complement of the second is included in the complement of the first.

2. The last section helps to show the close relationship between the interpreted formulae of the system of truth-functions and those of the system of classes. But it also suggests that the special symbolism of the class system obscures, rather than emphasizes, that relationship. We are now to examine an alternative notation which has the opposite effect. By calling it an alternative notation, I mean simply that it is one in which formulae can be framed having exactly the same interpretation as any class-statement formulae of the kinds with which we have been concerned. We incidentally dispense with the special symbolism of the class system, and use instead only four devices in addition to the familiar constants of the propositional calculus. These devices, which are explained in what follows, are :

      (i) individual variables
     (ii) predicative variables
    (iii) existential quantification
    (iv) universal quantification.

In discussing the class system we considered two kinds of statement-formulae; first, those exemplified by class-membership sentences; second, those exemplified by positively and negatively existential sentences. The general class-membership formula is ' $x \varepsilon \alpha$ '. It is exemplified by such a sentence as ' John is a member of the class of fathers '; to which we attach the same meaning as to the ordinary English sentence ' John is a father '. In the new notation we preserve the character of the variable ' x ' unchanged. That is to say, any expression which is a possible value of ' x ' in some class-membership formula is a possible value of ' x ' in some formula of the new kind. But we dispense with the class-membership constant ' ε ' and the class-expression variables ' α ', ' β ', &c., replacing them with a

---

[1] See Chapter 4, p. 110, footnote.

new type of variable, to which we give the name ‘predicative variable’ and for which we use the letters ‘f’, ‘g’, ‘h’, &c. To the variable ‘x’ and other variables of the same type, for which we use other small letters at the end of the alphabet, we give the name ‘individual variables’. The predicative variable is normally written first, followed by the individual variable, in what we shall call a predicative formula, e.g., ‘fx’, ‘gy’, &c. The range of individual expressions, i.e., of possible values of individual variables, has already been given.[1] We may define a predicative expression as any expression which, together with some individual expression, can form a sentence capable of being used to make a statement. Thus ‘is a father’, ‘lives in a glass house’, ‘is red’ are examples of predicative expressions. Predicative variables are, then, variables of which the possible values are predicative expressions. Thus any class-membership sentence, and any standard English sentence with the same meaning, alike exemplify a predicative formula.

Exemplifications of predicative formulae are sentences capable of being used to make statements. Such formulae can therefore be treated as a kind of statement-variables, i.e., can figure as variables in truth-functional formulae. Thus such expressions as ‘$fx \cdot gy$’, ‘$\sim(fx \vee fy)$’, ‘$fx \supset \sim gx$’, ‘$\sim(fx \cdot \sim gx)$’ are admissible exemplifications of the formulae ‘$p \cdot q$’, ‘$\sim(p \vee q)$’, ‘$p \supset \sim q$’, ‘$\sim(p \cdot \sim q)$’. Of particular interest among these complex predicative formulae are those in which the same individual variable is repeated, as in ‘$\sim(fx \cdot \sim gx)$’. For these give us a means of paraphrasing in our new notation all those class-membership formulae in which the expression following ‘ε’ is itself a compound class-formula. This is obvious when we remember how we defined the product, sum, and complement symbols of the class system.[2] Since ‘$x\varepsilon(\alpha + \beta)$’ is the defined equivalent of ‘$x\varepsilon\alpha \vee x\varepsilon\beta$’, it can be paraphrased as ‘$fx \vee gx$’. Similarly, ‘$x\varepsilon\alpha\beta$’ becomes ‘$fx \cdot gx$’; ‘$x\varepsilon\bar{\alpha}$’ becomes ‘$\sim fx$’; ‘$x\varepsilon\alpha * \beta$’ or ‘$x\varepsilon\alpha \times \bar{\beta}$’ becomes ‘$fx \supset gx$’ or ‘$\sim(fx \cdot \sim gx)$’; and ‘$x\varepsilon\alpha ** \beta$’ becomes ‘$fx \equiv gx$’. To take

---

[1] See Chapter 4, p. 104. This range must be understood to exclude expressions like ‘nobody’, ‘nothing’, ‘everything’, which would yield a sentence having the force of a denial or assertion of existence. Otherwise, the limits are only those imposed by the requirement of significance. For further discussion, see Chapter 5, pp. 144–146.

[2] See Chapter 4, p. 107.

a slightly more complicated example, ' $x\varepsilon(\overline{\alpha + \beta} \times \gamma)$ ' is replaced by ' $\sim (fx \vee gx) \,.\, hx$ '.

It is evident, then, that both the formal structure and the sense of any class-membership formula, however complicated, are preserved in the new notation, which at the same time dispenses with the special symbolism of classes and emphasizes the fact that such formulae are simply specializations of the formulae of the truth-functional system.

All class-statements we considered, except class-membership statements, were assertions or denials that some class was empty; i.e., exemplifications of positively or negatively existential formulae. For the paraphrase of these, we introduce the device of quantification. To assert that a class was empty, we equated the appropriate class-expression to ' 0 '. To deny that it was empty we cancelled the ' equals ' -sign of the equation. The formula ' $\alpha = 0$ ' could be read ' Nothing is a member of the class of α ' or ' It is not the case that anything is a member of the class of α '; and the formula ' $\alpha \neq 0$ ' could be read ' There is at least one thing which is a member of the class of α '. The formula corresponding in the new notation to ' $\alpha \neq 0$ ' is ' $(\exists x)(fx)$ ', which can be read ' There is at least one thing (person) which (who) f '; and the formula corresponding to ' $\alpha = 0$ ' is the negation of ' $(\exists x)(fx)$ ', i.e., ' $\sim((\exists x)(fx))$ ', which can be read ' There is nothing (nobody) which (who) f '. As no ambiguity results from the omission of the outside brackets the formula is commonly written ' $\sim(\exists x)(fx)$ '. These formulae adapt themselves easily to the cases where a compound class is asserted or denied to be empty. Thus ' $\alpha\beta = 0$ ' may be paraphrased as ' $\sim(\exists x)(fx \,.\, gx)$ '; ' $\alpha + \beta \neq 0$ ' as ' $(\exists x)(fx \vee gx)$ '; ' $\overline{\alpha} = 0$ ' as ' $\sim(\exists x)(\sim fx)$ '; ' $\alpha\overline{\beta} = 0$ ' as ' $\sim(\exists x)(fx \,.\, \sim gx)$ '; and ' $\overline{\alpha + \beta} \times \gamma \neq 0$ ' as ' $(\exists x)[\sim(fx \vee gx) \,.\, hx]$ '.

As the last example shows, brackets now serve to indicate the scope both of the propositional constants and of the quantifying symbol ' $(\exists x)$ ', which, for obvious reasons, is called the *existential* quantifier. The importance of a clear indication of the scope of quantifier and propositional constants respectively in a formula or sentence containing both, may be illustrated by the following examples. Suppose in the formulae ' $(\exists x)(fx \,.\, gx)$ ' and ' $(\exists x)(fx) \,.\, gx$ ' we give ' f ' the value ' is red ' and ' g ' the value ' is round '. Then from the first formula we obtain the *sentence*, ' There is at least one thing which is both red and round ', whereas from the second formula we obtain ' There is at least one thing which is red and x is round '. This last expression is not a sentence, but the conjunction of a sentence and a formula. Both the above formulae are different from ' $(\exists x)(fx) \cdot (\exists x)(gx)$ '. If we make in this last the same substitutions as before, we obtain the conjunctive sentence ' There is at least one thing which is red and there is at least one thing which is round '. The truth of the statement made by this sentence is compatible with the falsity of the statement made by ' $(\exists x)(x$ is red $.$ x is round) '.

How the class-inclusion and class-identity formulae are to be paraphrased is easily seen when it is remembered that ' $\alpha \subset \beta$ ' is equivalent to ' $\alpha\bar{\beta} = 0$ ' and that ' $\alpha = \beta$ ' is equivalent to ' $\alpha\bar{\beta} = 0 \cdot \beta\bar{\alpha} = 0$ '. The respective paraphrases are ' $\sim(\exists x)(fx \cdot \sim gx)$ ' and ' $\sim(\exists x)(fx \cdot \sim gx) \cdot \sim(\exists x)(gx \cdot \sim fx)$ '.

In the class system the device of equation to ' 0 ' to indicate that a class was empty was supplemented by the device of equation to ' 1 ' to indicate that the complement of a class was empty. Thus ' $\alpha = 1$ ' was defined as equivalent to ' $- \alpha = 0$ '. And the further rule was introduced that ' $- \alpha = 1$ ' was to be equivalent to ' $\alpha = 0$ '. In the new notation we have the parallel complication of a second quantifier, known as the universal quantifier, written ' (x) ', and definable in terms of the first. The sense of the universal quantifier is given by the two following definitions :

$$' (x)(fx) ' \quad =_{Df} ' \sim(\exists x)(\sim fx) '$$
$$' (x)(\sim fx) ' =_{Df} ' \sim(\exists x)(fx) '$$

These definitions [1] are exactly parallel to the rules for ' $\alpha = 1$ ' and ' $- \alpha = 1$ '; for the two defining expressions are respectively the paraphrases of ' $- \alpha = 0$ ' and ' $\alpha = 0$ '. Just as we are tempted to read ' $\alpha = 1$ ' as ' Everything is a member of the class of α ', so we are tempted, and sometimes encouraged, to read ' $(x)(fx)$ ' as ' Everything f ' or ' For every x, fx '; and this is often convenient. But when we have questions of interpretation in mind, it is safer, as we shall see, to read it in terms of its *definiens*.

---

[1] In a strict deductive development of the system, only one definition is necessary.

These two definitions yield, of course, the two equivalences

$$\textbf{(1)} \quad (x)(fx) \quad \equiv \; \sim(\exists x)(\sim fx)$$
$$\textbf{(2)} \quad (x)(\sim fx) \equiv \; \sim(\exists x)(fx)$$

and from these we can directly obtain the two further equivalences

$$\textbf{(3)} \quad \sim(x)(fx) \quad \equiv \; (\exists x)(\sim fx)$$
$$\textbf{(4)} \quad \sim(x)(\sim fx) \equiv \; (\exists x)(fx)$$

by using the laws and inference-procedures of the propositional calculus. Thus in the truth-functional law

$$(p \equiv \sim q) \supset (\sim p \equiv q)$$

we substitute ' $(x)(fx)$ ' for ' p ', ' $(\exists x)(\sim fx)$ ' for ' q ', obtaining

$$[(x)(fx) \equiv \sim(\exists x)(\sim fx)] \supset [\sim(x)(fx) \equiv (\exists x)(\sim fx)] \quad \text{(i)}$$

and from (1) and (i) we obtain (3) by the Rule of Inference. To obtain (4) we substitute ' $(x)(\sim fx)$ ' for ' p ', ' $(\exists x)(fx)$ ' for ' q ' and proceed as before.

From (1) to (4) we can obtain by substitution an indefinite number of more complicated equivalences. Equivalence (2), for instance, is exemplified in the following cases :

$$\textbf{(5)} \quad \sim(\exists x)(fx \,.\, gx) \quad \equiv \; (x)[\sim(fx \,.\, gx)]$$
$$\textbf{(6)} \quad \sim(\exists x)(fx \vee gx) \quad \equiv \; (x)[\sim(fx \vee gx)]$$
$$\textbf{(7)} \quad \sim(\exists x)(fx \,.\, \sim gx) \equiv \; (x)[\sim(fx \,.\, \sim gx)]$$

The justification for these substitutions might not at first seem obvious. But if we consider the formulae ' x is green and round ' and ' x is green or round ', we see that both the expressions, ' green and round ' and ' green or round ', answer to our description of a predicative expression and that hence both formulae exemplify the predicative formula ' fx '. We see also that these formulae are the ordinary English versions of ' x is green . x is round ', ' x is green $\vee x$ is round ', which respectively exemplify ' $fx \,.\, gx$ ' and ' $fx \vee gx$ '. All complex predicative formulae can thus be regarded as exemplifications of a simple predicative formula, just as all complex class-membership formulae are exemplifications of ' $x \varepsilon \alpha$ '.

Consider now the two formulae ' $\sim(\exists x)(fx \,.\, \sim gx)$ ' and ' $(x)(fx \supset gx)$ '. Bearing in mind the sense of ' $\supset$ ', we may read the latter as ' For every x, it is not the case that fx and not-gx '.

But this is precisely how we should read '$(x)[\sim(fx . \sim gx)]$', which we have just seen ((7) above) to be the equivalent of '$\sim(\exists x)(fx . \sim gx)$'. On these interpretational grounds alone, then, we are tempted to conclude that '$(x)(fx \supset gx)$' and '$\sim(\exists x)(fx . \sim gx)$' are equivalent. This temptation is reinforced when we notice that

$$\sim(fx . \sim gx) \equiv fx \supset gx$$

is merely a specialization of the truth-functional law

$$\sim(p . \sim q) \equiv p \supset q.$$

For we have only to write the universal quantifier ' for every x ' in front of each of the two equivalent predicative formulae, to obtain

$$(8) \quad (x)[\sim(fx . \sim gx)] \equiv (x)(fx \supset gx)$$

Does this introduction of '(x)' make any difference to the correctness of the equivalence? One would be inclined to say that it did not; and we shall see later on that this is correct, i.e., that the rules of the system allow us to prove this equivalence. Now, taking (8) together with (7), we can easily prove

$$(9) \quad \sim(\exists x)(fx . \sim gx) \equiv (x)(fx \supset gx)$$

—an equivalence to which we shall frequently refer hereafter— and we may use this anticipated result to warrant our reading '$(x)(fx \supset gx)$' as ' There is nothing which f and not-g '. Analogously we may anticipate the proofs of

$$(10) \quad \sim(\exists x)(fx \lor gx) \equiv (x)(\sim fx . \sim gx)$$
$$(11) \quad \sim(\exists x)(fx . gx) \equiv (x)(\sim fx \lor \sim gx)$$

which will make a similar use of the truth-functional laws '$\sim(p \lor q) \equiv \sim p . \sim q$' and '$\sim(p . q) \equiv \sim p \lor \sim q$'.

3. In the last section I have briefly set out the elements of a new notation, in which it is possible to frame formulae having the same interpretation as any law of the class system (as we here understand the latter). We shall see later that the new notation admits of a more comprehensive use; that, in it, formulae can be framed which do not admit of paraphrase in class terms. The wider logical system which can be constructed in the new notation is sometimes called the predicative (or functional) calculus. Evidently then, all the laws of the class

calculus can be obtained from the laws of the predicative calculus by paraphrase; but not conversely.

In the first section we sought to make clear the reasons for the formal parallelism between the class system and the propositional calculus by deriving the (interpreted) laws of the former from the (interpreted) laws of the latter. The derivation was clumsy, involving a lot of purely notational changes. One of the advantages claimed for the notation of predicative formulae and quantifiers was that it made the relationship between the two sets of interpreted laws more perspicuous. To make this claim good, we ought to be able to effect the derivation of the laws in the new notation more simply and more swiftly.

Let us return to our previous examples.[1] From

$$\text{(i) } p \cdot q \supset p \lor q$$

we obtain by substitution

$$\text{(ii) } fx \cdot gy \supset fx \lor gy$$

and, as before, by further specialization

$$\text{(iii) } fx \cdot gx \supset fx \lor gx.$$

Now to assert any complex predicative formula as a law is to assert that any significant sentence obtained from it by substitution is analytic, whatever values are given to the individual and predicative variables. Suppose our law is of the form 'fx'. Then, by a step corresponding to that from (5) to (6) in the original derivation of Section 1, we may assert as a law the corresponding formula of the pattern '$(x)(fx)$' (i.e., 'Everything f', or 'There is nothing which not-f'). To do this is, as before, to write into the law-formula itself the permitted generality of substitution with regard to the variable 'x'. We have, then, the general rule that from any complex predicative formula of one individual variable, asserted as a law, we can derive as a law the expression which results from universally quantifying that formula without modifying it in any other way.[2] From (iii) we derive, by the application of this rule, the law

$$\text{(iv) } (x)(fx \cdot gx \supset fx \lor gx).$$

This can be read 'There is nothing which both f and g and not either f or g', which is the paraphrase in predicative terms

[1] See Section 1, pp. 126–128.
[2] This operation may be called 'generalization'.

of the original conclusion ' $\alpha\beta \subset \alpha + \beta$ ' (i.e., ' There is nothing which is a member of the class of $\alpha\beta$ and not a member of the class of $\alpha + \beta$ ').

The parallel derivation to the other example given in Section 1 is as follows :

$$\text{(i) } (p \supset q) \supset (\sim q \supset \sim p)$$
$$\text{(ii) } (fx \supset gx) \supset (\sim gx \supset \sim fx)$$
$$\text{(iii) } (x)[(fx \supset gx) \supset (\sim gx \supset \sim fx)]$$

The retention of a similar notational pattern throughout results in an obvious gain in simplicity and clarity.

As in Section 1, additional special rules are required for further formal development. I list a number of formulae which we shall expect to hold good as laws of the system, but which we have not yet the means of deriving :

$$\text{(12) } (x)(fx \,.\, gx) \supset (x)(fx \lor gx)$$
$$\text{(13) } (x)(fx \supset gx) \supset (x)(\sim gx \supset \sim fx)$$
$$\text{(14) } (x)(fx \supset gx) \,.\, (x)(gx \supset hx) \supset (x)(fx \supset hx)$$
$$\text{(15) } (x)(fx \supset gx) \,.\, (x)(fx \supset hx) \supset (x)(fx \supset gx \,.\, hx)$$

If we translate these into words, we shall find that they are paraphrases of the following laws of the class system :

$$\text{C}(a) \quad \alpha\beta = 1 \supset \alpha + \beta = 1$$
$$\text{C}(b) \quad \alpha \subset \beta \supset \bar{\beta} \subset \bar{\alpha}$$
$$\text{C}(c) \quad \alpha \subset \beta \,.\, \beta \subset \gamma \supset \alpha \subset \gamma$$
$$\text{C}(d) \quad \alpha \subset \beta \,.\, \alpha \subset \gamma \supset \alpha \subset \beta\gamma$$

The obvious starting-points for derivation from the laws of the propositional calculus are :

$$\text{P}(a) \quad p \,.\, q \supset p \lor q$$
$$\text{P}(b) \quad (p \supset q) \supset (\sim q \supset \sim p)$$
$$\text{P}(c) \quad (p \supset q) \,.\, (q \supset r) \supset (p \supset r)$$
$$\text{P}(d) \quad (p \supset q) \,.\, (p \supset r) \supset (p \supset q \,.\, r)$$

We have just seen how from P(a) and P(b) we derive

$$(x)(fx \,.\, gx \supset fx \lor gx)$$

and
$$(x)[(fx \supset gx) \supset (\sim gx \supset \sim fx)].$$

By analogous steps we derive from P(c) and P(d)

$$(x)[(fx \supset gx) \,.\, (gx \supset hx) \supset (fx \supset hx)]$$

and
$$(x)[(fx \supset gx) \,.\, (fx \supset hx) \supset (fx \supset gx \,.\, hx)].$$

The next step consists in turning these universally quantified implications between predicative formulae into ordinary implications between universally quantified formulae. It is for this step that we need the additional rules. Examples are the rules that the following formulae [1] are analytic :

$$\text{I} \quad (x)(fx \supset gx) \supset [(x)(fx) \supset (x)(gx)]$$
$$\text{II} \quad (x)(fx \cdot gx) \equiv (x)(fx) \cdot (x)(gx)$$

The assertion of the first as a law may be expressed as follows : ' The formula " There is nothing which f and not g " entails the formula " If there is nothing at all which not f, there is nothing at all which not g " '. The assertion of the second as a law may be expressed : ' The formula " There is nothing which not both f and g " is logically equivalent to the formula " There is nothing which not f and there is nothing which not g " '. For example, ' There is nothing which is precious and not perishable ' entails ' If there is nothing which is not precious, then there is nothing which is not perishable '; and ' There is nothing which is not both precious and perishable ' is logically equivalent to ' There is nothing which is not precious and there is nothing which is not perishable '.

The use of these additional laws is a simple exercise in the deductive procedure outlined for the propositional calculus. E.g., to obtain (12), substitute in I ' $fx \cdot gx$ ' for ' fx ' and ' $fx \vee gx$ ' for ' gx ', obtaining

$$(x)(fx \cdot gx \supset fx \vee gx) \supset [(x)(fx \cdot gx) \supset (x)(fx \vee gx)]$$

We have already established the first half of this implication; so, by the Rule of Inference, we can derive the second half, which is (12), as a law. The derivation of (13) follows the same pattern. For (14) and (15) we may, for simplicity's sake, use the additional rule of inference that equivalent expressions may be substituted for one another. Then, having transformed

$$(x)[(fx \supset gx) \cdot (gx \supset hx) \supset (fx \supset hx)]$$

into

$$(x)[(fx \supset gx) \cdot (gx \supset hx)] \supset (x)(fx \supset hx)$$

by the use of I, we transform this into

$$(x)(fx \supset gx) \cdot (x)(gx \supset hx) \supset (x)(fx \supset hx)$$

by the use of II and the rule permitting interchange of equivalent functions. Similarly for (15).

---

[1] In the strict development of the system, these formulae are derived as theorems.

The general procedure by which the equivalences assumed at the end of the previous section are justified should now be obvious.   From I and II we can derive

III $(x)(fx \equiv gx) \supset [(x)(fx) \equiv (x)(gx)]$.

Then, having derived, for example,

$$(x)[\sim(fx \, . \sim gx) \equiv fx \supset gx]$$

from ' $\sim(p \, . \sim q) \equiv p \supset q$ ' by substitution and generalization, we use the law III to obtain from this result the formula

$$(x)[\sim(fx \, . \sim gx)] \equiv (x)(fx \supset gx)$$

and hence to justify the equivalence

$$\sim(\exists x)(fx \, . \sim gx) \equiv (x)(fx \supset gx).$$

Similarly for the other cases.

In this section I have not tried to do more than give informal illustrations of some methods by which theorems of the predicative calculus can be proved.   There are other techniques of proof, some swifter in application, and more elegant, than these.[1]   I have been concerned primarily to stress the intimate relations between the class and the predicative systems, and between both these and the system of truth-functions.

4. I remarked earlier that the notation of predicative formulae and quantifiers was more comprehensive than that employed in the simple class system; that whereas all the formulae which could be framed in the latter notation could be paraphrased by formulae framed in the former, the converse did not hold; and that, consequently, the predicative calculus admits of a greater formal development than the class calculus.   The point is sometimes expressed by saying that the predicative notation allows for a more thoroughgoing analysis of the logical form of certain statements than the simple class notation.   I want to illustrate certain ways in which this is so.   But I introduce them by consideration of a class of cases for which it is not impossible to find paraphrases in class terms.

So far we have considered in detail examples only of those predicative formulae which contain a single individual variable;

---

[1] See Reichenbach, *Elements of Symbolic Logic*, Chapter IV, and Quine, *Methods of Logic*, Parts II and III.

though we have seen that it is permissible to frame such formulae with two or more. Let us consider what sort of interpretation we might give to a formula containing two individual variables both of which also appeared in a parenthesis of quantification. Of course, the interpretation of such an expression as '$(x)(fx) \supset (\exists y)(gy)$' presents no problem. For the two individual variables form part of two independently quantified formulae, neither of which includes the other in its scope. But suppose we write '$(x)[(\exists y)(fx \supset gy)]$'. What interpretation, if any, could we give to this expression?

Suppose we were asked to exhibit as exactly as possible in our symbolism the form of the sentence ' No one loves without suffering '. We might paraphrase it as ' There is no one who both loves and does not suffer' and conclude that the appropriate formula was ' $\sim(\exists x)(fx . \sim gx)$' or '$(x)(fx \supset gx)$'. Suppose now that we were asked to do the same for the sentence ' No one loves without *somebody* suffering '; where there is no implication that the lover and the sufferer are necessarily the same. We may paraphrase initially by ' There is no one who loves without anybody suffering '. But it is not so clear what step to take next. The example clearly resembles the previous one in that if we begin with the negatively existential quantifier, the whole of the relative clause beginning with ' who ' must come within the scope of that quantifier. But clearly we need, in the analysis of the relative clause, an additional negatively existential quantifier to do justice to ' without anybody suffering ' (i.e., ' with nobody suffering '). These considerations might induce us to adopt the rule that ' $\sim(\exists x)[x$ loves $. \sim(\exists y)(y$ suffers$)]$' was to be regarded as the closest possible paraphrase of the sentence in our notation. Formulae or sentences, like this one, in which one quantifier includes another in its scope, may be reformulated so that their quantifiers occur together at the beginning of the sentence or formula in question. Care must be observed, however, in making this step. The formula exemplified by our doubly quantified sentence is ' $\sim(\exists x)[fx . \sim(\exists y)(gy)]$'. If we simply transferred ' $\sim(\exists y)$ ' to a position immediately after ' $\sim(\exists x)$ ', obtaining the formula ' $\sim(\exists x)\{\sim[(\exists y)(fx . gy)]\}$', we should be changing the scope of the negation sign preceding ' $(\exists y)$ ' and hence changing the sense of the expression. Before transferring the quantifier we must eliminate the negation sign

which precedes it. This is an easy matter; for ' $[fx \, . \, \sim(\exists y)(gy)]$ '
is of the form ' $p \, . \, \sim q$ ' and hence is equivalent to, e.g., the
corresponding expression of the form ' $\sim(\sim p \vee q)$ ', i.e., to
' $\sim[\sim fx \vee (\exists y)(gy)]$ '. Replacing the former by the latter in
the original formula, we have ' $\sim(\exists x)\sim[\sim fx \vee (\exists y)(gy)]$ ',
which, by the definition of the universal quantifier, is equivalent
to ' $(x)[\sim fx \vee (\exists y)(gy)]$ '. The second quantifier can now be
safely transferred to a position immediately following the
first, yielding ' $(x)(\exists y)(\sim fx \vee gy)$ '. This is equivalent to
' $(x)(\exists y)(fx \supset gy)$ ', the formula for the possible interpretation of
which we inquired at the end of the previous paragraph.

Our symbolic paraphrase of ' Nobody loves without somebody
suffering ' left open the possibility of the lover and the sufferer
being different persons; but it also left open the possibility that
they were the same. Suppose we had now to deal with ' Nobody
loves without somebody *else* suffering '. Let us approach this
by way of another example. Suppose first that we are to express ' There is at least one creature which can swim and there
is at least one creature, not identical with the first, which can
fly '. We might try ' $(\exists x)(\exists y)(x$ can swim $. y$ can fly) '. But
this is true if there is just one creature who can do both. We
might adopt the convention that the use of different variables
in the same formula implied difference of identity where existence was asserted; but this would be inconvenient, e.g., it
would limit our freedom in substituting for variables. Instead
the new formula ' $x = y$ ' is introduced, with the sense ' x is
identical with (the same person/thing as) y '. The formula
' $\sim(x = y)$ ' accordingly has the sense ' x is not identical with
y '. Now we can complete the paraphrase of our sentence as
follows : ' $(\exists x)(\exists y)[x$ can swim $. y$ can fly $. \sim(x = y)]$ '.
Similarly, we can render the form of ' Nobody loves without
somebody else suffering ' by ' $(x)(\exists y)[fx \supset \sim (x = y) . gy]$ '.

For some examples of multiply quantified formulae we can
find paraphrases in the class notation without the use of quantification. For example, ' Nobody loves without somebody
suffering ', which exemplifies ' $(x)(\exists y)(fx \supset gy)$ ', can be paraphrased ' It is not the case both that the class of lovers is not
empty and that the class of sufferers is empty ', which exemplifies ' $\alpha \neq 0 \supset \beta \neq 0$ '. But one cannot find a corresponding
paraphrase for ' $(x)(\exists y)[fx \supset \sim (x = y) . gy]$ '. In general,

wherever a multiply quantified formula is equivalent to a formula consisting of two or more independently quantified formulae linked by truth-functional connectives, it will be possible to find a class-paraphrase not employing quantification. Thus ' $(x)(\exists y)(fx \supset gy)$ ' is equivalent to ' $(\exists x)(fx) \supset (\exists y)(gy)$ '. But where this condition does not hold, such a paraphrase cannot be found. The qualifying phrase ' not employing quantification ' is essential; for it would obviously be possible to substitute class-membership formulae such as ' $x\varepsilon a$ ' for predicative formulae such as ' fx ' throughout all the quantified formulae we have considered.[1]

The last example, employing the constant ' $=$ ', introduces us to a way in which the notation we are considering is definitely more comprehensive than that of the simple class system. We originally defined a predicative variable as a variable which could take predicative expressions as its values; and a predicative expression as any expression which, together with an individual expression, could form a sentence capable of being used to make a statement. Now it is obvious that many ordinary sentences, e.g., ' *The cat* is between *the door* and *the window* ', ' *Tweedledum* hates *Tweedledee* ', ' *Tact* is rarer than *kindness* ', contain more than one individual expression. We can, for example, correctly regard both ' hates Tweedledee ' and ' Tweedledum hates ' as predicative expressions, possible values of ' f ' in a formula of the pattern ' fx '. But the existence of such cases suggests an extension of the sense of ' predicative expression ' to ' any expression which, together with *one or more* individual expressions, could form a sentence capable of being used to make a statement '. Thus we shall regard ' is between . . and ', ' hates ', ' is rarer than ' as predicative expressions; and ' x is between y and z ', ' x hates y ', ' x is rarer than y ' as predicative formulae, respectively exemplifying the general formulae ' $fxyz$ ' and ' fxy '. Predicative expressions used to form sentences exemplifying simple predicative formulae with more than one individual variable are sometimes called

---

[1] It is also to be noted that when we have successfully reduced a multiply quantified formula to a truth-function of independently quantified formulae, the need for separate individual variables disappears. Thus ' $(\exists x)(fx) \supset (\exists y)(gy)$ ' can be rewritten as ' $(\exists x)(fx) \supset (\exists x)(gx)$ ' without any ambiguity in the reference of the quantifying parentheses in the two halves of the expression.

relational predicates, and are distinguished into dyadic (' two-place '), triadic (' three-place '), &c., predicates, according to the number of individual expressions they commonly require to form a sentence. Two points to notice are these. First, any sentence exemplifying a simple relational formula, e.g., ' fxy ', also exemplifies ' fx '. Second, the order of the variables in a relational formula is not indifferent, but conventionally mirrors the order of the individual expressions in the sentences exemplifying the formula. Thus ' $fxy \equiv fyx$ ' is not an analytic formula : for some values of ' f ' it would yield, with universal quantification of ' x ' and ' y ', a necessarily or contingently true sentence, for others a false or self-contradictory one.

Conjoining the device of relational predicate variables with that of multiple quantification yields, then, a further range of exemplifiable formulae. The relative scope of quantifiers, as indicated by their order, may often, though not always, make a difference to the sense of sentences exemplifying such formulae. The sentence ' $(\exists x)(y)(x$ loves $y)$ ' does not mean the same as ' $(y)(\exists x)(x$ loves $y)$ ', though the ordinary English sentence ' Somebody loves everything ' might do ambiguous duty for both; but ' $(\exists x)(\exists y)(x$ loves $y)$ ' and ' $(\exists y)(\exists x)(x$ loves $y)$ ' are equivalent.

One further extension of the system remains to be mentioned. We have seen that a predicative formula like ' $fx \supset gy$ ' may yield a sentence either by substitution of individual and predicative expressions for individual and predicative variables (e.g., ' Tom loves $\supset$ Mary suffers '); or by substitution of predicative expressions alone, coupled with the use of quantifiers related to the individual variables (e.g., ' $(x)(\exists y)(x$ loves $\supset y$ suffers) '). In such an expression as the latter, the variables ' x ' and ' y ', in their occurrences before ' loves ' and ' suffers ' respectively, are sometimes spoken of as *bound* variables; presumably because they are not, in such a sentence, *free* to take individual expressions as values, but function rather as relative pronouns (' who ', ' which ') referring back to words like ' nothing ', ' nobody ', ' somebody '.[1] Now the notation itself almost

---

[1] The distinction between ' bound ' and ' free ' variables is useful for making the point, which should be obvious, that an expression is a formula, as opposed to a sentence, only if it contains at least one free variable. If all the variables in a correctly formed expression are bound, that expression is a sentence.

irresistibly suggests the possibility of binding not only individual variables, but also predicative variables, in a predicative formula. Consider the function '$fx \supset fy$', which would be exemplified by 'Tom suffers $\supset$ Mary suffers'. If we retained these values for the individual variables and bound the predicative variable by the use of the universal quantifier instead of replacing it by a predicative expression, we should obtain the sentence '$(f)(f\,\mathrm{Tom} \supset f\,\mathrm{Mary})$' which is equivalent to '$\sim(\exists f)(f\,\mathrm{Tom} \,.\, \sim f\,\mathrm{Mary})$' and which might be read 'There is nothing which is true of Tom and is not true of Mary'.

When we reach this stage in the development of the system, however—the stage of quantification of predicative variables—we move progressively further away from approximations to forms of statement which we are likely to employ in ordinary speech. The considerable further development of which the system is capable has interested logicians primarily because it seemed to provide a means of defining the basic concepts of mathematics. Into this province, of mathematical logic proper, I shall not enter.

II. THE PREDICATIVE SYSTEM AND ORDINARY SPEECH: PRELIMINARIES

5. When we had completed the exposition of the system of truth-functions, we discussed the relations between that system and the logic of ordinary speech. This discussion involved a comparison between the rules determining the sense of the constants of the system and the behaviour of certain words like 'not' and 'if' as these are ordinarily used. It was evidently false to say that the constants of the system meant the same as the words with which they were compared. The latter had no such neatly systematic relations to one another as the rules of the system ensured for the former.

Suppose we undertake a similar comparison for the system we have described in this chapter, which, as we have seen, may be held to include the simple class system of Chapter 4. It has certain features in common with the truth-functional system, and certain additional features. One of these additional features is that it makes use of two types of variable in addition to the one type used in the propositional calculus. The values which the variables of that calculus could take were clauses of the kind which can stand as complete sentences. How shall we characterize, more exactly than hitherto, the variables which we have called ' individual variables ' and ' predicative variables ', i.e., the distinction between individual and predicative expressions? We cannot put much weight on the word ' individual '. For we should not ordinarily say that sympathy was an individual, or that the fact that it rained yesterday was an individual; but there seems no reason for denying that ' Sympathy is a rare virtue ', ' The fact that it rained yesterday is now forgotten ' can be regarded as exemplifications of ' x is a rare virtue ', ' x is now forgotten ', and hence of ' fx '. It seems clear that the distinction between individual and predicative expressions is intended to reflect some fairly radical feature of the structure of sentences of the kind that can be used to make statements; and, taking the hint of ' predicative ', one might be inclined to think that the distinction was intended to coincide with that between the grammatical subject and the grammatical predicate of a singular sentence. This will not do as it stands, for various reasons : e.g., (i) it would prevent our recognizing the grammatical object of a sentence as the value of the second individual variable in a sentence exemplifying a relational predicative formula; (ii) it would force us to admit ' nothing ', ' nobody ', ' everything ' as individual expressions, whereas we want to relate these to quantifiers; (iii) it would, on the authority of some grammars, force us to admit the ' it ' of ' It is raining ' as an individual expression. Why should this last consequence matter? Well, it is a rule of the system that any sentence of the form ' fx ' entails the corresponding sentence of the form ' $(\exists x)(fx)$ '; but we do not wish to say that ' It is raining ' entails ' There is at least one thing which is raining '. We might try to meet these and other difficulties *seriatim*; e.g., by (i) requiring of an individual expression that it should be grammatically capable of filling the role of subject of a singular verb, but not that it should actually be doing so in any sentence in which it is appearing as an individual expression; (ii) ruling out such expressions as ' nothing ' by *fiat*; (iii) requiring that in any sentence in which an expression appears as a grammatical subject of a predicate ' f ', it should, in order to count as an individual expression in that appearance, be a possible answer to a possible question of the form 'What (who) *f*?' The third requirement would deal with the third difficulty; for there is no question 'What is raining?' to which 'It' is an answer. Such expedients are clearly unsatisfactory. I mention them, and the difficulties which suggest them, only in order to make the point that it is not easy to formulate a criterion for 'individual expression' which is both neat and accurate. Nor perhaps is it necessary. So long as we do not subject our description to too critical a scrutiny, we *can* describe a very easily recognizable distinction in ordinary language which the distinction between individual and predicative variables may not unnaturally be taken to reflect. In making ordinary statements, we are constantly concerned to *refer* to a particular person, object or place, to a particular episode, situation or institution, to a particular quality or fact, and to *ascribe* to it some property or to *describe* or *classify* it in some way; or, even more loosely and vaguely, to *say something about* it. Or we may be concerned, in making one and the same statement, to refer to two or more particular objects or qualities, &c., and to say that they are related in some way; as when we say that Tom is taller than Dick or that tact is rarer than kindness. We may distinguish, then, roughly, between the referring role which expressions may have in statements and the ascriptive or descriptive or classificatory role; and we may say that in so far as an expression fills the first role in a singular statement, it appears as an individual expression; and in so far as an expression fills the second role, it appears as a predicative expression.

It is important to notice that the above description does not put any limits on the sorts of thing which can be referred to. It puts no premium on concreteness. It would be correct to say, for all languages in which the distinction between substantival and non-substantival expressions exists, that whenever we refer, in the sense in which we are here using the word 'refer', we use a noun, pronoun, noun-phrase, or noun-clause, i.e., a substantive or substantival expression. To this extent the distinction between individual and predicative expression is a simple grammatical one; but only to this extent. It is tempting, but would be incorrect, to say that whenever we use a substantive or substantival expression, we are referring. It would be incorrect for reasons already noted. ' Nothing ' and ' nobody ' are substantival expressions; but when we say ' Nobody ', we are not referring to anybody. And ' it ' in ' It is raining ' is a substantival expression; but when we say ' It is raining ', we are not using ' it ' to refer to something which we then describe as ' raining '. Thus not all grammatically substantival expressions can have a referring use; and not all uses of substantival expressions, like ' it ', which can be used referringly, are referring uses. But the vast majority of substantival expressions *can* be used referringly, and the vast majority of the uses of such expressions *are* referring uses. So qualities, situations, facts, events, &c., can be referred to, as well as things or persons. And from the fact that something can be referred to, no philosophical conclusions follow about its nature. All that is shown is the existence of a linguistic need for a substantive. These points are reflected in the ways in which we find ourselves reading sentences embodying quantifiers and, hence, bound individual variables. In the place of a specific referring expression, we need some very general noun to follow the phrase ' There exists (does not exist) at least one . . .'. But sometimes the standard reading for, say, the negatively existential quantifier, viz., ' There is nothing which . . .', seems inappropriate. We find ourselves instead reading ' There is nobody who . . .', ' There is no creature which . . .' or, perhaps, ' There is no quality which . . .'. The choice of the phrase following ' There is . . .' is dictated by a consideration of the general category to which anything must belong if the predicative expression which follows is to be applicable to it. The range of such categories will be not less extensive than the range of categories to which objects of reference may belong.

6. The distinction between individual and predicative expressions and, hence, between individual and predicative variables can, then, be explained in terms of the distinction between the referring role which expressions can play in language, on the one hand, and the ascriptive, descriptive, or classificatory roles, on the other. But the explanation of this distinction, though it is a necessary preliminary to a comparison of the logical system described in this chapter with the logic of ordin-

ary speech, does not itself take us any distance in that comparison. If we confined ourselves to supplementing the symbols and rules of the truth-functional system with these two further types of variable, we should not be able to produce any further logical laws except such as were, in the strictest sense, merely more limited versions of laws of the propositional calculus (e.g., '$fx . gx \supset fx \lor gx$'). There would hence be no scope for comparisons over and above those already made in Chapter 3. All the laws *peculiar* to the system discussed in this chapter involve quantification. It is therefore the logic of what might be called the constants of quantification—'$(\exists x)$' and '(x)'—which we must compare with the behaviour of expressions in ordinary use. With the interpretation of these constants we are already familiar : '$(\exists x)(fx)$' is to be read ' There is (exists) at least one thing (person, &c.) which (who) f'; its negation as ' There is (exists) nothing (nobody) which (who) f'; '$(x)(fx)$' as ' There is (exists) nothing (nobody) of which (whom) it is not true that it (he) f'; and its negation as ' There is (exists) at least one thing (person) of which it is not true that it (he) f'. Now these expressions, ' There is at least one thing which . . .', ' There is nothing which . . .' &c., do occur in ordinary speech; but rarely. And we might think it strange that the whole of modern formal logic, after it leaves the propositional logic and before it crosses the boundary into the analysis of mathematical concepts, should be confined to the elaboration of sets of rules giving the logical interrelations of formulae which, however complex, all begin with these few rather strained and awkward phrases.

I hope to explain this strangeness later on. First, I must admit that many would say I have exaggerated it.[1] For, they would claim, there are large and important classes of sentences in ordinary use which in fact have the same meaning as sentences exemplifying the positively and negatively existential formulae of the quantificational logic;[2] and the notation of quantifiers

---

[1] So I have; but less than it is customary to minimize it. And the reasons why the strangeness is not quite so great are not quite the reasons customarily assumed. See the three following chapters.

[2] Formulae (or sentences) beginning with ' $\sim(\exists x)$' or with '(x)' may be called ' negatively existential ', since they are to be read ' There exists nothing which . . .' &c.; formulae (or sentences) beginning with '$(\exists x)$' or with ' $\sim(x)$' may be called ' positively existential ', since they are to be read ' There exists at least one thing which . . .' &c.

has the merit of making it possible to exhibit the logical relations of such sentences more systematically and more perspicuously than would be possible without it. Thus it is sometimes claimed that the large and important class of <u>general statements</u> (i.e., <u>statements to the effect that all or none of the members of a</u> <u>certain class have a certain property or are members of another</u> <u>class</u>) are really negatively existential statements. Those naturally made by means of a sentence beginning with ' all ' are said to be really of the form ' $(x)(fx \supset gx)$ ' or, its equivalent, ' $\sim(\exists x)(fx \cdot \sim gx)$ '; those naturally made by means of a sentence beginning with ' no ' or ' none of the ' to be of the form ' $(x)(fx \supset \sim gx)$ ' or ' $\sim(\exists x)(fx \cdot gx)$ '. Statements naturally made in sentences beginning with the words ' some ', ' something ', or ' somebody ', on the other hand, are said to be positively existential. Some of these claims are clearly the same as some mentioned in Chapter 4.[1] Let us note briefly now, in the case of one of them, how plausible, and how unplausible, it is. Suppose someone says ' All the books in his room are by English authors ' (S1). An acceptable paraphrase of this would be ' There is not a (single) book in his room which is not by an English author ' (S2). If in the formula ' $\sim(\exists x)(fx \cdot \sim gx)$ ' we give the value ' is a book in his room ' to ' f ' and ' is by an English author ' to ' g ', we obtain the sentence ' There is nothing which is both a book in his room and not by an English author ' (S3). And these two sentences, S2 and S3, seem very close. Yet, by the rules of the system, ' $\sim(\exists x)(fx)$ ' entails ' $\sim(\exists x)(fx \cdot \sim gx)$ '; so that to use the sentence employing quantification and read as S3 would be to make a true statement even if the room in question had no books in it at all. But it would seem grotesque to maintain that anyone saying ' All the books in his room are by English authors ' had made a true statement if the room referred to were empty of books; and a bad joke to argue ' There's not a book in his room; so there's not a book in his room which is not by an English author '. This reminds us that approximate interpretations in ordinary language of the symbolic expressions of a system (such as the interpretation incorporated in S3) may be misleading; that they may have to be corrected, re-understood, in the light of the rules of the system. For here we have two ordinary

[1] See p. 110.

English sentences (S1 and S2) which seem interchangeable, and of which one seems very like the reading (S3) proposed for a sentence of the form ' $\sim(\exists x)(fx . \sim gx)$ '. Yet it seems to be a necessary condition of the truth of a statement made by the use of either of the former that there should be books in the room referred to; while, so far from the fulfilment of this condition being necessary to the truth of the quantificational statement, the truth of the latter is entailed by the non-fulfilment of the condition.

To save the quantificational analysis in such cases, some have thought it enough to stipulate for the fulfilment of the existential condition, at least to the extent of one member of the subject class; offering a sentence of the form ' $\sim(\exists x)(fx . \sim gx) . (\exists x)(fx)$ '. This has the effect, for our example, of adding the clause ' and there is at least one book in his room '. We might still hesitate, on more than one ground, to say that the result gives the meaning of the original sentence.[1]

A claim more striking than those so far mentioned is sometimes made on behalf of this symbolism : viz., that many sentences which we should at first sight take to be straightforward exemplifications of a simple predicative formula really require analysis in quantificational terms if their form is to be made explicit. Thus the form of ' A man fell over ' is to be revealed by writing ' $(\exists x)(x$ is a man $. x$ fell over$)$ '; and the form of ' The King of England smiled ' is to be disclosed by the expression ' $(\exists x)[x$ is King of England $. (y)(y$ is King of England $\supset x = y) . x$ smiled$]$ '. Similar treatment is to be accorded to all sentences with singular subjects introduced by the indefinite or definite article. These claims I shall discuss later.[1]

Among other things, then, it is claimed for the modern quantificational system that it formalizes the logic of ordinary sentences beginning with ' all ', ' some ', and ' no '. But there is another and older system for which a similar claim used to be made, viz., the system of categorical propositions which we owe to Aristotle, and which employs such comparatively familiar-looking schemata as ' all s is p ' and ' some s is p '. It is orthodox modern doctrine that when the older system is cleared of obscurities and contradictions, it emerges as simply a small part of quantificational logic, all its formulae being interpretable in

[1] See Chapter 6.

terms of formulae of the latter. This doctrine, however, usually rests upon an unvoiced assumption that the quantificational system is in some sense the ' correct ' one. We cannot in fact be sure how the Aristotelian formulae are to be interpreted until we have studied the rules of the Aristotelian system. It might be possible to find for the system a consistent interpretation in which its constants approximate fairly closely to the ' all ' and ' some ' of ordinary speech, while its formulae differ in meaning from the formulae of the quantificational logic to which they are commonly assimilated. So we shall postpone a full examination of the claim that the quantificational system formalizes the logic of general statements, until we have examined the traditional system. Then we may compare both together with our ordinary uses of ' all ', ' some ', &c.

7. One final point must first be made. I have said that the existential quantifier is to be read ' There is (exists) at least one thing (person) which (who) . . .' Now in ordinary speech we commonly indicate the time-reference of a verb by difference of tense. We distinguish between ' There exists . . .' and ' There existed . . .', between ' There is . . .' and ' There will be . . .'; and in contexts in which such distinctions are relevant we take ' There is . . .' to apply, roughly, to the time of speaking or writing. In some contexts the question of time-reference does not arise. For example, the sentence ' There is at least one prime number between 16 and 20 ' does not mean that there is one at the moment. Nor does it mean that there always has been, is now, and always will be one such prime number. For it makes no sense to speak of such a number beginning or ending or going on and on. We might say that in this context ' There is . . .' is timeless; and so, in such a context, is ' $(\exists x)$ '. But consider contexts in which the question of time-reference does arise. How are we to express in the symbolism of quantifiers the difference between ' There is ', ' There was ', ' There will be '? We might rely upon putting the tense-indication into the dependent clause following the quantifier. For example, we might try writing the sentence ' There was at least one woman among the survivors ' in the form ' $(\exists x)(x$ is a woman . x was among the survivors) '. But to say ' There *is* at least one person who is a woman and was among the survivors ' is at least

to suggest that the person is alive at the time the sentence is uttered : and no such suggestion is carried by the original sentence. Changing the second 'is' to 'was' will not help; it will merely prompt the question 'What became of her then? Has she changed her sex?' Nor can the difficulty be evaded by declaring '($\exists x$)' in this sentence to be timeless; it is not true that when we speak of persons and incidents the question of time-reference does not arise. One possible resource is to say that '($\exists x$)', in contexts where it is not timeless, is ambiguously tensed, meaning either 'There is' or 'There was' or 'There will be'; and that we must rely on the context, or introduce some special indication, to remove, where necessary, the ambiguity. It is not always necessary to remove it; or, rather, temporal indefiniteness is not always temporal ambiguity. For there is a further distinguishable use of the grammatically present tense in which no particular reference to the time of utterance as opposed to any other time is intended, even though temporal happenings bear directly upon the truth of what is said. If, to revert to an earlier example, I say 'No one loves without somebody suffering', I do not intend to assert merely that no one at the moment loves without somebody suffering. I intend to assert rather that no one has so loved, no one will so love, and no one now so loves. So the negation of '($\exists x$)', interpreted this time *disjunctively* as 'There is or was or will be', will serve my turn; nor should we, in such a context as this, speak of '($\exists x$)' as temporally ambiguous any more than we speak of this quite common use of the present tense in ordinary language with a general temporal reference as ambiguous. Sentences in which the present tense is used in this way might be called 'temporally unrestricted' or 'omnitemporal' sentences.

From the point of view of time-reference, then, it seems that the device of quantification is reasonably well adapted to deal with the timeless sentences of, e.g., mathematics, and with temporally unrestricted sentences; but rather ill-adapted to deal with those sentences in which a time-reference, relative to the moment of utterance, is given by the choice of tense of the verb. The point is not unimportant. We shall see it later as a particular instance of a more general limitation on the scope of formal logic.

6

SUBJECTS, PREDICATES, AND EXISTENCE

I. THE TRADITIONAL SYSTEM OF CATEGORICAL PROPOSITIONS [1]

1. TRADITIONAL formal logic had in the main two parts, of which one was considerably more developed than the other. The less developed part dealt rather summarily with the hypothetical and disjunctive forms of proposition.[2] It consisted mainly in listing a few forms of valid inference (e.g., ' If p then q; but not-q; ∴ not-p ') and pointing out certain common fallacies (e.g., that of inferring in accordance with the pattern ' If p then q; and q; ∴ p '). The more developed part treated of the logical relations of certain formulae of which the variables took as values, not complete sentences, but parts of sentences. The first of these two parts invites comparison with the modern propositional calculus; the second with the modern predicative calculus. But whereas close formal connexions are, as we have seen, established between the propositional and predicative calculuses, no such connexion is traced in the traditional logic between its two parts. It is the second and more developed part, the traditional system of categorical propositions, that we are to be concerned with.

In this system four forms of proposition, or statement-formulae, are recognized. They are referred to respectively as the A, E, I, and O forms; and may be written as follows :

> All x is y
> No x is y
> Some x is y
> Some x is not y

I have said that the system invites comparison with the predicative calculus. But there are important differences between

---

[1] I am largely indebted, in the formal part of this chapter, to Dr. Miller's excellent monograph, *The Structure of Aristotelian Logic*.

[2] Inferences of the kind dealt with by this part of the traditional logic are sometimes called ' hypothetical syllogisms '.

them. One such difference is that in the traditional system there is no distinction in the type of variables. For the role of variables I have selected the small letters ' x ', ' y ', ' z ', &c., and this may recall the individual variables of the quantificational system; but in fact they are more closely analogous to the predicative variables of that system or to the class variables of the class system. Expressions which can replace variables in the above formulae to form sentences are called *terms*; and we may therefore call ' x ', ' y ', and ' z ' *term-variables*. It would commonly be said by exponents of the system that such sentences as

> All alcohol is poisonous
> All elephants are long-lived
> All tigers growl
> All the guests sat down

are sentences of the A form. And this calls for comment. For obviously, except for the first, none of these sentences exemplifies the formula ' All x is y ' in the straightforward sense of being obtainable from it by substitution of words for the variables. The formula does not allow for differences in tense and grammatical number; nor for the enormous class of ' all '-sentences which do not contain, as their main verb, the verb ' to be '. We might try to recast the sentences so that they at least fitted into one of the two patterns ' All x is y ' or ' All x are y '; but the results would be, as English, often clumsy and sometimes absurd. Moreover, there is another difficulty of the same kind. The development of the system requires that we should frequently be able to take two terms as identical when they occur in different parts of sentences; e.g., that we should recognize as identical the second term in ' All the officials left before midnight ' and the first term in ' All those who left before midnight were sober '. Further contortions of the language would be necessary to secure exact verbal identity in all such cases. It seems preferable therefore to regard the four formulae not as patterns to be strictly exemplified in order for a statement to qualify as of the corresponding form, but rather as representative patterns in terms of which are to be traced the logical relations of large classes of statements having resemblances indicated, though not rigidly defined, by those patterns.

The examples I gave call for a further comment. We are here, for the first time, dealing with a formal system in which the constants ('all ', ' some ', &c.) are words occurring in ordinary speech. This alone does not guarantee that they have within the system just the sense which they have in ordinary speech; does not guarantee that the sentence 'Some tigers growl ', for example, taken as a sentence of the I form has the very same sense as it would have in its ordinary employment. We cannot be sure of the interpretation of the constants of the system, until we have studied the rules of the system, seen what inference-patterns are recognized as valid within it, &c.[1] The same study will reveal how far the laws of the traditional system parallel the laws of the class and predicative calculuses, and hence how far the constants of the old system are inter-interpretable with those of the new.

In any given sentence exemplifying one of these formulae, the first term is called the *subject* and the second the *predicate*.   I may sometimes apply these names, by an obvious extension, to the first and second term-variables respectively; and I may sometimes refer to the variables as 'terms ' for the sake of brevity.

By prefixing ' non- ' to any term or term-variable, we obtain a negative term or term-variable. Thus we may have, as variants of the A form

$$\text{All non-}x \text{ is } y$$
$$\text{All } x \text{ is non-}y$$
$$\text{All non-}x \text{ is non-}y$$

An example of a sentence of the E form containing one negative term would be ' No non-fiction is saleable '.

The A and E forms are said to be *universal*; the I and O forms *particular*. The A and I forms are called *affirmative*; the E and O forms *negative*. The distinction between universal and particular forms is called a distinction of *quantity*; that between affirmative and negative forms a distinction of *quality*. It should be noted that the presence of negative terms

---

[1] Equally, of course, we must not simply ignore the ordinary sense of the words in deciding on the interpretation of the constants. It will be a matter of adjusting the interpretation to the rules in the light of the ordinary sense. The ordinary sense provides a point of departure.

does not imply a negative form; e.g., ' All non-x is non-y ' is of the A, i.e., an affirmative, form.

The four forms may conveniently be symbolized as follows : ' xAy ', ' xEy ', ' xIy ', xOy '. (In the light of the previous remarks concerning exemplification, this symbolization may be seen as more than a mere notational convenience.)   A negative term may be symbolized by writing the variable with a dash (e.g., ' x' '); so that we shall have, as special cases of the A form ' $x'Ay$ ', ' $x'Ay'$ ', and ' xAy' '.

2. We have next to inquire what inference-patterns are recognized as valid in the system, and what logical relations hold between its formulae; or, in other words, what are the laws of the system.   One respect in which the older system is in marked contrast with the newer ones is its relative formal poverty.   The number of different formulae admitted is notably small; and so is the number of valid inference-patterns.   Whereas I have given only a tiny selection of the indefinite range of laws which could be established in the newer systems, it will be quite a short task to list all those recognized in the traditional logic.   In writing down the laws of the old system, it will be convenient to use some of the symbolism of the new.   This will not in the least change their character; it will simply save space. For instance, instead of writing : ' The inference-pattern

$$xAy$$
$$yAz$$
$$\therefore \ xAz$$

is valid ', I shall simply write down the first-order formula

$$xAy \,.\, yAz \supset xAz$$

numbering it as one of the laws or analytic formulae of the system.   Similarly, instead of writing

'xAy ' is the contradictory of ' xOy '

I shall write down, as an analytic formula

$$xAy \equiv \, \sim xOy.$$

Where, as in the last case, a law simply relates two formulae in which the terms themselves, the quality of the terms, and their order are all identical, we can simplify the expression of the law still further : instead of the above equivalence, we can write

$$A \equiv \sim O.$$

To write this as an analytic formula is the same as to say that any sentence of the A form is the contradictory of the *corresponding* sentence of the O form.

The laws of the traditional system fall into three main groups. These are :

> (1) The laws of immediate inference, which detail various valid transformations of statements of the four forms;
> (2) The laws of the square of opposition, which give certain logical relations between formulae in which the terms, their quality, and their order are the same;
> (3) The laws of the syllogism, which list valid inference-patterns each involving three formulae.

(1) *Immediate Inferences*

(a) *Simple conversion* consists in transposing the subject and predicate, the quantity and quality remaining unchanged. The simple conversion of E and I statements and of these only is valid in the system. Thus

> (i) $x\mathrm{E}y \supset y\mathrm{E}x$
> (ii) $x\mathrm{I}y \supset y\mathrm{I}x$

are laws of the system, and the corresponding inference-patterns are valid; but

$$x\mathrm{A}y \supset y\mathrm{A}x$$
$$x\mathrm{O}y \supset y\mathrm{O}x$$

are not laws of the system, and the corresponding inference-patterns are invalid.

(b) *Conversion per accidens* consists in transposing the subject and predicate of a statement and changing its quantity from universal to particular, the quality remaining unchanged. We have here as laws

> (iii) $x\mathrm{A}y \supset y\mathrm{I}x$
> (iv) $x\mathrm{E}y \supset y\mathrm{O}x$

It should be noted that while (i) and (ii) yield equivalences, (iii) and (iv) do not. Using the machinery of proof of the propositional calculus, we can, for example, derive from (i), by substitution of 'y' for 'x' and 'x' for 'y', the expression '$y\mathbf{E}x \supset x\mathbf{E}y$'. Taking this together with (i) and using the definition of equivalence, we have '$x\mathbf{E}y \equiv y\mathbf{E}x$'. A parallel result cannot be obtained for (iii) and (iv).

(c) *Obversion* (or *Permutation*) consists in negating the predicate and changing the quality of the statement, subject and quantity remaining the same. Any statement of one of the four forms can be validly obverted. Thus we have

$$(\text{v}) \quad x\mathbf{A}y \supset x\mathbf{E}y'$$
$$(\text{vi}) \quad x\mathbf{E}y \supset x\mathbf{A}y'$$
$$(\text{vii}) \quad x\mathbf{I}y \supset x\mathbf{O}y'$$
$$(\text{viii}) \quad x\mathbf{O}y \supset x\mathbf{I}y'$$

As an example of the entailment of '$x\mathbf{A}y'$' by '$x\mathbf{E}y$', we may take the entailment of ' All democrats are non-Fascists ' by ' No democrats are Fascists '.

(d) *Contraposition* and *Inversion* consist in successive applications of certain of the above operations. E.g., contraposition consists in (1) obverting, (2) converting the result, and (3) obverting again; and can be validly carried out in just those cases where each successive operation is valid. Thus the contrapositive of A is the result of the final step in the sequence

$$x\mathbf{A}y$$
$$x\mathbf{E}y' \text{ (by obversion)}$$
$$y'\mathbf{E}x \text{ (by conversion)}$$
$$y'\mathbf{A}x' \text{ (by obversion)}$$

and we have, as a law of contraposition,

$$x\mathbf{A}y \supset y'\mathbf{A}x'$$

These laws will not be separately listed.

(2) *The Square of Opposition*

The doctrine of the Square of Opposition concerns the logical relations between any two statements of different forms having the same subject and predicate. Since the terms, their position, and quality are identical in the related statements, we can symbolize the laws of the doctrine simply by using the letters A, E, I, O. The doctrine is as follows : A is the contradictory of O, and E of I; A and E are contraries, and I and O subcontraries; A entails I, and E entails O.   Expressing these relations as laws, we have

$$
\begin{array}{lll}
\text{(ix)} & xAy \equiv \sim xOy & \text{or } A \equiv \sim O \\
\text{(x)} & xEy \equiv \sim xIy & \text{or } E \equiv \sim I \\
\text{(xi)} & \sim(xAy \cdot xEy) & \text{or } \sim(A \cdot E) \\
\text{(xii)} & xIy \lor xOy & \text{or } I \lor O \\
\text{(xiii)} & xAy \supset xIy & \text{or } A \supset I \\
\text{(xiv)} & xEy \supset xOy & \text{or } E \supset O
\end{array}
$$

(3) *The Syllogism*

The doctrine of the syllogism is the main achievement of traditional logic. So far we have been concerned with the logical relations between only two statement-formulae at a time. The doctrine of the syllogism is concerned with a certain class of inference-patterns involving three statement-formulae, two as premises and one as conclusion. The class of inference-patterns in question may be specified as follows : (*a*) one term of one premise is to be identical with one term of the other; (*b*) the other two terms of the premises are to be identical with the terms of the conclusion. A syllogism is an argument or inference exemplifying an inference-pattern, whether valid or invalid, which answers to this description.[1] The theory of the syllogism prescribes which of all the possible inference-patterns answering to this description are to count as valid. An example of such a pattern was given on p. 155.

Now there is a relatively small number of inference-patterns, valid or invalid, of the kind described. This number is determined by two factors : (*a*) the number of different statement-forms, which is four; (*b*) the number of logically significant variations in the relative positions of the terms. That the relative positions of the terms may make a difference to the validity of the inference-pattern can readily be seen. For example, the inference-patterns

$$
\begin{array}{cc}
xAy & xAy \\
yAz & zAy \\
\hline
\therefore \quad xAz & \therefore \quad xAz
\end{array}
$$

both consist entirely of A forms; and the only difference be-

---

[1] By some writers the word 'syllogism' is so used that 'valid syllogism' is pleonastic.

tween them is in the order of the terms in the second premise. But, assuming that the ' all ' of the system approximates in sense to the ' all ' of ordinary speech, we should be inclined to regard inferences of the left-hand pattern as valid, and those of the right-hand pattern as invalid.   There are four logically significant variations in the arrangement of the terms : (*a*) the term common to both premises (the *middle term*) may be the subject of both; (*b*) it may be the predicate of both; or (*c*) it may be the subject of one and the predicate of the other—and this case subdivides into (i) the case where it is the subject of the premise of which the predicate is also the predicate of the conclusion, and (ii) the case where it is the subject of the premise of which the predicate is the subject of the conclusion.   These four cases are called the four *figures* of the syllogism, and are commonly represented as follows (where ' *m* ' stands for the middle term, ' *p* ' for the term which is the predicate of the conclusion, and ' *s* ' for the term which is its subject) :

Figure 1	2	3	4
m p	*p m*	*m p*	*p m*
s m	*s m*	*m s*	*m s*
s p	*s p*	*s p*	*s p*

It might seem that reversing the order of the premises would increase the number of variations.   But the premises together form a conjunctive statement, the order of the conjuncts of which is, for the present purpose, logically indifferent.   Indeed, I shall commonly write the premises in the reverse order to that conventionally illustrated above, the better to bring out analogies with laws already considered of the predicative and class calculuses.

It is easy to see that in each figure there are sixty-four arithmetically possible forms or *moods* of syllogism.   For the first premise may have any of the forms A, E, I, O; for each of these four possibilities, the second premise may also have any of the four forms; and for each of these sixteen possibilities, the conclusion may have any one of the four forms; which yields sixty-four moods in each figure.   Since there are four figures, there are altogether 256 possible moods of the syllogism. Of these 256 only twenty-four are recognized as valid; the rest are invalid. The valid moods are normally listed as follows :

1st Figure	AAA,	EAE,	AII,	EIO,	AAI,	EAO
2nd Figure	EAE,	AEE,	EIO,	AOO,	EAO,	AEO
3rd Figure	AAI,	IAI,	AII,	EAO,	OAO,	EIO
4th Figure	AAI,	AEE,	IAI,	EAO,	EIO,	AEO

where the first letter in each case stands for the premise containing the term which is the predicate of the conclusion (the *major premise*), the second letter for the premise containing the term which is the subject of the conclusion (the *minor premise*), and the third letter for the conclusion. Reversing the order of the premises, we could write the corresponding laws as follows (I select the first mood of each figure as an illustration) :

$$(\text{xv}) \quad xAy \,.\, yAz \supset xAz$$
$$(\text{xxi}) \quad xAy \,.\, zEy \supset xEz$$
$$(\text{xxvii}) \quad yAx \,.\, yAz \supset xIz$$
$$(\text{xxxiii}) \quad yAx \,.\, zAy \supset xIz$$

It will be seen that I have allowed for the numbering of the remaining laws, to some of which I shall later refer.

3. In the last section I have made no mention of any general method of testing inference-patterns for validity, nor have I attempted to derive any one law from any other. I have not in fact sought to show that the laws mentioned were connected with one another in any of the ways which justify the application of the name 'system' to the propositional, class, and predicative calculuses. I have simply given a *list* of the laws of the traditional logic. But plainly the laws listed are not all independent of one another. For example, our list contains the laws

(xi) $xAy \supset xIy$ (Square of Opposition)

(xv) $xAy \,.\, yAz \supset xAz$ (1st mood of 1st figure of the syllogism)

(xix) $xAy \,.\, yAz \supset xIz$ (5th mood of 1st figure of the syllogism)

But if we had two statements of the forms ' xAy ' and ' yAz ' as premises, we could obviously derive the corresponding statement of the form ' xIz ' by the use of the first two laws alone, without the direct application of the third. Law (xv) yields the conclusion ' xAz ' and (xi) enables us to derive from this the conclusion ' xIz '.　Given the other two laws, law (xix) is super-fluous.　We should therefore expect there to be a procedure for deriving (xix) from the other two laws; and it is not difficult to see how the application of the machinery of proof of the pro-positional calculus would enable us to do this.

Now there do exist, in the traditional expositions of the sub-ject, two doctrines, each of which represents a partial system-atization of the laws.　One is the doctrine of *reduction*; the other that of *the rules of the syllogism.*　The first is roughly analogous to the modern deductive method of systematizing; the second to a testing method.　The second consists of a set of higher-order statements laying down the conditions to which a given syllogistic inference-pattern must conform if it is to be valid.　These statements are few in number, and the validity of any pattern can be determined simply by consulting them to see if the pattern conforms to the rules.

The doctrine of the rules is of less logical interest than that of reduction.　The general theory of the latter is that, by the use of the procedures of immediate inference and of the laws of the Square of Opposition, all the inference-patterns of the second, third, and fourth figures can be ' reduced ' to those of the first. By a further application of these or similar methods, those of the first figure can be reduced to one.　The logical interest of re-duction lies in the close analogy between it and deduction.　To reduce one inference-pattern to another is, in effect, to deduce the law corresponding to the first from the law corresponding to the second.　It is this analogy which I wish to bring out by taking two examples, one of each kind of reduction recognized (*direct* and *indirect* reduction) and exhibiting them as deductions of the kind familiar in the propositional calculus.　I shall make use of the rules of inference and some of the laws of the proposi-tional calculus, together with the supplementary rule that logically equivalent expressions may be substituted for one another in any formula.　By means of the latter rule we shall, for example, be able directly to substitute for an I or E formula its simple converse (see p. 156).

(1)　Direct reduction of one syllogism to another is traditionally described as follows : to reduce a form of syllogism B to a form of syllogism A is to show that from the premises of B or premises obtained from them by conversion, there follows in A either the conclusion of B or a conclusion from which the conclusion of B follows by conversion.   I take as an example the direct reduction of

$$xEy \cdot zAy \therefore xEz \text{ (2nd figure, 2nd mood)}$$

to

$$xAy \cdot yEz \therefore xEz \text{ (1st figure, 2nd mood)}$$

and this I want to exhibit as the deduction of

$$\text{(xxii) } xEy \cdot zAy \supset xEz$$

from

$$\text{(xvi) } xAy \cdot yEz \supset xEz$$

From (xvi) we obtain, by substituting for ' yEz ' and ' xEz ' the equivalent (converse) formulae ' zEy ' and ' zEx ',

$$xAy \cdot zEy \supset zEx$$

from which, by substitution on variables ('x' for 'z' and 'z' for 'x'), we obtain

$$zAy \cdot xEy \supset xEz$$

from which, by the law '$p \cdot q \equiv q \cdot p$' and the rule permitting substitution of equivalent expressions, we obtain

$$xEy \cdot zAy \supset xEz$$

which is the law to be derived.

(2) Indirect reduction is traditionally described as follows: to reduce indirectly one form of syllogism to another is to use the second to show that the falsity of the conclusion in the first is inconsistent with the truth of its premises.   I take as an example the reduction of

$$xOy \cdot zAy \quad \therefore \quad xOz \quad \text{(2nd figure, 4th mood)}$$

to $\qquad xAy \cdot yAz \quad \therefore \quad xAz \quad \text{(1st figure, 1st mood)}$

and this I shall exhibit as the deduction of the law corresponding to the first inference-pattern from the law corresponding to the second.   From

$$(a) \ xAy \cdot yAz \supset xAz$$

by Square of Opposition (ix) and substitution of equivalents, we obtain

$$(b) \sim xOy \mathbin{.} yAz \supset \sim xOz$$

From (b) by '$(p \supset \sim q) \supset \sim (p \mathbin{.} q)$' and Rule of Inference we obtain

$$(c) \sim [(\sim x\, Oy \mathbin{.} yAz) \mathbin{.} xOz]$$

From (c) by '$(p \mathbin{.} q) \mathbin{.} r \equiv (r \mathbin{.} q) \mathbin{.} p$' and substitution of equivalents we obtain

$$(d) \sim [(xOz \mathbin{.} yAz) \mathbin{.} \sim xOy]$$

From (d) by '$\sim (p \mathbin{.} \sim q) \supset (p \supset q)$' and Rule of Inference we obtain

$$(e) \ xOz \mathbin{.} yAz \supset xOy$$

From (e) by substitution of 'y' for 'z' and 'z' for 'y' we obtain

$$(f) \ xOy \mathbin{.} zAy \supset xOz$$

which is the law to be derived. Other reductions could, in ways similar to these, be exhibited as deductions.

What these examples help us to see is that it would be possible to present the whole body of laws of the traditional logic as a calculus or deductive system in the contemporary style. Such a calculus would require, as special axioms or postulates, a suitable selection of the special laws of the traditional system, including some laws of Immediate Inference and of the Square of Opposition and at least one syllogistic law; it would require suitable rules of inference; and it would presuppose the propositional calculus, i.e., would accept and make use of the theorems of the latter.

II. THE ORTHODOX CRITICISMS OF THE SYSTEM

4. The most interesting questions which have arisen about the traditional logic are questions concerning the interpretation of the system. One might be inclined to think that there could scarcely be a problem here; that, with certain reservations regarding the word 'some', the rules listed give a perfectly acceptable account of the logical powers of the words which figure as the constants of the system, as these words are most commonly used in ordinary speech; and that hence the solution

of the interpretation-problem is simply to equate the constants of the system with those words in their standard or typical employment. I shall try to show in the end that, with a few reservations, this naïve view is also the correct one. It has been so frequently disputed, however, that it has become orthodoxy to deny it; and, indeed, to go further and maintain that the constants of the system cannot be given any interpretation such that (a) they have roughly the same meaning as in ordinary speech and (b) all the rules of the system hold good together for that interpretation. It is, in other words, maintained that no consistent interpretation can be found for the system as a whole which approximates to the naïve interpretation. I want to show that this thesis is false; and false in an important way. For in seeing just how it is false, we come to notice an important general feature of the ordinary use of language which is systematically neglected in modern formal logic. For the proper purposes of that logic, this neglect is unimportant; it becomes important only when it impairs our understanding of ordinary speech.

Criticisms of the traditional system have centred round the question of whether or not, in using a sentence of one of the four forms, we are to be regarded as committing ourselves to the existence of anything answering to the description given by the first term of the sentence. It is felt that this question cannot be left unanswered; for the answer to it makes a difference to the validity of the laws. It is argued that the usage of the ordinary words (e.g., ' all ') corresponding to some of the constants of the system varies in this respect. Everyone agrees that it would be absurd to claim that the man who says ' All the books in his room are by English authors ' has made a true statement, if the room referred to has no books in it at all. Here is a case where the use of ' all ' carries the existential commitment. On the other hand, it is said, we sometimes use ' all ' without this commitment. To take a classic example : the statement made by ' All moving bodies not acted upon by external forces continue in a state of uniform motion in a straight line ' may well be true even if there never have been or will be any moving bodies not acted upon by external forces. The consistency-problem for the traditional system is then posed as follows. We must decide, with regard to each of the four forms, whether it carries the existential commitment or whether it does not.   But, for any plausible decision, i.e., any decision which keeps the constants of the system reasonably close in sense to their use as words of ordinary speech, we find that some of the laws of the traditional system become invalid.   It has generally been assumed that, in the case of the particular forms, i.e., I and O, only one decision was reasonable, viz., that they did carry the existential commitment; and that whichever decision was made for one of the universal forms, the same decision should be made for the other.   So the problem reduced itself to a dilemma.   Either the A and E forms have existential import or they do not.   If they do, one set of laws has to be sacrificed as invalid; if they do not, another set has to go. Therefore no consistent interpretation of the system as a whole, within the prescribed limits, is possible.

5. The detail of the dilemma is usually presented by way of an attempt to interpret the traditional system in terms of the class or predicative calculus.   And this procedure seems not unreasonable.   For the calculuses have the following characteristics.   First, the presence or absence of existential commitment is explicit in their formulae from the start; since all or nearly all of these formulae are either positively or negatively existential.   Second, they provide formulae which at least come fairly close in meaning to typical uses of forms of sentence in ordinary speech beginning with ' all ', ' some ', and ' no '. Third, there are striking formal analogies between laws of these systems and many laws of the traditional system.   The first of these points is obvious.   The second and third may be illustrated together.   We should normally accept ' All the books in his room are by English authors ' and ' At least one of the books in his room is not by an English author ' as contradictories.   The second sentence seems very close in form to ' $(\exists x)(fx \, . \sim gx)$ ', which is the contradictory of ' $(x)(fx \supset gx)$ '; and the first sentence would commonly be accepted as an instance of the form ' xAy ', which has as its contradictory ' xOy '.   It is true that we should hesitate to accept ' There is at least one thing which both f and not-g ' as a paraphrase of ' Some x's are not y '; which is the way we are told to read ' xOy '.   For to say, e.g., that some tigers are not fierce would normally be taken to

imply that there was more than one tiger which was not fierce. But then we should experience precisely the same hesitation over the proposed reading of ' xOy ', given that it is the contradictory of ' xAy '; for the contradictory of the statement that all tigers are fierce is the statement that at least one tiger is not fierce. The formulae ' $(\exists x)(fx . \sim gx)$ ' and ' xOy ', whatever their differences, have in common this particular discrepancy from the ordinary form ' Some x's are not y '. Once this degree of parallelism between the two kinds of formulae is admitted, striking formal analogies present themselves : e.g., that between the law of the first mood of the first figure

$$xAy . yAz \supset xAz$$

and the law of the transitivity of class-inclusion

$$\alpha \subset \beta . \beta \subset \gamma \supset \alpha \subset \gamma$$

or, in its quantificational form, the law

$$(x)(fx \supset gx) . (x)(gx \supset hx) \supset (x)(fx \supset hx).$$

To proceed with the working out of the dilemma. We saw that it consisted in having to decide whether the A and E forms were to have or to lack existential import as far as their subject-terms were concerned. This decision is to be taken in the shape of the adoption of one of two alternative interpretations of the four forms in terms of the class or quantificational formulae. It is already agreed that the I and O forms are to be regarded as having existential import, so their translation is a simple matter. For ' xIy ', ' xOy ', we adopt the positively existential readings ' $(\exists x)(fx . gx)$ ', ' $(\exists x)(fx . \sim gx)$ '; or, in class terms, ' $\alpha\beta \neq O$ ' and ' $\alpha\bar{\beta} \neq O$ ' respectively. For A and E, we are to choose between, on the one hand, conjoining the negatively existential formula (' $\sim (\exists x)(fx . \sim gx)$ ' for A) with an assertion of existence as far as the first ' term ' is concerned (' $(\exists x)(fx)$ '); or, on the other hand, adopting the negatively existential formula alone. For each of these alternative interpretations we are to try to determine how many of the laws of the traditional system hold good.[1]

---

[1] I summarize the steps which lead to (and from) this procedure. An ambiguity is noticed in the ordinary use of ' all '. This causes a doubt about the precise interpretation of the constants and formulae of the traditional system. To resolve this doubt, we try to find an unambiguous

I take first the second of the above alternatives. This yields the following table of translations :

Table 1

A	xAy	$\alpha\bar{\beta} = 0$	$\sim(\exists x)(fx . \sim gx)$
		or $\alpha \subset \beta$	or $(x)(fx \supset gx)$
E	xEy	$\alpha\beta = 0$	$\sim(\exists x)(fx . gx)$
		or $\alpha \subset \bar{\beta}$	or $(x)(fx \supset \sim gx)$
I	xIy	$\alpha\beta \neq 0$	$(\exists x)(fx . gx)$
		or $\sim(\alpha \subset \bar{\beta})$	or $\sim(x)(fx \supset \sim gx)$
O	xOy	$\alpha\bar{\beta} \neq 0$	$(\exists x)(fx . \sim gx)$
		or $\sim(\alpha \subset \beta)$	or $\sim(x)(fx \supset gx)$

Now to examine which of the laws hold good for this translation.

Conversion. Simple conversion of E and I obviously holds for this interpretation. Since ' $\alpha\beta = \beta\alpha$ ' is a law of the class system, ' $\alpha\beta = 0$ ' (' xEy ') and ' $\beta\alpha = 0$ ' (' yEx ') are equivalent, and so are ' $\alpha\beta \neq 0$ ' (' xIy ') and ' $\beta\alpha \neq 0$ ' (' yIx '). But, of course, ' $\alpha\bar{\beta} = \beta\bar{\alpha}$ ' is not a law, so the transposition of terms in A and O would, as under the traditional laws, be invalid. Similarly, in the predicative notation, ' fx ' and ' gx ' are validly interchangeable in ' $\sim(\exists x)(fx . gx)$ ' and ' $(\exists x)(fx . gx)$ ', but not in ' $\sim(\exists x)(fx . \sim gx)$ ' nor in ' $(\exists x)(fx . \sim gx)$ '.

Conversion per accidens, however, is no longer valid for this interpretation. We cannot infer from ' $\alpha\bar{\beta} = 0$ ' to ' $\beta\alpha \neq 0$ '. Or, in the other notation, we cannot infer from ' There is nothing which both f and not-g ' to ' There is at least one thing which both g and f '. A statement of the first form may be true

---

interpretation of the old system by exhibiting it as a part or fragment of the class or quantificational logic, translating each formula of the old system into some analogous formula of the new, which, however, has the merit of making its existential commitment explicit. If we fail to find a translation for each of the four forms such that *all* the laws of the traditional logic hold good for that translation, we are invited to conclude that the old system *as a whole* cannot be consistently interpreted in any way which approximates to the intentions of its exponents; that this inconsistency is due to an ambiguity in the forms, passed on from ordinary speech and concealed by the use of ordinary words as constants of the system; and that the best we can do for the old system is to choose the interpretation which will salvage as many of its laws as possible, and represent it as a misunderstood fragment of a system whose structure is now happily clear.

while the corresponding statement of the second form is false. Similarly, for the move from E to its limited converse O.

The class and predicative analogues of *obversion* are obviously valid :

$xAy \supset xEy'$ $\alpha\bar{\beta} = 0 \supset \alpha\bar{\beta} = 0$
$$\sim(\exists x)(fx \cdot \sim gx) \supset \sim(\exists x)(fx \cdot \sim gx)$$

$xEy \supset xAy'$ $\alpha\beta = 0 \supset \alpha\bar{\bar{\beta}} = 0$
$$\sim(\exists x)(fx \cdot gx) \supset \sim(\exists x)(fx \cdot \sim\sim gx)$$

$xIy \supset xOy'$ $\alpha\beta \neq 0 \supset \alpha\bar{\bar{\beta}} \neq 0$
$$(\exists x)(fx \cdot gx) \supset (\exists x)(fx \cdot \sim\sim gx)$$

$xOy \supset xIy'$ $\alpha\bar{\beta} \neq 0 \supset \alpha\bar{\beta} \neq 0$
$$(\exists x)(fx \cdot \sim gx) \supset (\exists x)(fx \cdot \sim gx)$$

Contraposition. The laws of contraposition for A and O remain valid, while the ' weakened ' contraposition of ' xEy ' to ' $y'Ox'$ ' breaks down. The formula for A is :

$xAy \supset y'Ax'$ $\alpha \subset \beta \supset \bar{\beta} \subset \bar{\alpha}$ $(x)(fx \supset gx) \supset (x)(\sim gx \supset \sim fx)$

Square of Opposition. It is the old laws of the Square of Opposition which suffer the heaviest casualties :

(1) The rule that A is the contradictory of O of course continues to hold : ' $\sim(\exists x)(fx \cdot \sim gx)$ ' is the contradictory of ' $(\exists x)(fx \cdot \sim gx)$ '.

(2) Similarly, for the rule that E is the contradictory of I.

the other logical relations cease to hold.

(3) A and E are no longer contraries. Corresponding statements of the forms ' $\sim(\exists x)(fx \cdot \sim gx)$ ' and ' $\sim(\exists x)(fx \cdot gx)$ ' (or ' $\alpha\bar{\beta} = 0$ ' and ' $\alpha\beta = 0$ ') can be true together, namely in the case where the corresponding statement of the form ' $\sim(\exists x)(fx)$ ' (or ' $\alpha = 0$ ') is true.

(4) Similarly, I and O are not subcontraries : statements of the forms ' $(\exists x)(fx \cdot gx)$ ' and ' $(\exists x)(fx \cdot \sim gx)$ ' will be false together when the corresponding statement of the form ' $\sim(\exists x)(fx)$ ' is true.

(5) A does not entail I. To say that the class $\alpha\bar{\beta}$ is empty is not to say that the class $\alpha\beta$ has members.

(6) E does not entail O. Saying that there is nothing which both f and g is not to commit oneself to saying that there is at least one thing which both f and not-g.

The Syllogism.   There is no need to go into the detail of which of the accepted moods of the syllogism will be invalid on this interpretation.   It is apparent from the previous cases that all those moods in which the truth of the premises, as now interpreted, allows of a certain class being empty, while the truth of the conclusion requires that class to have members, will be invalid.   An obvious example is AAI in the first figure.

The features of the proposed interpretation which are responsible for this outbreak of invalidity in the accepted laws are fairly obvious.   In every case mentioned the breakdown of the law has been a direct consequence of one or both of two facts : first, that statements of the A and E forms, as we have interpreted them, are true in those cases where the subject-class is empty; second, that statements of the I and O forms in this interpretation cannot be true if the subject-class is empty.   In the predicative notation : ' $\sim(\exists x)(fx)$ ' entails the truth of ' $\sim(\exists x)(fx . \sim gx)$ ' and ' $\sim(\exists x)(fx . gx)$ ' and the falsity of ' $(\exists x)(fx . \sim gx)$ ' and ' $(\exists x)(fx . gx)$ '.

The prospects for the alternative interpretation, in which one of these features is eliminated, might seem a little fairer.   Moreover, by adding an existential commitment to the universal forms, this interpretation may seem to possess the additional advantage of bringing us a little closer to the most frequent uses of ' all ' and ' no ' forms in ordinary speech.   So let us try substituting for Table 1 the revised translation-table below :

Table 2

xAy	$\alpha\bar{\beta} = 0 . \alpha \neq 0$	$\sim(\exists x)(fx . \sim gx) . (\exists x)(fx)$
xEy	$\alpha\beta = 0 . \alpha \neq 0$	$\sim(\exists x)(fx . gx) . (\exists x)(fx)$
xIy	$\alpha\beta \neq 0$	$(\exists x)(fx . gx)$
xOy	$\alpha\bar{\beta} \neq 0$	$(\exists x)(fx . \sim gx)$

It is true that this second interpretation saves the validity of some of the traditional laws which have to be sacrificed on the first; but not of all.   And this limited success is gained at the cost of rendering yet other laws of the old system invalid.   For instance, of the laws of the Square of Opposition, the new interpretation saves

A ⊃ I $\sim(\exists x)(fx . \sim gx) . (\exists x)(fx) \supset (\exists x)(fx . gx)$

E ⊃ O $\sim(\exists x)(fx . gx) . (\exists x)(fx) \supset (\exists x)(fx . \sim gx)$

$\sim$(A . E) $\sim[\sim(\exists x)(fx . \sim gx) . (\exists x)(fx) . \sim(\exists x)(fx . gx)]$

That is, it preserves the two entailments of particular by universal forms and the rule that A and E are contraries. But it fails to save the rule that I and O cannot both be false. And it renders invalid the laws ' A $\equiv$ $\sim$O ' and ' E $\equiv$ $\sim$I '. For if O is negated to yield its contradictory, we obtain ' $\sim$$(\exists x)(fx \cdot \sim gx)$ '; we do not also obtain the positively existential component of the new A form. A and O are no longer contradictories, but only contraries; since, while both cannot be true for a given example, both may be false, in the case where the positively existential component of A is false. Similarly, E and I are only contraries.

The new interpretation preserves the validity of the conversion *per accidens* of A to I, but not that of E to O. Moreover, it renders invalid the simple conversion of E. The formula ' $\alpha\beta = O \cdot \alpha \neq O$ ' and ' $\beta\alpha = O \cdot \beta \neq O$ ' are by no means equivalent. To say ' Nobody is both an architect and an angel; and there is at least one architect ' is not the same as to say ' Nobody is both an angel and an architect; and there is at least one angel '. And with the validity of the simple conversion of E goes the validity of a number of forms of syllogism.

The dilemma, then, is a clear one. It rests upon the assumption that the only two unambiguous interpretations of the system for which its constants approximate in sense to their ordinary use are the two just considered. Unless this assumption can be shown to be mistaken, the conclusion must be accepted that there is no consistent and acceptable interpretation of the system as a whole.

III. SUBJECTS AND PREDICATES

6. This conclusion, and the assumption upon which it rests, are in fact mistaken. It is perfectly possible to find interpretations for the A, E, I, and O forms for which all the laws of the traditional system hold good together. There are at least two distinct, though related, methods by which this can be done. One has only a limited and formalistic interest; the other illuminates some general features of our ordinary speech. But though they are very different in certain respects, the ways in which they operate to save the consistency of the system are closely related. I give the formalistic solution first, partly for

the sake of completeness and partly for the light it casts on the second, or realistic, solution.

The first method consists simply in a further elaboration of the kind of interpretation in class or quantificational terms which we have been considering.　It is a kind of *ad hoc* patching up of the old system in order to represent it, in its entirety, as a fragment of the new.　The method is to encounter every breakdown in a traditional law by amending the class or predicative interpretation suggested in such a way as to secure its validity. For example our second attempt at providing a translation in terms of positively and negatively existential formulae left us with three laws of the Square of Opposition invalid.　So we begin with the *ad hoc* prevention of these breakdowns.　Thus we want to make A and O contradictories.　Now, on Table 2, A is ' $\sim(\exists x)(fx \cdot \sim gx) \cdot (\exists x)(fx)$ ' and O is ' $(\exists x)(fx \cdot \sim gx)$ '. The contradictory of an expression of the form ' $\sim p \cdot q$ ' is the corresponding expression of the form ' $p \lor \sim q$ '.　We accordingly decide to make O of this form by re-interpreting it as ' $(\exists x)(fx \cdot \sim gx) \lor \sim(\exists x)(fx)$ '.　A and O are now contradictories.　Similarly, we re-interpret I as

$$(\exists x)(fx \cdot gx) \lor \sim(\exists x)(fx)$$

so that it is the contradictory of E, which is

$$\sim(\exists x)(fx \cdot gx) \cdot (\exists x)(fx).$$

It is evident that we have, by this manœuvre, saved the law that I and O are subcontraries (i.e., that corresponding statements of these forms cannot both be false).　This law broke down for the previous interpretations because corresponding statements of these forms *could* both be false, in the case where the corresponding statement of the form ' $\sim(\exists x)(fx)$ ' was true. But on the new interpretation the truth of this statement is a sufficient condition of the truth of both I and O statements; since ' $q \supset p \lor q$ ' is analytic.　Nor do we sacrifice any of the other laws of the Square of Opposition in saving these three. A and E have not been altered, so they remain contraries.　The laws ' $A \supset I$ ' and ' $E \supset O$ ' remain valid.　For the old form of I entails the new form of I, and A entails the old form of I; hence A entails the new form of I.　Similarly, E entails the new O.

Further amendments, however, are required. Although we have saved all the laws of the Square of Opposition, we have not altered E of Table 2; so its simple conversion remains invalid. Moreover, the amendments so far made render invalid the simple conversion of I. If we transpose the terms (i.e., the predicative variables) in the formula ' $(\exists x)(fx \cdot gx) \vee \sim(\exists x)(fx)$ ' we obtain ' $(\exists x)(gx \cdot fx) \vee \sim(\exists x)(gx)$ '; and these formulae are by no means equivalent. For ' $\sim(\exists x)(fx) \cdot (\exists x)(gx)$ ' entails the first and is inconsistent with the second.

The reason for the breakdown of the conversion of E was that ' $\sim(\exists x)(gx)$ ' [or ' $\beta = O$ '] was consistent with

$$\sim(\exists x)(fx \cdot gx) \cdot (\exists x)(fx) \quad [\text{or } \alpha\beta = O \cdot \alpha \neq O]$$

but not with its simple converse

$$\sim(\exists x)(gx \cdot fx) \cdot (\exists x)(gx) \quad [\text{or } \beta\alpha = O \cdot \beta \neq O].$$

The term-symmetry of E can obviously be restored, and the breakdown prevented, by adopting the interpretation

$$\sim(\exists x)(fx \cdot gx) \cdot (\exists x)(fx) \cdot (\exists x)(gx) \quad [\text{or } \alpha\beta = O \cdot \alpha \neq O \cdot \beta \neq O]$$

Similarly, the term-symmetry of I can be restored by re-interpreting it as

$$(\exists x)(fx \cdot gx) \vee \sim(\exists x)(fx) \vee \sim(\exists x)(gx)$$

which also maintains its status as the contradictory of E. Adopting these readings for E and I will obviously force us to make further alterations in the other forms in order to preserve their logical relations. Since, by the rule of obversion, ' xAy ' is equivalent to ' xEy' ', we can obtain the appropriate interpretation for A simply by negating the second term (' g ' or ' β ') throughout the latest form of E; which gives us

$$\sim(\exists x)(fx \cdot \sim gx) \cdot (\exists x)(fx) \cdot (\exists x)(\sim gx)$$
$$[\text{or } \alpha\bar{\beta} = O \cdot \alpha \neq O \cdot \bar{\beta} \neq O]$$

Finally, O, as the contradictory of A, must be re-interpreted as

$$(\exists x)(fx \cdot gx) \vee \sim(\exists x)(fx) \vee \sim(\exists x)(\sim gx).$$

So we have, as our final interpretation :

Table 3

A $\sim(\exists x)(fx \, . \sim gx) \, . \, (\exists x)(fx) \, . \, (\exists x)(\sim gx)$
E $\sim(\exists x)(fx \, . \, gx) \, . \, (\exists x)(fx) \, . \, (\exists x)(gx)$
I $(\exists x)(fx \, . \, gx) \vee \sim(\exists x)(fx) \vee \sim(\exists x)(gx)$
O $(\exists x)(fx \, . \sim gx) \vee \sim(\exists x)(fx) \vee \sim(\exists x)(\sim gx).$

For this interpretation, all the laws of the traditional logic hold good together; and they hold good within the logic of classes or quantified formulae; as a part of that logic.

So the consistency of the system can be secured in this way. But the price paid for consistency will seem a high one, if we are at all anxious that the constants ' all,' ' some ', and ' no ' of the system should faithfully reflect the typical logical behaviour of these words in ordinary speech. It is quite unplausible to suggest that if someone says ' Some students of English will get Firsts this year ', it is a sufficient condition of his having made a true statement, that no one at all should get a First. But this would be a consequence of accepting the above interpretation for I. Note that the dropping of the implication of plurality in ' some ' makes only a minor contribution to the unplausibility of the translation. We should think the above suggestion no more convincing in the case of someone who said ' At least one student of English will get a First this year '. The third table of translations, then, does, if anything, less than the other two to remove our sense of separation from the mother tongue.

7. So let us start again, taking the latter as our guide. And let us not be bound by the assumption from which all these difficulties have arisen; namely, that whatever interpretation we give to the four forms, it must be an interpretation in explicitly existential terms; that all statements of the four forms must be positively or negatively existential, or both. Suppose someone says ' All John's children are asleep '. Obviously he will not normally, or properly, say this, unless he believes that John has children (who are asleep). But suppose he is mistaken. Suppose John has no children. Then is it true or false that all John's children are asleep? Either answer would seem to be misleading. But we are not compelled to give either answer.

We can, and normally should, say that, since John has no children, the question does not arise. But if the form of the statement were

$$\sim(\exists x)(fx \, . \sim gx) \qquad \text{[Table 1]}$$

the correct answer to the question, whether it is true, would be 'Yes'; for ' $\sim(\exists x)(fx)$ ' is a sufficient condition of the truth of ' $\sim(\exists x)(fx \, . \sim gx)$ '. And if the form of the statement were either

$$\sim(\exists x)(fx \, . \sim gx) \, . \, (\exists x)(fx) \qquad \text{[Table 2]}$$
$$\text{or} \qquad \sim(\exists x)(fx \, . \sim gx) \, . \, (\exists x)(fx) \, . \, (\exists x)(\sim gx) \qquad \text{[Table 3]}$$

the correct answer to the question would be that the statement was false; for ' $\sim(\exists x)(fx)$ ' is inconsistent with both these formulae. But one does not happily give either answer simply on the ground that the subject-class is empty. One says rather that the question of the truth or falsity of the statement simply does not arise; that one of the conditions for answering the question one way or the other is not fulfilled.

The adoption of any of the explicitly existential analyses, whether it be a negatively existential one (Table 1) or a conjunction of negatively and positively existential components (Tables 2 and 3), forces us to conclude that the *non-existence* of any children of John's is sufficient to determine the truth or falsity of the general statement; makes it true for the first analysis, false for the other two. The more realistic view seems to be that the existence of children of John's is a necessary precondition not merely of the truth of what is said, but of its being *either* true *or* false. And this suggests the possibility of interpreting all the four Aristotelian forms on these lines : that is, as forms such that the question of whether statements exemplifying them are true or false is one that does not arise unless the subject-class has members.

It is important to understand why people have hesitated to adopt such a view of at least some general statements. It is probably the operation of the trichotomy 'either true or false or meaningless', as applied to statements, which is to blame. For this trichotomy contains a confusion : the confusion between sentence and statement.[1] Of course, the sentence ' All John's children are asleep ' is not meaningless. It is perfectly signi-

[1] See Chapter 1, p. 4.

ficant. But it is senseless to ask, of the *sentence*, whether it is true or false. One must distinguish between what can be said about the sentence, and what can be said about the statements made, on different occasions, by the use of the sentence. It is about statements only that the question of truth or falsity can arise; and about these it can sometimes fail to arise. But to say that the man who uses the sentence in our imagined case fails to say anything either true or false, is not to say that the sentence he pronounces is meaningless. Nor is it to deny that he makes a mistake. Of course, it is incorrect (or deceitful) for him to use this sentence unless (*a*) he thinks he is referring to some children whom he thinks to be asleep; (*b*) he thinks that John has children; (*c*) he thinks that the children he is referring to are John's. We might say that in using the sentence he *commits himself* to the existence of children of John's. It would prima facie be a kind of logical absurdity to say 'All John's children are asleep; but John has no children'. And we may be tempted to think of this kind of logical absurdity as a straightforward self-contradiction; and hence be led once more towards an analysis like that of Table 2; and hence to the conclusion that the man who says 'All John's children are asleep', when John has no children, makes a false statement. But there is no need to be led, by noticing this kind of logical absurdity, towards this conclusion. For if a statement S presupposes a statement S′ in the sense that the truth of S′ is a precondition of the truth-or-falsity of S, then of course there will be a kind of logical absurdity in conjoining S with the denial of S′. This is precisely the relation, in our imagined case, between the statement that all John's children are asleep (S) and the statement that John has children, that there exist children of John's (S′). But we must distinguish this kind of logical absurdity from straightforward self-contradiction. It is self-contradictory to conjoin S with the denial of S′ if S′ is a necessary condition of the truth, simply, of S. It is a different kind of logical absurdity to conjoin S with the denial of S′ if S′ is a necessary condition of the *truth or falsity* of S. The relation between S and S′ in the first case is that S entails S′. We need a different name for the relation between S and S′ in the second case; let us say, as above, that S *presupposes* S′.

Underlying the failure to distinguish sentence and statement, and the bogus trichotomy ' true, false, or meaningless ', we may detect a further logical prejudice which helps to blind us to the facts of language.   We may describe this as the belief or, perhaps better, as the wish, that if the uttering of a sentence by one person, at one time, at one place, results in a true statement, then the uttering of that sentence by any other person, at any other time, at any other place, results in a true statement.   It is, of course, incredible that any formal logician should soberly believe this.   It is, however, very natural that they should wish it were so; and hence talk as if it were so.   And to those tempted to talk as if it were so, the distinction I have insisted upon between sentence and statement will not occur or will seem unimportant.   Why this wish-belief should be natural to formal logicians, and what further effects it has, I shall discuss later.

What I am proposing, then, is this.   There are many ordinary sentences beginning with such phrases as ' All . . .', ' All the . . .', ' No . . .', ' None of the . . .', ' Some . . .', ' Some of the . . .', ' At least one . . .', ' At least one of the . . .' which exhibit, in their standard employment, parallel characteristics to those I have just described in the case of a representative ' All . . .' sentence.   That is to say, the existence of members of the subject-class is to be regarded as presupposed (in the special sense described) by statements made by the use of these sentences; to be regarded as a necessary condition. not of the truth simply, but of the truth or falsity, of such statements.   I am proposing that the four Aristotelian forms should be interpreted as forms of statement of this kind.   Will the adoption of this proposal protect the system from the charge of being inconsistent when interpreted?   Obviously it will. For every case of invalidity, of breakdown in the laws, arose from the non-existence of members of some subject-class being compatible with the truth, or with the falsity, of some statement of one of the four forms.   So our proposal, which makes the non-existence of members of the subject-class incompatible with either the truth or the falsity of any statement of these forms, will cure all these troubles at one stroke.   We are to imagine that every logical rule of the system, when expressed in terms of truth and falsity, is preceded by the phrase ' Assuming that the statements concerned are either true or false, then . . .'   Thus the rule that A is the contradictory of O states that, *if corre-*

sponding statements of the A and O forms both have truth-values,
then they must have opposite truth-values; the rule that A
entails I states that, *if corresponding statements of these forms
have truth-values*, then if the statement of the A form is true,
the statement of the I form must be true; and so on. The suggestion that entailment-rules should be understood in this way
is not peculiar to the present case.[1] What is peculiar to the
present case is the requirement that, in order for any statement
of one of the four forms to have a truth-value, to be true or false,
it is necessary that the subject-class should have members.

That the adoption of this suggestion will save the rules of the
traditional system from breakdown is obvious enough for all the
rules except, perhaps, those permitting, or involving the validity
of, the simple conversion of E and of I. That the subject-
class referred to in a statement of either of these forms must be
non-empty in order for the statement to be true or false does not
guarantee, in the case of the truth of an E statement or the
falsity of an I statement, the non-emptiness of the predicate-
class. This was the reason why the final interpretations of
Table 3 required three components for each form instead of two.
But, whilst this is true, it does not constitute an objection, nor
lead to the breakdown of the rules as we are now to understand
them. Thus perhaps a statement of the form ' xEy ' might be
true while the corresponding statement of the form ' yEx ' was
neither true nor false. But all that we require is that so long as
corresponding statements of the forms ' xEy ' and ' yEx ' are
both either true or false, they must either be both true or both
false. This is secured to us by interpreting ' xEy ' as the form
of hosts of ordinary statements, beginning with ' No . . .' or
' None of the . . .', of the kind described in this section.

Similar considerations hold for I; though mention of I reminds us of one not unimportant reservation we must make,
before simply concluding that the constants ' all ', ' some ',
' no ' of the traditional system can be understood, without
danger to any of the rules, as having just the sense which these
words have in the hosts of ordinary statements of the kind we
are discussing. And this is a point already made : viz., that
' some ', in its most common employment as a separate word,

---

[1] Compare the discussion of the truth-functional system, Chapter 3,
pp. 68–69.

carries an implication of plurality which is inconsistent with the requirement that O should be the strict contradictory of A, and I of E. So ' some ', occurring as a constant of the system, is to be interpreted as ' At least one . . .' or ' At least one of the . . .', while ' all ' and ' no ', so occurring, can be read as themselves.

The interpretation which I propose for the traditional forms has, then, the following merits : (*a*) it enables the whole body of the laws of the system to be accepted without inconsistency ; (*b*) with the reservation noted above, it gives the constants of the system just the sense which they have in a vast group of statements of ordinary speech ; (*c*) it emphasizes an important general feature of statements of that group, viz., that while the existence of members of their subject-classes is not a part of what is asserted in such statement, it is, in the sense we have examined, presupposed by them. It is this last feature which makes it unplausible to regard assertions of existence as either the whole, or conjunctive or disjunctive parts, of the sense of such ordinary statements as ' All the men at work on the scaffolding have gone home ' or ' Some of the men are still at work '. This was the reason why we were unhappy about regarding such expressions as ' $(x)(fx \supset gx)$ ' as giving the form of these sentences ; and why our uneasiness was not to be removed by the simple addition of positively or negatively existential formulae. Even the resemblance between ' There is not a single book in his room which is not by an English author ' and the negatively existential form ' $\sim(\exists x)(fx \,.\, \sim gx)$ ' was deceptive. The former, as normally used, carries the presupposition ' books-in-his-room ' and is far from being entailed by ' not-a-book-in-his-room ' ; whereas the latter is entailed by ' $\sim(\exists x)(fx)$ '. So it is that if someone, with a solemn face, says ' There is not a single foreign book in his room ' and then later reveals that there are no books in the room at all, we have the sense, not of having been lied to, but of having been made the victim of a sort of linguistic outrage. Of course he did not *say* there *were* any books in the room, so he has not said anything false. Yet what he said gave us the right to assume that there were, so he has misled us. For what he said to be true (or false) it is necessary (though not sufficient) that there should be books in the room. Of this subtle sort is the relation between ' There is not a book

in his room which is not by an English author ' and ' There are
books in his room '.[1] What weakens our resistance to the
negatively existential analysis in this case more than in the case
of the corresponding ' All '-sentence is the powerful attraction
of the negative opening phrase ' There is not . . .'.

To avoid misunderstanding I must add one point about this
proposed interpretation of the forms of the traditional system.
I do not claim that it faithfully represents the intentions of its
principal exponents. They were, perhaps, more interested in
formulating rules governing the logical relations of more im-
posing general statements than the everyday ones I have mostly
considered; were interested, for example, in the logical powers
of scientific generalizations, or of other sentences which approximate more closely to the desired conditions that if their utterance by anyone, at any time, at any place, results in a true
statement, then so does their utterance by anyone else, at any
other time, at any other place. We have yet to consider how
far the account here given of certain general sentences of common speech is adequate for all generalizations.

8. It is illuminating at this point to consider another orthodox
criticism of the traditional logic. It is frequently said that the
traditional logicians confused two quite different relations,
namely those of class-inclusion and class-membership; that
they mistakenly assimilated class-membership statements to

---

[1] Some will say these points are irrelevant to logic (are ' merely pragmatic '). If to call them ' irrelevant to logic ' is to say that they are not
considered in formal systems, then this is a point I should wish not to
dispute, but to emphasize. But to logic as concerned with the relations
between general classes of statements occurring in ordinary use, with the
general conditions under which such statements are correctly called ' true '
or ' false ', these points are not irrelevant. Certainly a ' pragmatic ' consideration, a general rule of linguistic conduct, may perhaps be seen to
underlie these points: the rule, namely, that one does not make the
(logically) lesser, when one could truthfully (and with equal or greater
linguistic economy) make the greater, claim. Assume for a moment that
the form ' There is not a single . . . which is not . . . ' were *introduced*
into ordinary speech with the same sense as ' $\sim(\exists x)(fx . \sim gx)$ '. Then
the operation of this general rule would inhibit the use of this form where
one could truly say simply ' There is not a single . . . ' (or ' $\sim(\exists x)(fx)$ ').
And the operation of this inhibition would tend to confer on the introduced
form just those logical presuppositions which I have described; the form
would tend, if it did not remain otiose, to develop just those differences
I have emphasized from the logic of the symbolic form it was introduced
to represent. The operation of this ' pragmatic rule ' was first pointed
out to me, in a different connexion, by Mr. H. P. Grice.

class-inclusion statements. The point of this criticism is that, when presented with a singular categorical statement such as one made in the words 'Caesar is dead', which would now be classified as a singular predicative or class-membership statement, traditional logicians commonly assigned it to the A form. Its negation 'Caesar is not dead' they assigned to the E form. The explanatory observations which customarily accompany this decision are not of interest. Its justification, if it has one, must clearly lie in some close analogy between the formal powers of such a statement and those of other statements of the class to which it is assigned.

Now if general statements of the A form were in fact class-inclusion statements (i.e., statements of the form ' $\alpha \subset \beta$ ' or ' $(x)(fx \supset gx)$ '—or even ' $\sim(\exists x)(fx \cdot \sim gx) \cdot (\exists x)(fx)$ '), the modern criticisms would obviously be correct. The formal powers of these negatively (or negatively and positively) existential statements *are* very different from those of statements of the class-membership or simple predicative kind. When we are provided with a logical symbolism adequate for expressing the forms of statements of certain kinds, we can say that two such statements are of the same form only if one of them exemplifies some symbolic formula which the other also exemplifies. Then, and only then, will there be some analogy between their formal powers; i.e., some law or inference-pattern which applies to them both. So to say that simple predicative statements are of a totally different form from class-inclusion statements is to point to such obvious facts as that ' fx ' and ' $(x)(fx \supset gx)$ ' do not exemplify one another; that there is no common formula which they both exemplify; that such a law as

$$(x)(fx \supset gx) \cdot (x)(gx \supset hx) \supset (x)(fx \supset hx)$$

is irreducibly different in form from such a law as

$$fy \cdot (x)(fx \supset gx) \supset gy$$

and so on.

The validity of this criticism of the procedure of the traditional logicians, however, depends wholly upon the assumption that statements of the A form are correctly regarded as class-inclusion statements, in the sense given to this phrase by modern logicians. Since the assumption is false, the criticism is wholly invalid. This is not to say that the traditional procedure was in fact justified; it is to say merely that the question cannot be settled by contemplating the symbolism of the predicative calculus.

The formal analogies which struck the traditional logicians are obvious enough. If one says, for example, of all the members of a certain group, that they have a certain characteristic; and that everything which has that characteristic has a certain further characteristic; then it follows that all the members of the group in question have the second characteristic. Similarly, if one says of a certain individual thing, that it has a certain characteristic; and that everything which has that characteristic has a certain further characteristic; then it follows that the individual thing in question has the second characteristic. Analogous conclusions follow here from analogous premises; and whether one is speaking of an individual or all the members of a group makes no difference to the validity of the inference. So the traditional logicians were induced by this analogy to say that both types of inference were of the pattern ' $xAy . yAz$ $\therefore xAz$ '. It is in their adoption of this method of emphasizing a few such formal analogies that the assigning of singular predicative statements to the A form consists. It must be admitted that the method is, in certain ways, ill-chosen. If statements of a certain class are to be called statements of the A form, we shall expect the formal analogies between them and other statements of that form to be thoroughgoing; whereas we do not, in the case of singular statements, find a plausible analogy to, e.g., the rule that A entails I. Nevertheless, the partial formal analogy exists; and it was not absurd to mark it in the traditional way.

The importance of the modern criticism, however, does not lie in the opportunity which it gives of defending the traditional procedure on a comparatively trivial point. It lies in revealing a curious implication of the assumption that the modern systems are adequate for the logic of common speech. I remarked earlier [1] that the distinction between individual and predicative expressions—a distinction made in the quantificational logic— may best be understood in terms of the distinction between the referring role, and the ascriptive or classificatory role, which expressions may play in the making of ordinary statements.

[1] See Chapter 5, Section 5.

Let us give the logical title of ' subject-predicate statements ' to statements in making which we use one part of our sentence to play the referring role and the remainder to play the ascriptive or classificatory role.   The title is a reasonable one; for we commonly use the grammatical subject of such a sentence to play the former role, and the grammatical predicate to play the latter role.   Now, of course, the quantificational logic allows a place for *some* referring expressions; viz., those which can appear as values of individual variables.   It allows a place for *some* subject-predicate statements : viz., singular class-membership or predicative statements (of the form ' $x\varepsilon\alpha$ ' or ' fx ', where ' x ' takes an individual expression as a value); statements which are not either positively or negatively existential.   The curious assumption implicit in regarding the quantificational logic as adequate for the analysis of ordinary categorical statements in general is, roughly speaking, the assumption that the only subject-predicate statements are statements in the singular; that all other categorical statements are positively or negatively existential.   But of course we can *refer to*, and *talk about*, the members of a group collectively in just the same way as we can refer to and talk about an individual member of a group.   Compare a statement made in the words ' Miss Robinson has gone home ' with a statement made in the words ' All the members of the Robinson family have gone home '.   The grammatical subject of each sentence is used to refer; in the one case, to an individual, in the other, to the members of a group.   Such a reference cannot be made unless there is such an individual, or there are members of such a group.   So each statement carries a presupposition of existence; but neither statement is existential.   If one started either of these sentences and were prevented from finishing it, one would have made no statement, and, *a fortiori*, no statement which is or entails an existential statement; but one might have succeeded in referring to some individual or the members of some group, which one could not do unless such an individual, or some members of such a group, existed.   My proposals for the interpretation of the traditional system have largely taken the form of pointing out that many ordinary statements beginning with the words ' all ', ' no ', ' at least one ' are what they are traditionally called, viz., subject–predicate statements.

What that system does is to give a very incomplete account of the logical relations of statements of this kind, allowing, under the names of quantity and quality, for limited formal variations.

9. In here insisting on resemblances between the singular and plural statements which I have classified together under the subject–predicate title, I do not wish to deny that they exhibit differences. I wish mainly to emphasize their common contrast with negatively and/or positively existential statements; and I use the orthodox criticism discussed in the last section to throw into relief the odd assumption it embodies, that the only categorical statements to be contrasted in this way with existential statements are statements in the singular. It is instructive to notice a further result of this assumption; instructive because it illustrates how the tension between linguistic fact and logical dogma may breed ingenious error.

If ' Jack Straw is happy ' (S_1) is a sentence which would be used to make a subject–predicate statement, so, obviously, is ' Jack Straw and Mary Straw are both happy ' (S_2). S_2 is a sentence in the plural. But it raises no serious difficulties for the dogma; for it can correctly be represented as equivalent to a conjunction of singular sentences, i.e., to ' Jack Straw is happy and Mary Straw is happy '; which exemplifies the formula '$fx . fy$'. But if S_1 and S_2 are subject–predicate sentences, it seems odd to maintain that ' All the Straws are happy ' (S_3) is not; that it is of a totally different, namely a positively and/or negatively existential, form. So an attempt is sometimes made to repeat for S_3 the manœuvre which worked for S_2, to represent S_3 as also a conjunction of singular sentences, i.e., as equivalent to some sentence such as ' Jack Straw is happy and Mary Straw is happy and William Straw is happy and . . .' and so on.[1] Now even if, in a given case, one is in a position to complete the inventory, it is obvious that the statement made by the use of the resulting conjunctive sentence neither entails nor is entailed by the original general statement; and so is not equivalent to it. To secure the entailment one way, one has to add to the singular statements the general statement that these are all the Straws there are. To secure the entailment

[1] The suggested equivalence has appealed to logicians for other reasons besides.

7

the other way, one has to destroy the singular statements by obliterating individual mention of individual Straws. So the enterprise of making the statements equivalent is hopeless. But the interest of the suggestion lies in the fact that, because of the pull of the unadmitted real resemblance between S_1 and S_3, the real differences are denied. The differences are that S_3 does, and S_1 and S_2 do not, explicitly speak of the totality of a collection; that S_3 does not, and S_1 and S_2 do, explicitly mention particular individuals. One sees aright when one sees that both statements that do, and statements that do not, explicitly speak of particular individuals may be subject–predicate statements, and neither assert nor deny, but presuppose, the existence of things referred to by, e.g., the grammatical subjects of sentences used to make them. Compare the case of a statement which *un*explicitly speaks of a particular individual; viz., a statement made in the words " One (at least one) of the Straws is happy ' (S_4). A parallel manœuvre is to declare this sentence to be equivalent to a disjunction of singular sentences the use of which would involve explicitly mentioning particular individuals : ' Jack Straw is happy or Mary Straw is happy or . . .' and so on. And this manœuvre fails too, for the entailment holds only in one direction. S_4 resembles S_1 and S_2 in being a subject–predicate sentence and differs from them in not being used to speak explicitly of a particular individual. It is a mistake either to exaggerate the resemblance by declaring it to be equivalent to a sentence which is used to speak explicitly of particular individuals; or to exaggerate and distort the difference by declaring it to be an existential sentence.

10. I have described how the logical character of sentences whose use to make statements presupposes the existence of something referred to by their grammatical subjects can go unnoticed because (or partly because) of the operation of the bogus trichotomy ' true, false, or meaningless '; and how this error operates in the realm of general statements. As the last paragraph suggests, this error does not operate in that realm alone; but by invading that of singular statements as well, tends to limit still further the class of referring expressions or logical subjects.

A classical illustration of this is provided by Russell's ' Theory of Definite Descriptions '. According to this theory, the form of the sentence ' The King of France is wise ' is revealed by writing it as an explicitly existential sentence, viz., ' $(\exists x)$ [x is King of France . $(y)(y$ is King of France $\supset x = y)$. x is wise]'; i.e., ' There is a person of whom it is true that he and that no one else is King of France and that he is wise '. It is argued that this analysis provides the only acceptable means of reconciling the fact that the sentence is meaningful with the fact that there does not happen to be a king of France. For suppose it is a subject–predicate sentence. Then (so the argument goes), if it is not meaningless, it is either true or false. It is true if the King of France is wise and false if the King of France is not wise. But the statement that the King of France is wise and the statement that the King of France is not wise are alike true only on the condition that there is a king of France. Hence, if it is a subject–predicate sentence, either it is meaningless or there is a king of France. The argument is sometimes put more briefly. If the sentence is of the subject–predicate form, then, if it is not meaningless, it must be *about* something; so either it is meaningless or there is a king of France for it to be about. The conclusion is drawn that it is not a subject–predicate sentence; and the existential analysis is adopted instead. On that analysis, the sentence is straightforwardly false (and hence significant) if there is no king of France; since ' $\sim(\exists x)(fx)$ ' entails ' $\sim(\exists x)[fx . (y)(fy \supset x = y) . gx]$ '. The theory is generalized to cover all apparent subject–predicate statements in the singular beginning with the definite article.

These arguments lose their power if we keep in mind the distinction between sentence and statement, and the conception of subject–predicate statements, which I have earlier outlined. For a sentence of the statement-making type to have meaning, it is not necessary that every use of it, at any time, at any place, should result in a true or false statement. It is enough that it should be possible to describe or imagine circumstances in which its use would result in a true or false statement. For a referring phrase to have meaning, it is not necessary that on every occasion of its use there should be something to which it refers.

Sometimes we begin a singular statement about a person or thing with a name (' Robinson ') or a ' the '-phrase (' the President ', ' the chair ') or a pronoun (' he ', ' it '). Sometimes we begin such a statement with expressions which we are inclined to call more indefinite : with words or phrases like ' someone ', ' something ', ' one of them '; or with phrases which start with the indefinite article (' a man ', ' a table '). Statements of the latter class are also currently assimilated to existential statements. Thus ' A man fell over the edge ' would be said to mean ' $(\exists x)(x$ is a man $.$ x fell over the edge) '; and ' Someone fell over the edge ' would be said (perhaps) to mean ' $(\exists x)(x$ is a person $.$ x fell over the edge) '. These translations may well strike us at first as pointlessly perverse; we may well fail to understand how anything except a determination to caricature all ordinary statements in terms of the symbolism of quantificational logic could induce anyone to propose them. We might wonder next whether the point of the translations was to try to bring out the logical differences between, e.g., statements made by sentences beginning with the definite article, and statements made by sentences beginning with the indefinite article. But it is wildly absurd to suggest that the difference between ' A man fell over the edge ' and ' The man fell over the edge ' is that the truth of a statement made by the use of the first sentence is consistent with the existence of more than one man, while the truth of a statement made by the use of the second is not. Yet this is just the logical difference between ' $(\exists x)(x$ is a man $.$ x fell over the edge) ' and ' $(\exists x)[x$ is a man $.$ $(y)(y$ is a man $\supset x = y)$ $.$ x fell over the edge] '. It is not in these terms, or in any qualification of them which adheres to the principle of existential analysis, that we shall come to understand the difference. We begin to understand it when we consider such facts as that a paragraph in a novel or a newspaper which begins with the sentence ' A man approached the edge ' may end with the sentence ' The man fell over the edge '; where the point of the change from ' a ' to ' the ' may be to indicate (though not to state) that the man referred to in the last sentence is the same as the man referred to in the first. We tend generally to speak of *the* ϕ when we can safely rely upon some feature of the situation in which we write or speak to single out some one ϕ for our hearers' or readers' attention. It may be proximity or contemporaneity or (as in the above example) the linguistic context, which we thus rely upon to enable our hearers or readers to pick up the reference, to identify the object referred to (even if only as *the man referred to at the beginning of the paragraph*). The use of 'the' helps the identification by indicating (though not stating) that we *are* placing this reliance upon what may, in a broad sense, be called contextual features. This is, of course, a very rough description; and we may, and do, use 'the' for other purposes as well. We tend to speak, on the other hand, of *a φ* when these conditions are not fulfilled; and the use of 'a' serves then to indicate that we do not expect our audience to be enabled by contextual features to identify the object of our reference. 'A', too, may be, and is, used for other reasons as well.

Consider also the ways in which we might dissent from a statement made in the words 'A man fell over the edge'. We might say 'He didn't fall; he jumped'; or we might say : 'It wasn't a man; it was a woman wearing trousers'; or we might say : 'Nobody fell over; you've been seeing things'. The importance of the pronouns 'he' and 'it' in the first two dissenting remarks is that they take up the reference to a definite person, indefinitely made by the phrase 'a man'. The first remark denies what is said about the subject of the reference; the second remark accepts what is said about the subject of the reference, but corrects the description of that subject. These examples emphasize a logical resemblance between indefinite and definite referring expressions. The third dissenting remark is different from either of the other two. One could make it, and in making it, *contradict* the original statement, without admitting that any reference had been made at all in the original statement. For the original statement to be false, it is not necessary that a reference should have been made. So this example brings out a difference between 'a man', as used in the original sentence, and definite referring expressions; and a difference between that sentence and typical subject–predicate sentences. If someone says 'The President fell over the edge', one may reply 'No one fell over' and from this correctly move to 'So he can't have done'. But if someone says 'A man fell over the edge', it will not generally be appropriate to move, in reply, from 'No one fell over' to 'So he can't have done'.

It is by consideration of such facts as these (of many more than these) that one comes to understand the roles of 'a' and 'the' in introducing singular statements. The jejune existential analysis cannot possibly do justice to more than a few of such facts, and then only at the cost of falsifying others. Nevertheless, one must try to understand the motives for the existential analysis in the case of indefinite referring expressions ('a man') as well as in the case of definite descriptions ('the King of France'). For logical dogmas are seldom just perverse.

We have detected already the belief, underlying the Theory of Definite Descriptions, that a genuine logical subject, a true referring expression, can have a meaning only if there exists an object to which it applies. 'The King of France', which failed to satisfy this condition, was degraded from the status of referring expression. Now why is this belief so firmly held? The answer seems to be that the meaning of any genuine referring expression is taken to be *identical with the object to which it applies.*[1] Its meaning is what it stands for; and what it stands for is what it refers to. This simple and only too natural equation is fatal to the claims of phrases like 'a man' as referring expressions. For while there are plenty of men, there is plainly no single object which is the meaning of the phrase. And yet the phrase is not one we should ordinarily call ambiguous. It has the same meaning in immense numbers of sentences. So the conclusion seems to follow that it is not a referring expression. So the available logical apparatus of predicates and quantifiers must be employed to show that the sentences in which it seems to play something like a referring role are not really subject–predicate sentences at all, but existential sentences.

We have just seen that there is something to be said for this conclusion, as well as something to be said against it; that sentences like 'A man fell over the edge' do not behave in all respects, though they behave in some respects, like subject–predicate sentences. But though there is something to be said for the conclusion, there is nothing to be said for the reasoning by which it is arrived at. It rests once more upon the fatal confusion between sentence and statement, meaning and reference. For a singular referring expression to have a meaning, it suffices that it should be possible in suitable circumstances to use it to refer to some one thing, person, place, &c. Its meaning is the set of linguistic conventions governing its correct use so to

---

[1] The phrase 'the object to which it applies' contains implicitly the whole of the confusions here discussed, the whole of a persistent and mistaken theory of meaning.

refer.   For the great majority of referring expressions, these conventions are such that a given expression may be used on different occasions to refer to different individual things, persons, places, &c.   A moment's reflection shows this to be true no less of the phrase ' the King of France ', or ' the '-phrases in general, than of ' a man ' or ' a '-phrases in general.   Sentences and phrases and words have meanings, in virtue of which they may be used to make statements and to refer to things.   But the meanings of sentences are not the statements they are used to make, and the meanings of words and phrases are not the things they are used to refer to.   Only the grossest equivocation with words like ' mean ' and ' refer ' can continue to obscure these facts.

The doctrines I am here criticizing have a curious consequence for the interpretation of the symbolism of the predicative calculus.   In discussing that symbolism, we began by distinguishing individual from predicative variables; and since a variable is explained as a gap-sign in a formula capable of being exemplified by a sentence, this distinction in type of variable seemed to involve a distinction between types of expression; [1]   namely, the distinction between individual and predicative expressions. We then explained how sentences could be framed from predicative formulae by binding individual variables to form existential sentences, as well as by replacing the variables by individual expressions.   We should therefore expect to find two basic types of sentence exemplifying formulae of the predicative calculus : viz., predicative sentences containing individual expressions and not involving quantification; and existential sentences containing quantifiers and not containing individual expressions; as well as mixed sentences containing both.   The curious consequence of the doctrines just examined is that ordinary language, if that doctrine is sound, contains no individual expressions at all, and consequently that there do not exist any sentences at all of the first type.

For where are genuine individual referring expressions to be found, having the characteristics required if the doctrines just examined are correct?   It might be thought that proper names would fill the bill.   But even a proper name does not satisfy

---

[1] More strictly, a distinction between expressions as playing certain kinds of role in sentences.   See Chapter 5, Section 5.

the requirement that in order for a sentence in which it occurs to be significant there must exist just one individual which (or who) is its meaning.   One can significantly ask, using a proper name, ' Did N exist ? ' ;   the same name can be borne by many different creatures or things ; and in no case is the meaning of a name identical with a creature or thing which bears it.   To bestow a name is not to give a word a meaning.   Names, then, do not satisfy the requirement ; and nor do (and nor could) any other expressions which language provides.   For the requirement itself is impossible, itself embodies the confusions already discussed.

The fact that these doctrines have this curious effect upon the interpretation of the symbolism of the quantificational logic does not in itself constitute a refutation of them.   Sufficient reasons for rejecting them have already been given.   But it does throw into relief an oddity in the way in which these doctrines (e.g., the Theory of Descriptions) are customarily presented.   It is often said that the verbal or grammatical form of a sentence such as ' The King of France is wise ' is *misleading* as to its logical form ; in that it looks like a subject–predicate sentence, while really being existential.   Of course, this could be true only if the majority, or a very large proportion, of the sentences which resemble this sentence in verbal or grammatical form really were of the logically subject–predicate form.[1]   But we have just seen that a consequence of the doctrine underlying the Theory of Descriptions is that there are no genuine referring expressions, and hence no genuinely subject–predicate sentences at all.   If the underlying doctrine is abandoned, the reasons for adopting the existential analysis disappear.   A way is then open for a more realistic conception of individual referring expressions, which permits us to re-admit definite descriptions, along with proper names and some pronouns, into that class. The curious consequences for the interpretation of the symbolism of the quantificational logic fail to hold ; and plenty of sentences can be seen as exemplifying ' fx '.   But at the same time the claims mentioned at the end of Section 6 of Chapter 5 have to be abandoned.

11. An immediate consequence of giving the sense I propose to ' subject–predicate statement ' is that the existential state-

---

[1] See Chapter 2, p. 51.

ments presupposed by subject–predicate statements will not themselves count as subject–predicate statements; and hence will fall outside the scope of the traditional system as I have recommended that it should be interpreted. For the four forms are to be so interpreted that the question of the truth or falsity of a statement exemplifying one of them does not arise unless there are things (or there is a thing) referred to by the subject-term. Consequently, if we tried to assimilate a statement of the pattern ' x's exist ' to any of the four forms, or to regard it as a subject–predicate statement at all, we should be faced with the absurd result that the question of whether it was true or false could arise only if it were true; or, that, if it were false, the question of whether it was true or false did not arise. This gives a new edge to the familar philosophical observation that ' exists ' is not a predicate. When we declare or deny that ' there are ' things of such-and-such a description, or that things of such-and-such a description ' exist ', the use of the quoted phrases is not to be assimilated either to the predicative or to the referring use of expressions.

It might seem that this raises a difficulty. For no restriction was placed on the range of possible objects of reference. Can we not, then, besides referring to the members of a class, refer to the class itself, and describe it, for example, as having few, many, ten, some, or no members? If so, we are faced with two related problems. One is that if we treat such a statement as a subject–predicate statement, we seem committed to saying that it presupposes that the class referred to by the subject-term exists. Now, it is not clear what the assertion that a class exists could mean, if not that it has members. But this may be precisely what the putative subject–predicate statement in question either affirms or denies; and in this case, we should be faced with the unacceptable conclusion that the statement in question presupposes its own truth or falsity. The second difficulty is this. If the statement that the class of x's has members is to be accorded the status of subject–predicate proposition, it seems unsatisfactory to withold this status from the undeniably equivalent statement that x's exist. These are schoolmen's difficulties and call for schoolmen's solutions. Both could be dealt with shortly in the following way. Pending the provision of a standard sense to the putative statement that a class exists, other than the interpretation of it as being to the effect that the class has members, we can say that there simply are no existential statements related to subject–predicate statements about classes or properties as the statement that x's exist is related to a subject–predicate statement about the x's; and that consequently the presupposition-rule does not apply to subject–predicate statements of the former kind. (Alternatively, we could rule that to say that the class of x's, or the property of being (an) x, existed, meant something, but something different from the assertion that there were members of the class or things possessing the property; that it meant, e.g., no more than that the class-expression or property-name in question, and all its acknowledged synonyms, were in fact significant.) The second difficulty can be met as follows. To say that the class of x's has members is to ascribe the property of having members to the class. It is not to predicate anything of the members, the x's. Similarly, in the equivalent statement that x's exist, nothing is predicated of the x's. But to deny that the statement that x's exist is a subject–predicate statement is simply to say that the statement that x's exist, unlike the statement that x's are fat or thin, predicates nothing of the x's. From the fact that a statement is equivalent to another statement of a certain form, it does not follow that it is itself a statement of that form.

Since the genesis of all these difficulties is largely terminological, it might seem that they could be dealt with by a simpler terminological operation than this; viz., by excluding statements of which the grammatical subjects are used to refer to classes or properties from the logical category of subject–predicate statements. But this would be a pity, in so far as the logic with which the terminology of subjects and predicates is traditionally associated treats of some formal analogies which range over statements of the kind in question as well as over statements of which the grammatical subjects are used to refer to persons, animals, objects, and institutions.

12. It is obvious that the traditional system gives only a very limited account of the logical relations of subject–predicate statements. It would be possible to add to it in various ways. Other variations in quantity besides that between the universal (' all ' and ' no ') and particular (' at least one ') forms could be

introduced; though to do so would be to detract from the simplicity of the system without much compensating gain in richness. It would be possible, following the example of the analogues in the predicative calculus, to produce a set of rules permitting such transformations as that of ' All x is either y or z ' into ' All x which is not y is z '. Those exponents of traditional logic who claimed that the rules of immediate inference and of the categorical or hypothetical syllogisms provided an exhaustive canon of formal reasoning were curiously blind on this point. To exhibit a piece of argument as exemplifying one of the recognized forms, it was often necessary to transform one of the premises. For example, the form of inference from ' All x is either y or z ' and ' All z is s ' to ' All x which is not y is s ' can be represented as syllogistic only by transforming the first premise into ' All x which is not y is z '. Such a transformation is just as much a piece of valid formal deduction as the ensuing syllogistic inference. Its principle has as much right to a place in the canon as the appropriate syllogistic principle. But all such prior manipulation of the premises was dismissed under the heading of ' putting the premises into logical form '.[1]   If all deductive inferences which fall outside the recognized patterns of the system are thus declared to be not really inferences, but something else, then the claim to completeness becomes trivially impregnable.

Some of the foregoing sections may appear to wear the guise of a defence of the traditional system. But the appearance is, at least in part, misleading. First, it is, as I have suggested, far from clear that the exponents of the system would welcome such a defence. Second, it would be a mistake to claim that the traditional system does, or that any formal system could, give a comprehensive account of the logic of subject–predicate statements. And this not only for the reasons just given. Any comprehensive account would include, for example, a discussion of the differences between singular sentences beginning with definite and with indefinite descriptive phrases. We have seen that these differences are misrepresented by the recommended translations in quantificational terms; but they cannot be represented at all by any formal feature of the traditional

---

[1] For some elaboration (and qualification) of the remarks of this paragraph, see Chapter 7, Section 10.

system.[1] Nor are such matters amenable to treatment in terms of anything which could be called a formal system. The two points I have been mainly concerned to establish are, one, relatively trivial and, one, important. The relatively trivial point is that some orthodox criticisms of the traditional system are mistaken. The important point is that, underlying both these criticisms and such doctrines as the Theory of Descriptions, we find a radical misconception of certain general logical features of the use of language, as well as of certain logically interesting features of the use of particular types of expression. The reasons for this misconception (or neglect) I shall discuss further.[2] But it would be mistaken in fact, and in principle, to represent the traditional system as succeeding in an enterprise in which the modern logic fails, or vice versa.

[1] Compare what might be called a ' natural syllogism ' with the stiffly unreal examples of the text-books. A piece of dialogue might run :

—A man has just drunk a whole bottle of methylated spirits.
—No one who takes a dose like that ever survives it.
—So he'll die.

Note how the indefinite first term yields to the definite pronoun ' he ' in the conclusion; and how the tense alters at each step. Unlike other departures from the strict schema (such as ' die ' for ' not survive it ' and ' takes a dose like that ' for ' drinks a whole bottle, &c.') these two cannot be eliminated without destroying the sense of the original.

[2] In Chapter 8.

CHAPTER 7

GENERAL STATEMENTS AND RELATIONS

I. GENERAL STATEMENTS

1. OF general subject–predicate statements, of the form ' all s are p ', I have said that the question of their truth or falsity arises only if there are s; and have implied that, if the question does arise, then such a statement is true if there are no s which are not p, and false if there is an s which is not p. Even this needs qualification, unless it is to be taken as a restrictive definition. For there are many cases of subject–predicate statements beginning with ' all ' which it would be pedantry to call ' false ' on the strength of one exception or a set of exceptions. If the circumstances in which the exceptions appear are themselves very exceptional, we may feel that they do not count against our statement; that it carried the unspoken, because unneeded, qualification ' in normal circumstances '. Nor will exceptions occurring in quite normal circumstances always require us to admit error : to generalize is to ' speak generally '. But in yet other cases, a single exception does constitute a refutation. And these, being the tidiest cases, are taken as the standard.

2. Not all general statements are subject–predicate statements. And not all general sentences which look as if they are used to make statements are so used. And not all general sentences which *are* used to make statements are quite so straightforwardly used as one might be tempted to suppose. There are, in fact, many differences among general sentences.

Some of these differences have been exploited in support of the claim that there are at least some general sentences to which the negatively existential analysis (' $(x)(fx \supset gx)$ ') is applicable. For example, it may be said that each of the following sentences viz.,

> All twenty-sided rectilinear plane figures have the sum of their angles equal to 2×18 right angles
> All trespassers on this land will be prosecuted

> All moving bodies not acted upon by external forces
> continue in a state of uniform motion in a straight line

might be truthfully uttered; but in no case is it a necessary
condition of their truthful utterance that their subject-class
should have members. Nor can it be said that the question of
whether or not they are truthfully uttered is one that arises only
if their subject-class has members. They are not subject–
predicate sentences. These facts, however, are very inadequate
to support the proposed analysis. If the proposed analysis were
correct, it would be a *sufficient condition* of the truthful utterance
of these sentences that their subject-classes had no members;
for ' $\sim(\exists x)(fx)$ ' entails ' $(x)(fx \supset gx)$ '. But this is very far
from being the case for these, or for any other, general sentences.

These sentences are different from one another. The first
is a proposition of mathematics. To accept it as true is to
accept it as necessarily true, as analytic. To the question,
whether or not it is an analytic truth of mathematics, the
further question, whether or not there exists in Nature (or in any
designs) a plane figure of these specifications is totally irrelevant.
To accept it as true is to accept an exemplification of the entailment formula :

> ' x is a rectilinear plane figure of n sides ' entails ' x has
> the sum of its angles equal to $(n - 2) \times 2$ right angles '.

This formulation reminds us of another which we accept as
equivalent :

> ' x is a rectilinear plane figure of n sides $\supset x$ has the sum
> of its angles equal to $(n - 2) \times 2$ right angles ' is analytic.

And from here the step is easy to the generalized analytic sentence ' $(x)(n)(x$ is a rectilinear plane figure of n sides $\supset x$ has the
sum of its angles equal to $(n - 2) \times 2$ right angles) '; of which
' (x) (x is a rectilinear plane figure of 20 sides $\supset x$ has the sum of
its angles equal to 18×2 right angles) ' is a specialization.
And this is of the form ' $(x)(fx \supset gx)$ '. So we can, after all,
make use of the quantificational symbolism for the formulation
of this sentence; but only (with safety) if we make it clear that
we are writing down an analytic sentence; and only then if we
bear in mind the reservations which attend the use of this

symbolism to express entailment.[1] The *unqualified* declaration that the negatively existential formula gives the form of the sentence is false.

The second sentence is an example of one of those which look as if they are used to make statements but are not. The land-owner who causes the sentence to be written on a board at the edge of his land is not making a prediction, but issuing a warning or a threat. He might be said to utter the sentence ' truthfully', or in good faith, if it corresponds to his intentions. But he makes neither a true nor a false statement; for he makes no statement at all.

The third sentence belongs to physical theory;[2] and I do not claim to treat it with a more than schematic realism. Suppose that *in every observed case* the extent of deviation of a moving body from continuance in uniform motion in a straight line is related by some constant relation to the magnitude and direction of the forces which operate upon it. And suppose this relation to be such that the assumption that it holds for types of cases not observed is equivalent, in the unencountered case of a body not acted upon by any external force, to the assumption that such a body will continue in uniform motion in a straight line. Then the evidence on the basis of which we conclude, if we do, that this relation holds for all moving bodies is the evidence on the basis of which we accept the statement in question as true. We see the point of the statement only when we see it as a part of the wider theory. For then we see that though the state-ment has no *direct* application, since there are, let us say, no bodies not acted upon by external forces, yet the question of its truth or falsity *can* arise, and it *can* correctly be called true, as a part, or consequence, of the general theory which does have direct application, since there are moving bodies. The sense in which we call such a general statement true may be compared with the sense in which we may call some conditional statements with unfulfilled conditions true; for they also may be logical consequences of accepted generalizations which have direct application (taken together, perhaps, with some other, non-general, statements).

[1] See Chapter 1, Section 15, and Chapter 8, Section 3.
[2] It may, for all I know, have ceased to do so. Or it may have become an analytic sentence. I shall assume that neither of these things is so; for my purpose in using it is illustrative.

3. It is customary to divide empirical general statements into restricted and unrestricted generalizations; or into generalizations about closed classes and generalizations about open classes; or, we may put it, into general reports and forecasts on the one hand, and laws on the other. The division is neither a clearly marked nor an exhaustive one. But it has a point, though its point is often misdescribed. The ideal law-statement may be initially and incompletely characterized as follows. Suppose S is a sentence expressing such a statement : then given that the utterance of S by some person at some time at some place results in a true statement, it follows necessarily that the utterance of S (unmodified in any particular, e.g., tense) by any other person at any other time at any other place results in a true statement. Thus no statement in which the reference of the words used depends in any way upon the situation in which they are uttered can be an ideal law-statement. This characterization seems precise, as far as it goes; but the line between restricted and unrestricted generalizations is not in practice so sharply drawn. There are many generalizations which people are tempted to say are unrestricted, about ' open classes ' and so on, which only approximate to this requirement. For instance ' All cats like fish ' would commonly be said to be such a generalization. But it would be possible to say : ' It *used to be true* that all cats like fish; but now X has bred a new strain of cats which detest fish.' When the pre-X talkers uttered the sentence, they made a true statement; but when the post-X talkers uttered it, they made a false one. So the class referred to was not ideally open. This is not to say that there are no ideal law-statements. But it is to say that if we attempt to make the characterization wide enough to include all those general statements which have been classified as unrestricted, it becomes a vague characterization, to be framed in terms of approximation to the ideal. We may speak, then, of law-statements, and quasi-law-statements, including under the latter head the statements which only approximate to the ideal. In making such statements we use the grammatically present tense. But the force of that tense in such statements is not to indicate that conditions are being reported which are contemporaneous with the report. Nor is it the timeless present of necessary statements. It is the omnitemporal present of law-statements, or, as in our

example, the quasi-omnitemporal present of some quasi-law-statements.

It is sometimes thought that law-statements, of the form ' all *s* are *p* ', which have direct application to instances, are not made true simply by the circumstance that there (omnitemporally) is no *s* which is not *p*; i.e., that the qualified truth-conditions laid down for general subject–predicate statements in the first paragraph of this chapter are inadequate for law-statements; that to accept them as true is to accept the further claim that there exists some necessary link between the characteristic of being an *s* and the characteristic of being a *p* which underlies their constant conjunction. A typical argument in support of such a view is the following.[1] Suppose one had very good grounds for believing that there had never been more than a very small number of members of a certain species (*s*); that there never would be any more; and that each member of the species, when adult, had a certain trivial characteristic (*p*) (as, for example, a number of men might all have noses just two inches long). Then the condition that there (omnitemporally) is no *s* which is not *p* may be accepted as fulfilled. But the statement that it was fulfilled would not be a law-statement. A sign of this is that it would not be legitimate to infer that if there were to be another *s*, it, too, would be *p*. So some unrestricted statements for which the truth-conditions described are adequate are not law-statements. So, it is concluded, no statements for which the truth-conditions described are adequate are law-statements.

The last step in the argument, however, is invalid. What follows is not that the truth-conditions of law-statements have been inadequately described, but merely that the characterization of law-statements so far given is inadequate in *some* respect. Nor is the respect far to seek. An *essential* part of the evidence for the conclusion that there (omnitemporally) is no *s* which is not *p* in our imagined case consists of evidence that the class of members of the species is limited in a very definite temporal sense; i.e., evidence that there will be no more members, and that there never were more than the limited number of which observations have been recorded. All we need to add to our characterization of natural laws is the requirement that such evidence as this shall not be an essential part of our grounds for

[1] Cf. *Kneale, Probability and Induction*, Pt. II.

accepting them.   Evidence which is both permissible and adequate to establish a law will then be adequate to establish also the related unfulfilled conditionals.   It should be added that ordinary speech unhesitatingly discriminates between these cases.   We should never use the omnitemporal present in a case such as that imagined.   We should say, instead, ' All the *s* there ever were, were *p* ; and there'll be no more '.

So if a law-statement which approximates to the form ' All *s* are *p* ' is one which has direct application (e.g., ' All mammals are vertebrates ', ' Metals expand when heated '), there is no reason to think that its truth-conditions are different from those described for other subject–predicate statements.   (To say this is not to deny that subject–predicate law-statements are different in *some* respects from other subject–predicate statements, for, as we have just seen, to call them *law-statements* is both to emphasize the unrestrictedness of their application and to say something about the nature of the evidence by which they are supported).   And if a law-statement of this form does not have direct application (e.g., ' Bodies not acted upon by external forces continue, &c.'), then its truth or falsity depends upon the truth or falsity of other law-statements with which it is deductively connected and which do have direct application.

The phrase ' direct application to instances ' in the above must be interpreted a little generously.   ' Metals expand when heated ' is a higher generalization about copper, zinc, gold, &c. (i.e., *kinds* of material) ; and ' All mammals are vertebrates ' is a higher generalization about the lion, the tiger, the whale, &c. (i.e., *species* of animal) ; whereas the ' instances ' are individual pieces of metal and individual animals.   The majority of law-statements, moreover, are like the first of these two examples rather than the second.   That is to say, they state that when one thing happens to something, another thing happens to it (' *expands* when *heated* ').   Law-statements of this kind are often expressed in ' if . . . then . . .' sentences, or ' whenever ' sentences, with two finite verbs (e.g., ' If potassium is brought into contact with water, combustion takes place ').   It would be possible, with some linguistic strain, to express such laws as subject–predicate generalizations about open classes of *events* : ' All instances of potassium being brought into contact with water are (or are followed by) instances of combustion '.

The strain, the necessity of using such highly general nouns as 'instances', is the result of the fact that language is richer in nouns for complex types of thing than in nouns for complex types of event. Nor is there any elucidatory virtue in such a manœuvre. For there is no special virtue in the simple subject–predicate form; and the account given of the truth-conditions of statements naturally made in that form has very simple parallels for law-statements more naturally made in the other forms I have mentioned.[1]

4. I spoke earlier of general sentences which, though used to make statements rather than to issue warnings or to lay down rules, are not so straightforwardly statement-making as they might seem. An example would be : '(All) M.P.s get £1,000 a year.' This is not falsified by the case of an M.P. whom the Treasury forgets to pay throughout his period in Parliament. Nor is the failure of falsification a simple instance (though it is a complex instance) of one of the qualifications mentioned in the first paragraph of this chapter; nor is it to be explained by saying that the sentence is used merely to lay down, or quote, a rule, or to say that the rule exists, without any commitment on the question of whether the rule is observed. (Compare : ' M.P.s are entitled to £1,000 a year.') Rather, it occupies a half-way position between stating the facts about the actual receipts and about the entitlements of M.P.s. A rebuttal of the assertion which operates by clearly separating these two elements would be : ' In theory they do; but in practice payments are so much in arrears that they never receive all they are entitled to '. This element of rule-acknowledgement is less distinctly present in many other general statements. E.g., 'All Smith's books are bound in calf ' hints at a policy, a private rule, of Smith's.

I mention these apparently trivial points for the following reason. It is possible to take examples of general sentences which clearly belong to sharply contrasting classes : e.g., analytic statements; ideal law-statements; rules of games or

---

[1] The discussion of law-statements in this chapter and the next must be taken to refer only to law-statements which directly apply to instances or are simply deducible from others which so apply. Perhaps only these (or only some of these) are aptly termed ' generalizations '. There are other, and higher-grade, laws and principles of scientific theory, of which the relation to the observed facts is far from being so simple.

of institutions; quite fortuitous collocations of fact. To the first and third of these classes the concept of empirical truth or falsity does not apply. To the second and fourth it does; and, I have sought to maintain, in fundamentally the same way. But the general sentences which can be neatly classified under one or another of such headings are probably the exception rather than the rule. The fact that general sentences are thus the confused meeting-place of many characters has both encouraged wrong assimilations [1] and fostered spurious distinctions. In particular, it is important to notice the shading continuity of that line which runs from high-grade natural law-statements to those ' all s are p ' statements which one has no good ground for making short of independent evidence, in the case of each individual member of the subject-class, that it is p. At various points in between these extremes lie the majority of empirical general statements. Seeing this should make us look for the difference between them in things which can alter gradually : in the character of our grounds for making them, and in the *extent* of our commitment in making them; and not in an abrupt cleavage in type of truth-conditions at some point near one end of the line.

II. RELATIONS

5. In discussing, in Chapter II, the kind of formal analogies between inferences which interested the logician, we saw that one such analogy was exhibited by inferences of patterns like the following :

> x is a descendant of y . y is a descendant of z $\therefore$ x is a descendant of z
> x is a part of y . y is a part of z $\therefore$ x is a part of z
> x entails y . y entails z $\therefore$ x entails z
> x is older than y . y is older than z $\therefore$ x is older than z
> $x = y$. $y = z$ $\therefore$ $x = z$.

We saw also that the logician's desire to codify formal analogies by adopting a representative verbal pattern to figure in a quoted rule encountered in this case a certain difficulty; the difficulty of the absence of any pervasive formal feature common

---

[1] Note the tell-tale word ' law '.

and peculiar to relational statements which can enter into valid inferences of patterns analogous to the above. Of course, all such inferences have a common formal feature, or there would be no question of detecting a formal analogy between them. They all exemplify the pattern

$$fxy \,.\, fyz \;\therefore\; fxz.$$

But the pattern will not serve the logician's turn. For, like the general pattern of syllogistic inference in the first figure

$$m - p, s - m \;\therefore\; s - p$$

it is at least as widely exemplified by invalid as by valid inferences. Whereas language supplies us with a small number of constants by means of which different valid forms of the first-figure syllogism can be specified (as, e.g., ' all m is p, all s is m $\therefore$ all s is p '), it provides us with no constants by means of which we can specify, in one formula, just that subset of inferences of the form ' $fxy \,.\, fyz \;\therefore\; fxz$ ' which are valid. We can, it is true, find some patterns which seem to qualify for the title of formal (i.e., exhibit the desired indifference to subject-matter) and which between them cover a good many of the statements entering into valid inferences of this form : e.g.,

x is more ϕ than y
x is ϕ-er than y
x has a greater (smaller) amount (degree) of ϕ than y
x has the same ϕ as y.

A good many specific formulae which can figure in valid inference-patterns of the sort we are concerned with either directly exemplify some one of the above or, with a greater or lesser degree of linguistic strain, can be translated into formulae which do so. But no amount of stretching of the language will enable these patterns to cover all the cases we are concerned with (e.g., ' x is an ancestor of y ', ' x includes y ', ' $p \supset q$ '). Moreover, there is, as we shall see, an important logical difference between the first three, which can be regarded as merely linguistic variants on each other, and the last. So we are as far as ever from the discovery of one truly representative pattern for relational statements with just the kind of logical powers we are here concerned with. And we are left with only the expedient of classifying together, under the name ' transitive ', all those relational predicates which yield analytic formulae if substituted for 'f' in the formula '$fxy . fyz \supset fxz$'. Non-transitive relational predicates may be divided into those which yield contingent formulae when substituted for 'f' in the above expression (e.g., 'loves'), and those which yield analytic formulae when substituted for 'f' in '$fxy . fyz \supset \sim fxz$' and hence yield self-contradictory formulae when substituted for 'f' in '$fxy . fyz \supset fxz$'. The latter are called intransitive relational predicates.

6. If we compare the two transitively relational formulae 'x has the same size as y' and 'x is greater than y', it is easy to detect the important logical difference which I mentioned just now. The first formula entails, while the second is incompatible with, the formula which results from the transposition of its individual variables. This difference exemplifies a further classification of relational predicates. Predicates which yield analytic formulae when substituted for 'f' in the expression '$fxy \supset fyx$' are called symmetrical. Non-symmetrical relation-words are those which yield either contingent or self-contradictory formulae when substituted for 'f' in this expression; and those which yield self-contradictory formulae are called asymmetrical. Of transitive relations, some are symmetrical, some are asymmetrical, and some are neither. All those which involve identity or equality in some respect are symmetrical (e.g., 'is congruent with' 'is synonymous with' 'is logically equivalent to' 'is a brother or a sister of'). Those which indicate relative positions in some kind of order are asymmetrical (e.g., 'greater, older, taller than' 'ancestor of'). An example of a transitive relation which is neither symmetrical nor asymmetrical is that of entailment : the formula 'the statement that p entails the statement that q' is consistent with, but does not entail the formula 'the statement that q entails the statement that p'. One might be tempted to think that all symmetrical relations were necessarily transitive; but the relation of resemblance provides a counter-example. Examples of intransitive asymmetrical relations, and of relations which are neither transitive nor intransitive and neither symmetrical nor asymmetrical, are not difficult to find.

7. Relation-words are classified by logicians in yet other ways, corresponding to other formal characteristics. These I shall

not discuss. But one further formal feature common to most dyadic predicates must be mentioned : viz., that for any statement to the effect that one thing stands in a certain relation to another, there is usually a logically equivalent statement to the effect that the second thing stands in some relation to the first ; or, in other words, a sentence of the form ' xRy ' commonly entails and is entailed by some sentence of the form ' yRx.' The two relations are called each other's converses. Obviously, an alternative way of saying that a given relational predicate is symmetrical is to say that it is its own converse. For a great many relational expressions of which the operative word is a verb, the converse can be formed simply by changing the voice from active to passive or vice versa : e.g., ' x teaches y ' is equivalent to ' y is taught by x '. In other cases we can form converses from pairs of opposed words or phrases : e.g., ' pupil of ', ' teacher of '; ' the square root of ', ' the square of '; ' parent of ', ' offspring of ', &c. Or we may have a choice; ' entails ' has as converses both ' is entailed by ' and ' follows from '. We are continually making transformations of a statement into its converse, in every kind of field ; and the formal similarity between such moves is legitimately of interest to the formal logician. The pattern which all such moves exemplify is

$$fxy \therefore gyx.$$

Even more obviously than in the case of the putative pattern for transitivity, we cannot cite this as a valid inference-pattern. Nor can we, as we did in the transitivity case, usefully employ the pattern as a basis for a formal contrast between some relational expressions and others. For even if it is the case that language fails to provide us with a natural-sounding converse for some relational expressions, the fact is without logical significance ; we could always invent such a converse without changing the sense of the relational expression for which we invent it. So the logical feature of relational expressions discussed in this section does not supply a basis for a further formal classification of relational statements, as into ' transitive ', ' symmetrical ', &c.

8. I have made the point that the formal analogies between statements which form the greater part of the subject-matter of this branch of logic cannot, owing to the absence of pervasive

constants, be exhibited by means of rules to the effect that certain quoted verbal patterns are analytic formula, valid inference patterns, &c. We have now to note a connected point which serves in part to explain this one : viz., that the formal analogies in question are in a certain sense more comprehensive than any others we have been concerned with. For example, of the analytic formulae

$$p \vee q \supset q \vee p$$
$$s\mathrm{E}p \supset p\mathrm{E}s$$
$$x \text{ is married to } y \supset y \text{ is married to } x$$

the first two belong to formal logic, and the last does not. To say that a statement is of the pattern ' $p \vee q$ ' (or ' $s\mathrm{E}p$ ') is to classify it with a group of statements to which it is formally analogous; to say that a statement is of the pattern ' x is married to y ' is to classify it with a group of statements to which it is non-formally as well as formally analogous. The formal analogy between ' $p \vee q$ ', ' $s\mathrm{E}p$ ', and ' x is married to y ' which leads us to declare them all symmetrical formulae is one which extends over formal constants belonging to different branches of logic (' $\vee$ ' and ' I ') and over non-formal constants (' is married to ') alike. In ceasing to look for representative constants, we begin to find more far-reaching analogies.

These examples show something else. They show how, in pursuing more extensive formal analogies, we have stretched the sense of the word ' relation '. The use of the word is natural enough so long as we consider examples like the formula ' x is next to y '. It is natural enough to say that in making a statement of this form we mention, or refer to, two persons or things and declare them to stand in a certain relationship. But this description, derived from singular subject–predicate statements, becomes highly unnatural if applied to a statement of the form ' $p \vee q$ ' simply in virtue of its being of this form. We are not, in saying something of the form ' $p \vee q$ ', mentioning two statements or two clauses, but using two of the latter to make one of the former. Nevertheless, the formal analogy—viz., the legitimacy of pivoting two similar bits of a sentence about a third dissimilar bit—is certainly present. The nomenclature of ' symmetrical relational statements ' is harmless so long as we put no more weight upon it than this.

9. I remarked earlier on the dogmatic claim to completeness made on behalf of the traditional formal logic by some of its exponents. Clearly the explicit recognition of the formal analogies discussed in this chapter, and hence of forms of inference not discussed within the traditional system, is incompatible with that claim. It is easy to see how the impossibility of framing valid representative schemata could delay the explicit recognition of these forms. But some of the types of argument involved (notably transitively relational inferences, or ' arguments *a fortiori* ') were too common to escape notice altogether. Consequently, the claim to completeness has sometimes been upheld by an attempt to assimilate relational inferences to the recognized forms of subject–predicate inference. There are obvious difficulties in this programme. For example, an inference of the form

$$x \text{ entails } y$$
$$y \text{ entails } z$$
$$\therefore x \text{ entails } z$$

exhibits a striking enough analogy to the first mood of the first figure of the syllogism; but is certainly not a syllogistic inference. For, regarded as subject–predicate statement-formulae, the two premises have no common term: their subject-term variables are respectively ' x ' and ' y '; their predicate-formulae are respectively ' entails y ' and ' entails z '. Similarly, the transformation of ' The Bank is next to the Post Office ' into ' The Post Office is next to the Bank ' has an analogy to some forms of immediate inference; but does not exemplify one of these forms. For, regarded as of the subject–predicate form, the two statements have no common terms at all. The analogy in each case is precisely one of those over-riding analogies to which the logic of relations draws attention; for ' $x\mathrm{A}y$ ' is a transitive, and ' $x\mathrm{E}y$ ' and ' $x\mathrm{I}y$ ' are symmetrical, formulae.

Attempts in the face of these difficulties to maintain the reducibility of, e.g., transitively relational inferences to syllogistic form have a certain interest. They have varied in subtlety. The relatively subtle type of reduction might be illustrated as follows. Any statement of the form ' x entails y ' is equivalent to the corresponding statement of the form ' All statements entailed by y are entailed by x '. If we apply this model of translation to the form of inference quoted, we obtain :

All statements entailed by y are statements entailed by x
All statements entailed by z are statements entailed by y
∴ All statements entailed by z are statements entailed by x

which is a syllogism in the first figure, the common term of the premises being ' statements entailed by y '. The original inference may now be said to have been ' re-exhibited ' in syllogistic form. This procedure fails, however, to make good the claim that the inference was all along a syllogism in disguise. On the contrary, the principle of the transitivity of entailment, which is manifestly the principle of the inference in its original form, is covertly made use of in the individual transformations of the premises and conclusions of the original inference into the premises and conclusions of its syllogistic replacement. The formula ' x entails y ' is equivalent to the formula ' All statements entailed by y are entailed by x ' only if ' entails ' is a transitive relation-word. But to say that ' entails ' is a transitive relation-word is just to say that inferences of the pattern ' x entails y . y entails z ∴ x entails z ' are valid.

I call this instance of an attempted reduction relatively subtle, because in it the principle of the original inference is covertly made use of. The cruder kind of attempt merely introduces the principle, or some necessary truth corresponding to it, as a further premise, to be added to those of the original inference. Thus, by way of a caricature of this kind of attempt, we might imagine someone saying that the form of the inference from ' The Bank is next to the Post Office ' to ' The Post Office is next to the Bank ' was revealed by writing it as a hypothetical syllogism :

If the Bank is next to the Post Office, the Post Office is next to the Bank
The Bank is next to the Post Office
∴ The Post Office is next to the Bank.

Of course he has produced a valid inference, and one of a different form from the original. But he has not revealed the real form of the original. He might claim to have done so, had he supplied a premise without which the original inference would have been invalid. But the original inference was valid as it stood, for ' next to ' is a symmetrical relational predicate. And to say this is to describe the form of the original transformation : it was the conversion of a symmetrical relational statement.[1]

10.[2] The argument of the previous section seems simple enough. But in part the appearance of straightforwardness is deceptive. For what does it mean to assert or deny that an argument is of a certain form ? One of the answers I have earlier given is that to assign an argument to a certain form is to say that it exemplifies, or, with some verbal adjustment, can be made to exemplify, a certain verbal pattern. When we are dealing with arguments or inferences or transformations as they occur in ordinary speech, the adjustment proviso is more often requisite than not. Then what are the limits of permissible adjustments ? Why did the adjustments made in the above ' reduction ' to syllogistic form exceed them ?

The answer given in the previous section has a complexity which must be examined. Suppose someone says that the real form of the move from ' Leslie is a father ' to ' Leslie is male ' is given by the pattern ' $p \cdot q \therefore p$ '; on the ground that ' Leslie is a father ' is equivalent to ' Leslie is a parent and Leslie is male '. One protests that the validity of the move in its original form is presupposed by the transformation of the premises into the equivalent conjunctive statement. This protest embodies a decision : a decision to refuse to say that an inference from p to q is of the form $a \therefore b$ when the adjustment of p which is necessary to make the inference exemplify the form $a \therefore b$ is one which presupposes the validity of the move from p to q. If one is asked : What, then, is the form of the original inference in this case? one may answer : The move from ' Leslie is a father ' to ' Leslie is male ' certainly resembles a host of other valid moves in being of the pattern ' $fx \therefore gx$ '; but logicians have not bothered to give a special name to this class of inferences; so there is no answer to the question other than that which consists in pointing out this resemblance.

<hr />

[1] In general, given any valid inference, it is possible to frame a different valid inference incorporating, as an additional premise, a necessary truth corresponding to the principle of the original inference; and in the early stages of the application of this process, the inference obtained may differ in form from its immediate predecessor. (But there is no hope of obtaining a valid inference with so many premises that it can dispense with a principle.)

[2] See Chapter 2, Part II.

In the case of the attempted reduction of ' x entails y . y entails z $\therefore$ x entails z ' to syllogistic form, we have the same grounds as in the above simple case for refusing to say that the inference is syllogistic in form.   But we also have, what we lack in the simple case, a name fresh from the logician's vocabulary for the class of resembling inferences to which this one belongs. So we can not only refuse to assign it to the proffered form, but also assign it instead to a different form viz., that of transitively relational inferences; to which wider class we can in fact also assign all inferences of the proffered form.

Consider now a case which differs from both these.   It is suggested that a move from p to q is of the form a $\therefore$ b.   On this occasion the necessary adjustment to, say, p does not presuppose the validity of the move to q, but does exemplify some other recognized pattern (e.g., a theorem derivable in some logical system).   Here, again, it is a reasonable decision to refuse to accept the proffered form.   Thus the existence of analogies in the predicative calculus to transformations of certain subject–predicate statements makes us uneasy about certain of those transformations formerly made under the heading ' putting the premises into logical form ' (cf. Chapter 6, Section 12).

Thus answers to questions about the logical forms of inferences, and hence of statements, must always be relative to the formal classifications recognized at the time the question is put; unless they embody decisions to accept further classifications or jettison existing ones.   And to ask whether the account which some system or systems provide of the forms of inference to be found in ordinary discourse is complete or not, must always be, if not to ask a trivial or confused question, either to ask specifically whether it is worth adopting certain proposed further classifications or to wonder generally whether further classifications will be adopted.   What governs our decisions on these matters? Well, obviously, it is required that the classification proposed should count as a formal one, vague though this notion is; i.e., that the resemblance noted should have the required kind of generality.   After this, the desideratum seems to be ' formalizability '; i.e., the possibility of framing representative formulae of which the relations can be determined by a systematic technique of testing or deduction.   We have already considered and shall consider further, the effects of this ideal.

CHAPTER 8

TWO KINDS OF LOGIC

I. FORMAL LOGIC: APPLICATIONS AND LIMITATIONS

1. LANGUAGE is used for a variety of purposes. The normal use of some sentences is to give orders; of others, to ask questions; of yet others, to take oaths, to convey greetings, to make apologies, or to give thanks. When sentences are used in any of these ways it makes no sense to inquire whether what is said is true or false. But the normal use of an indefinitely large number of sentences is to say things to which this inquiry is appropriate. Such sentences as these I have called, by an easily understood brachylogy, ' statement-making sentences '. To know the meaning of a sentence of this kind is to know under what conditions someone who used it would be making a true statement; to *explain* the meaning is to *say* what these conditions are. One way of giving a partial account of these conditions is to say what some of the entailments of the sentence are. For to say that one sentence entails another is to say that a statement made by the use of the first is true only if the corresponding statement made by the use of the second is true; and to say that one sentence entails and is entailed by another is to say that a statement made by the use of the first is true if, and only if, the corresponding statement made by the use of the second is true. This might make us think that to give the two-way entailments (the logical equivalents) of a statement-making sentence is all that can be done, in the way of *saying*, to give its meaning. And since the meaning of sentences can sometimes be explained simply by talking, we may think that, in such cases, this is all that ever *need* be done; that where talking can explain, this is the only kind of talking we can do and the only kind we need do.

To think this is to make a mistake, though a common one. Let us return to the point that to explain the meaning of a statement-making sentence is to say under what conditions someone who used it would be making a true statement: and let us call this ' giving the rules of use ' of the sentence. We

have just noticed the temptation to think that the only kind of
rules involved are entailment-rules.   I want to show, first, that
this view is false, and, second, that the fact of its falsity imposes
an unavoidable limitation on the scope and application of formal logic.   The limitation in question is not one to be deplored
or to be welcomed.   It is one to be noticed; for the failure to
notice it leads to logical mythology.

It is a fact I have remarked upon before, that the questions,
whom a sentence is uttered by, and where and when it is uttered,
may be relevant to the question of whether a true statement is
made by its utterance.   The same sentence in different mouths
may be used to make one true, and one false, statement (' My
cat is dead '); the same sentence in the same mouth at different
times may be used to make one true, and one false, statement
(' My cat is dead '); and so on.   (Not only is this true of the
majority of the statement-making sentences we use in ordinary
speech.   It is also an unavoidable feature of any language we
might construct to serve the same general purposes.   But I
shall not try to prove this; for it is with ordinary discourse that
I am concerned.)   Since this is so, the assertion that a sentence
S entails a sentence S' cannot be generally taken to mean that if
any statement made by the use of the first is true, then any
statement made by the use of the second would be true.   It must
rather be taken to mean the following : If, at some time, at
some place, in the mouth of some speaker, the utterance of S
results or would result in a true statement, then the utterance
of S' at that time, at that place, in the mouth of that speaker,
would result in a true statement.   So the entailments of S may
tell us to what *kind* of situation S may be correctly applied;
they do not give general instructions enabling us to determine
whether, in the mouth of a certain speaker, at a certain time, at
a certain place, S is being applied to a situation of that kind.
Such general instructions can be given; but not by entailment-
rules.   Entailment-rules, as the above schematic formulation
shows, abstract from the time and place of the utterance and
the identity of the utterer : so they cannot tell the whole story
about the conditions under which a sentence is used to make a
true statement, unless the sentence is one of which it is true
that, if its utterance by anyone, at any time, at any place
results in a true statement, then its utterance by anyone else,

at any other time, at any other place, results in a true statement.

Entailment-rules, then, must be supplemented by rules of another kind. We may call these ' referring rules '. Referring rules take account of what entailment-rules abstract from, viz., the time and place of the utterance and the identity of the utterer. Examples of referring rules are : the word ' I ' is correctly used by a speaker to refer to himself; the word ' you ' is correctly used to refer to the person or persons whom the speaker is addressing; one of the correct uses of the present tense is for the description of states of affairs contemporaneous with the describing of them; the past tense is correctly used to indicate that the situation or event reported is temporally prior to the report. Elucidation of some or all of the uses of such words as ' the ', ' a ', ' over there ', ' he ', ' they ', ' now ', ' here ', ' this ', ' those ' are elucidations of referring rules; so are some discussions of the uses of the many tenses of verbs. Consideration of these and other examples shows that the description I gave of the factors taken account of by referring rules (viz., time and place of utterance, and identity of the speaker) must be generously interpreted. These factors embrace many distinguishable features of what, in a wide sense of the word, might be called the *context* of an utterance. A referring rule lays down a *contextual requirement* for the correct employment of an expression. But the fact that the contextual requirement is satisfied is not a part of what is *asserted* by the use of a sentence containing an expression governed (in this use) by a referring rule : it is, rather, presupposed by the use of the expression, in the sense of ' presupposed ' which I introduced in Chapter 6. Thus, if someone says, ' He will die in the course of the next two months ', it is linguistically outrageous to reply, ' No, he won't ' *and then give as one's reason* ' He's dead already '. If the event has already taken place, the question whether it will take place within the next two months or not is a question which does not arise. ' He's dead already ' disputes the presupposition that his death lies in the future, that he is not dead already. But it does not *contradict* the original statement, since to do this would be to admit its presuppositions; and hence does not contradict anything entailed by the original statement. The fact that the fulfilment of the contextual requirement is not part of what is asserted by the use of a sentence containing an expression governed by a referring rule thus involves and is involved by the distinction between referring rules and entailment-rules.[1]

2. Formal logic is concerned with the meanings of sentences only in so far as these can be given by entailment-rules. Indeed, its concern is far more limited than this suggests, for only a relatively small subclass of highly general entailment-rules are of interest to the logician. Hence formal logic systematically ignores the referring element in ordinary speech. This fact helps to explain the preoccupation of formal logic with certain types of sentence; and helps to explain also the popularity among logicians of certain collateral doctrines such as I discussed in Chapter 6. From the logician's point of view, the ideal type of sentence is one of which the meaning is entirely given by entailment-rules; that is, it is one from which the referring element is absent altogether; that is, roughly, it is one of which it is true that if its utterance at any time, at any place, by any speaker, results in a true statement, then its utterance at any other time, at any other place, by any other speaker, results in a true statement. Almost the only types of contingent sentence (i.e., sentence the utterance of which would result in a contingent statement) which seem able fully to realize this ideal are positively and negatively existential sentences, of which some forms are studied by the predicative calculus, or sentences compounded of these. That sentences of this sort may realize the ideal is easily seen. For the main, though not the only, referring elements, of sentences which contain such elements, are of two types: (1) the time-indications, relative to the moment of utterance of the sentence, which are given by the tenses of verbs; (2) the logical subjects, i.e., the separate words or phrases used to pick out the object or objects, person or persons, &c., which are being referred to. Neither of these elements need be present in a sentence exemplifying one of the positively or negatively existential forms studied in the calculus. For (1), as we have already seen,[2] ' $(\exists x)$ ' must be interpreted as, if not temporally ambiguous, either timeless or omnitemporal; and (2) since such a sentence is existential, it need contain no

---

[1] See also pp. 174–176.   [2] Chapter 5, Section 7.

expression which functions as a logical subject. Of course, in so far as we attempt to cast ordinary empirical statements into one of these forms, we may find one or both of these types of referring element in the subordinate clauses of the resulting existential sentence. But the logician is concerned with the form; and here he seems to have found a form which *can* be exemplified by sentences entirely free from referring elements.

A qualification must be added here. It is not quite true that the only contingent sentences which answer to this ideal of independence of context of utterance are those sentences which are entirely free from referring elements. For law-sentences in general answer to this ideal; and therefore subject–predicate law-sentences answer to it; for although they contain a referring element of the second type, the reference is to an open class, and is therefore independent of contextual conditions.

All necessary statements may be said to answer, though in a different way, to the ideal of independence of context. For sentences embodying necessary statements are merely the analogues of higher-order sentences stating entailments, or else other logical relations which can be re-expressed as entailments. Their use is not to describe or report or forecast. They embody entailment-rules, and, like them, abstract from contextual conditions. So one does not in making them refer to any part of the world, or to any stretch or moment of the world's history ; [1] and the present tense, in which they are generally, though not necessarily, framed, is, not the omnitemporal, but the timeless present. We have already seen that, with certain safeguards,[2] the symbolism of modern logic may be used in writing some of them.

I shall return later to the consideration of the sentences which do answer to the logician's ideal. But first I want once more to stress the obvious fact that the vast majority of the statement-making sentences we ever have, or might have, occasion to use in ordinary speech do not answer to it. For in this contrast between the logically ideal type of sentence and the types we mostly employ is the final explanation of many facts which I have mentioned in earlier chapters ; particularly in the last three. For example, it explains how it is that many features of the use of ordinary speech which are sufficiently general to deserve consideration under such a title as ' The Logic

---

[1] But see footnote to p. 217.   [2] Cf. Chapter 7, pp. 196–197.

of Language ' are necessarily omitted from consideration under the narrower title ' Formal Logic '.   Here I may instance such features as the uses of ' a ' and ' the '; the presupposition-relation between certain subject–predicate statements and certain existence-statements; the functions of the various grammatical tenses.   Second, it explains the *acharnement* with which differing types of subject–predicate statements are assimilated to negatively and/or positively existential forms, with the result that both their general character and the differences between them are obscured.   This is a natural consequence; for the formal logician is reluctant to admit, or even envisage the possibility, that his analytical equipment is inadequate for the dissection of most ordinary types of empirical statement.   Third, it explains the myth of the logically proper name and reveals the full importance of the myth.   The logically proper name is envisaged as a type of referring expression which shall be free from the unideal characteristics which all referring expressions possess.   If there did exist a class of expressions the meaning of each of which was identical with a single object, then of course the use of any expression of that class to refer to the appropriate object would be independent of contextual conditions.   A contingent sentence of the form ' fx ', where the predicate replacing ' f ' was omnitemporal and the individual expression replacing ' x ' was an expression of this class, would have the ideal characteristic that, if its utterance at any time, at any place, in the mouth of any speaker, resulted in a true statement, then its utterance at any other time, at any other place, in the mouth of any other speaker, would result in a true statement.   Now the whole structure of quantificational logic, with its apparatus of individual variables, seems, or has seemed to most of its exponents, to require, for its application to ordinary empirical speech to be possible, that there should exist individual referring expressions which could appear as values of the individual variables.   That is to say, the whole structure has seemed to presuppose the existence of simple predicative sentences of the form ' fx '.   The belief in logically proper names made it possible to assume both that there were such sentences and that they were of the logically ideal type; and thus helped to preserve the illusion that formal logic was an adequate instrument for the dissection of ordinary speech.   In fact, there *are* such sentences, but they are *not* of the logically ideal type.   Finally, the preoccupation with the ideal type of sentence explains the persistent neglect of the distinction between sentence and statement.   For, in the case of sentences of the ideal type, the distinction really *is* unimportant.   Such a sentence whenever it is used, is used to make one and the same statement;   the contextual conditions of its use are irrelevant to the truth or falsity of that statement.   To this type of sentence the otherwise bogus trichotomy ' true, false, or meaningless ' may be harmlessly applied.

3. We have seen that there do exist sentences answering to the logical ideal.   Law-sentences are omnitemporal, analytic sentences are timeless;   analytic sentences abstract from references to particular objects or groups,[1] law-sentences, if they contain references at all, refer to open classes.   An obvious inquiry, therefore, is :   How far is the symbolic apparatus of modern logic adequate for the expression of the form, or the general logical powers, of these sentences?   Now the fact is that this symbolic apparatus can be, and is, made use of, not only within formal logic itself, but also in application to mathematics, and to systems of law-sentences.   The deductive relationships of the members of systems of contingent law-sentences can be exhibited by means of this apparatus.   So our question must be, not *whether* it is possible to use this apparatus for such purposes, but *how* it is possible to do so.   For there are certain prima facie difficulties about these uses of this apparatus.

The main difficulty may be put briefly.   The foundation of modern logic is the system of truth-functional formulae.   The character of the quantificational superstructure is thoroughly determined by the character of the foundation.   Such characteristic quantificational formulae as ' $(x)(fx \supset gx)$ ' ' $\sim(\exists x)(fx \cdot gx)$ ', &c., are, as we have seen, quasi-special-cases of truth-functional formulae.   Now one thing which is quite clear about both analytic statements and law statements is that they are not, in this thoroughgoing way, truth-functional. An analytic statement of the form ' if p then q ' is not made true by the circumstance that the antecedent of the conditional is

[1] Or if they seem to contain such references (e.g., ' If Leslie is a father, Leslie is male '), the question of what reference is made (or even of whether a reference is made at all) is entirely irrelevant to their truth.

8*

false.   A law-statement of the form ' there is no case of f which is not a case of g ' is not made true by the circumstance that ' there is no case of f'.   So we cannot, without reservations, adopt ' $p \supset q$ ' as the form of the first, or ' $(x)(fx \supset gx)$ ' as the form of the second.

We have already seen something of the method of circumventing this difficulty in the case of analytic statements.   If we make it clear, when employing the truth-functional symbolism for analytic sentences or formulae, that this is what we are doing; if, for example, for every such employment of the form

$$p \supset q$$

we bear in mind the invisible escort of quotation marks and the phrase ' is analytic '; then the above-noted troublesome consequence of the employment of this form no longer applies.   For while it is a rule of the system that the formula ' $\sim p$ ' entails the formula ' $p \supset q$ ' (i.e., that a statement of the form ' $\sim p$ ' entails the corresponding statement of the form ' $p \supset q$ '), it is by no means a rule of the system that a statement of the form ' $\sim p$ ' entails the statement that the corresponding statement of the form ' $p \supset q$ ' is analytic.   A similar move might seem to be available in the case of contingent law-statements.   That is, we are to make it clear, every time we employ the symbolism to express a law-statement, that this is what we are doing.   We shall not, as in the case of analytic formulae, employ quotation-marks; for a law-statement is a contingent assertion about the way the world goes, and not any kind of linguistic rule.   We may imagine rather that every time we employ the formula ' $(x)(fx \supset gx)$ ' to express a law-statement, we use it as a sort of shorthand for ' it is a natural law that $(x)(fx \supset gx)$ '.   As before, we escape the consequence that a law-statement expressed by means of the quantificational formula is made true by the circumstance that the corresponding statement of the form ' $\sim(\exists x)(fx)$ ' is true.   For while it is a rule of the system that ' $\sim(\exists x)(fx)$ ' entails ' $(x)(fx \supset gx)$ ', it is by no means a rule of the system that ' $\sim(\exists x(fx)$ ' entails ' it is a natural law that $(x)(fx \supset gx)$ '.

These are but preliminary manœuvres.   They might well seem pointless, or meaningless, ones, unless the logical relations between symbolic expressions all mentally supplied with the tag 'analytic', or between such expressions all supplied with the tag 'natural law', were exact replicas of the logical relations between the corresponding formulae unsupplied with either tag. Only if this parallel holds, it seems, shall we be justified in claiming to be able to apply the logical systems concerned to the realms of necessary truth or scientific law. The preliminary manœuvres might then appear to be justified as measures designed to bar the logical gates of these realms to intruders from non-scientific empirical discourse.

On the other hand, if the parallels are to hold, then we seem to encounter further difficulties. For example, we shall be committed to holding that the rule that '$\sim p$' entails '$p \supset q$' still applies where both the entailing and the entailed formulae (or sentences) of these forms are analytic; that is to say, that a statement to the effect that a formula of the form '$\sim p$' is analytic entails the statement that the corresponding formula of the form '$p \supset q$' is analytic. And this may seem a consequence only a little less embarrassing than that which we have avoided. To take an example. ' It is not the case that squares have just three sides ' is analytic. Then by the application of this rule ' It is not the case that squares have just three sides ', as analytic, entails, as analytic, any sentence whatever of the form ' Squares have just three sides $\supset q$ ', whatever value we may give to 'q'. So ' Squares have just three sides $\supset 5 = \sqrt{25}$ ' and ' Squares have just three sides $\supset$ Tom is a bachelor ' will be analytic sentences. So, if we allow the equivalence between the statement that a sentence of the form '$p \supset q$' is analytic and the statement that the first sentence of the truth-functional compound entails the second, we shall have to conclude that ' Squares have just three sides ' entails ' $5 = \sqrt{25}$ ' and ' Tom is a bachelor ' and any other sentence we like to mention. Generally, any self-contradictory statement will entail any statement whatever. And this goes flatly against our normal use of ' entails ' as the converse of ' is deducible from '.

We must remember, however, that what we set out to explain was the successful use of the symbolic apparatus of logic in the development of a system of necessary truth, i.e., a logical or mathematical system. A little reflection shows that the rule we are considering has no embarrassing consequences in such a

use of the symbolic apparatus.   One mitigating feature which
may first be mentioned is that since the expressions used in the
development of the system will be limited by the formation-rules
and definitions of the system, we shall never be able to derive,
from a formula of the form ' $\sim p$ ', a formula of the form ' $p \supset q$ '
in which the expressions replacing ' q ' lie outside the system
altogether.   So there will be nothing of that appearance of
lunatic irrelevance which characterized the example given in the
previous paragraph.   But a more important point is the
following.   Suppose our system is developed by the deductive
method.   Then, unless the system is inconsistent, in which
case the sooner this fact appears, the better, none of the axioms
will be self-contradictory or inconsistent with any other.   The
system may be supposed to use, as rules of inference, the Principle of Substitution and the Principle of Inference [1] and to presuppose the propositional calculus.   Among the axioms or
early theorems we may find expressions of the form ' $\sim p$ ', from
which we shall accordingly be able to derive corresponding
formulae of the form ' $p \supset q$ '.   But if the axioms or early
theorems contain, as analytic, a formula of the form ' $\sim p$ ',
they will not, unless the system is inconsistent, contain also the
expression which replaces ' p ' in this form.   Consequently, we
shall never be able to apply the Rule of Inference to a formula
of the form ' $p \supset q$ ' when it is derived from the corresponding
formula of the form ' $\sim p$ ' by use of the ' embarrassing ' rule ;
that is to say, from a formula of the form ' $p \supset q$ ', so derived,
we shall never be able to derive the expression which replaces
' q '.   So, as far as the development of the system is concerned,
the ' embarrassing ' rule is not embarrassing at all : it can never
force us to accept, as entailed directly or indirectly by the
axioms, any preposterously inconsequential theorem.   We
might put the point as follows.   As far as entailment within the
system is concerned (i.e., the direct or indirect derivability of
theorems from axioms), the meaning of ' entails ' is given not
simply by the rules for ' $\supset$ ' (or the quite analogous rules
for ' " . . . $\supset$ . . ." ' is analytic '), but by these rules *taken in
conjunction with the rules of inference of the system*.   The presupposed laws of the propositional calculus in themselves license
no derivations at all : it is the higher-order rules of inferences

---

[1] See Chapters 2 and 3, pp. 58–60 and 99–100.

of the system which permit, and limit, their use.　In particular, all breaking of new ground in the system (as opposed to the exemplifying of already established laws) takes place under the aegis of the Rule of Inference.　Entailment of F_2 by F_1 within the system, where F_1 is related in an earlier theorem to F_2 by means of ' $\supset$ ', requires that the rules of inference should permit F_2 to be detached from F_1 and asserted separately as a law.

This example is enough to show what I set out to show : namely how, in spite of the fact that the rules for ' $p \supset q$ ' (whether the constituents of the function are contingent or necessary) are by no means analogous to those for ' entails ', it is, nevertheless, perfectly possible to make use of the symbolic apparatus of truth-functions for the development of systems of necessary truth.　There still remains a question, not about the development of such a system, but about the application of the laws.　Where a formula of the form ' $p \supset q$ ' is derived as analytic within the system we shall sometimes, but not always, want to say that the first of its constituents entails the second ; i.e., that the analytic formula can itself be read, in the applications of the system, as a rule authorizing deductions.　We shall not, for example, want to say this, when the formula of the form ' $p \supset q$ ' is derived from the corresponding formula of the form ' $\sim p$ '.　The resolution of this quite different problem consists simply in the imposition of restrictions on the translation of the declaration that a formula of the form ' $p \supset q$ ' is analytic into the declaration that the first of its constituents entails the second.[1]

It is obvious that similar considerations, as regards ' entailment within the system ', apply to the deductive development of systems of natural law.　From the point of view simply of the development of a deductive system, the fact that the system is one of natural laws rather than necessary truths raises no special problem.

Nevertheless special problems do arise.　To begin with, the preliminary manœuvre suggested by the treatment of systems of necessary truth is highly suspect.　For in the discussions of Chapter 7, I was at pains to emphasize that to call a general

---

[1] See Chapter 1, p. 24.　The full discussion of these restrictions is too complicated to be undertaken here.

subject–predicate statement a law-statement was not to assign it a different kind of truth-conditions from any other general subject–predicate statement. It was merely to say something about the extent of its application and about the character of the evidence by which it was supported. A general subject–predicate statement to the effect that every case of f is a case of g, *whether it is a law-statement or not*, is contradicted by the *ordinary* contingent statement to the effect that at least one case of f is not a case of g.[1] The contradictory of a logically necessary statement is a self-contradictory statement; but the contradictory of a law-statement is an *ordinary* contingent statement (i.e., *not* a law-statement). So the preliminary manœuvre, which cuts off law-statements, when expressed in the symbolism of modern logic, from logical relations with ordinary contingent statements, must be abandoned or modified. The parallel with necessity was misleading. The problem of how the symbolic apparatus can be used for a system of law-statements remains.

But a little common sense resolves it. First we must notice that a general subject–predicate law-statement to the effect that every case of f is a case of g entails the corresponding *negatively* existential statement to the effect that $\sim(\exists x)(fx \cdot \sim gx)$ or $(x)(fx \supset gx)$. Both will be omnitemporal. These negatively existential consequences of subject–predicate law-statements may also be called law-statements. Next, we must recall that the condition of the acceptability of a law-statement which does not have direct application is its deductive relationship to law-statements which do. The only safeguard we need then adopt is the resolution not to include in the premises of our system any but law-statements. This will suffice to exclude any sentence of the form ' $(x)(fx \supset gx)$ ' which expresses a truth solely in virtue of the fact that the corresponding sentence of the form ' $\sim(\exists x)(fx)$ ' expresses a truth (unless this latter sentence expresses, not only a truth, but a law); but this effect is secured without setting up a spurious logical barrier between law-statements and contingent statements which are not law-statements. So the original manœuvre is modified, rather than altogether abandoned.

[1] Here we must allow for the qualifications of the first paragraph of Chapter 7.

We are left with a not very serious problem, which is the analogue of the application-problem in systems of necessary truth. Suppose we have a sentence of the form '$\sim(\exists x)(fx)$' which *does* express a law-statement. Then we shall be able to derive any corresponding sentence of the form '$(x)(fx \supset gx)$'. Shall we say that this sentence expresses a law or not? In the context of the system, where its derivation is apparent, it will not matter if we say this. But it might be misleading to say it outside that context; for it would suggest that our grounds for saying it were of a different kind. For example, it would be misleading to treat 'There is no moving body unaffected by external forces which does not continue, &c.' as a law solely on the ground that it was a law that there is no moving body unaffected by external forces. (I do not suggest that this latter statement is in fact a law, or even that it is true.) Here, as in the analogous case, a policy of restrictive rules is required.

I do not claim that this section does more than indicate the ways in which our puzzles about the use of the symbolic apparatus of modern logic in the development of systems of necessary truth or of natural law may be resolved. But the other specific problems which may arise will, I think, have analogies to those here discussed and be capable of resolution in analogous ways. The main points I have sought to establish are these: (1) that when we inquire what use can be made of the symbolic apparatus of logic we find that for certain general reasons it seems best adapted to the role of systematically exhibiting the logical relationships between sentences which answer to the ideal of independence of contextual conditions; (2) that the actually occurring sentences of this type are analytic sentences and law-sentences; (3) that analytic sentences and law-sentences seem to present certain obstacles to expression in a thoroughly truth-functional symbolism; (4) but that when we examine the actual process of constructing a system of such sentences by the use of the symbolism, we see how the obstacles either are, automatically, or can be, deliberately, overcome. If we are clear about all these points, we are prevented from many illusions which attend the too indiscriminate use, in philosophical analysis, of modern logical symbolism; and delivered from many puzzles about its legitimate uses.

4. We have seen [1] that at an early stage in the development of any logical system rules should be laid down prescribing what combinations of the symbols of the system are permissible. These are the formation-rules of the system. Expressions framed in accordance with them are called well-formed; and combinations of symbols which violate them are said to be ill-formed. Ill-formed expressions are without meaning : the deductive or testing technique of the system cannot be applied to them; and, when the system is interpreted, no sense is given to such expressions. The framing of formation-rules obviously presupposes the classification of the constants and variables of the system into different types. For to give formation-rules is to say what classes of symbols of the system can significantly figure in combinations of certain kinds with other types of symbols of the system. When the system is given a linguistic interpretation, this classification of expressions into types is obviously carried over into the domain of words and phrases : it applies to the verbal expressions which can figure as values of the variables of the system, and to the verbal expressions used to interpret its constants. So we may expect to find some restrictions on the significant combinations of the expressions of ordinary language, which are analogous to the formation-rules of a linguistically interpretable system. And, so long as we do not insist overmuch on their strictness, we do find such analogies. We find them, we may say, in the rules (some of the rules) of grammar. Grammarians, like logicians, classify expressions into types. Given that a sentence is to contain an expression of one grammatical type, then the rules of grammar will often lay down requirements concerning other types of expression it must contain and, sometimes, the method of their arrangement. If these requirements are not satisfied, then no sentence, or an ungrammatical sentence, is obtained. ' Ungrammatical ' is, roughly speaking, the linguistic analogue of ' ill-formed '. To take some examples. (1) The formation-rules of the propositional calculus require that '.' or 'v' should be flanked at least by two statement-variables in a well-formed expression. Grammar describes the role of conjunctions like

[1] Cf. Chapter 2, p. 62.

' or ' and ' and ' as that of joining two like clauses or phrases. (2) In a formal system which made a notational distinction between one-place and two-place predicates, there would be a formation-rule to the effect that a two-place predicate required at least two individual variables or expressions to figure in a well-formed expression. Compare this with the grammatical requirement that a transitive verb should have both a subject and an object. (3) Logic does not allow ' xyz ' as a well-formed expression. Grammar does not allow ' Tom, Dick, Harry ' as a sentence.

It is clear that the parallels could be multiplied. It is also clear that they cannot be pressed at all closely. Grammatical classifications are of many different kinds, are difficult to formulate clearly, and not always easy to apply. This is natural; for they deal with living or once-living languages and not with invented symbolisms. Formal classifications are precisely stated, and can be made as easy to apply as he who chooses the symbolism desires. No sense is given to expressions which violate the formation-rules of a system. But many ungrammatical sentences make sense, and so do many expressions which are not sentences at all, but which, if written, would be written between full stops; and context may confer upon a single word the force of a sentence. Even where the detailed analogies seem at their closest, they may break down : ' Either there will be war or not ' is a perfectly good sentence; but ' $p \vee \sim$ ' is an ill-formed expression.

Although the analogies cannot be pressed too closely, it is evident that, where they exist, they have a common root. Earlier [1] we saw how the *formal* distinction between individual and predicative variables reflects the *functional* distinction between referring to something and describing it; and how this is correspondingly reflected by the *grammatical* distinction between subject and predicate. The formation-rule that an individual variable must be escorted by a predicative variable, the grammatical rule that a sentence must have a predicate as well as a subject, have their root in the necessary fact that no statement is made by referring alone. Similarly, the grammatical need which conjunctions have for two clauses, the formal need which statement connectives have for two state-

[1] Cf. Chapter 5, Section 5.

ment-variables, alike reflect a cluster of tautologies : as that, for example, one cannot say that one thing is conditional upon another without indicating *both* what is conditional *and* upon what it is conditional. It might be asked why distinguish the root tautology from the formal or grammatical requirement? The answer is that the linguistic devices by which statements of different kinds are made might conceivably have been quite different from those we are familiar with. Both the grammatical rules and the formation-rules reflect, not only the root tauto-logy, but the kind of linguistic devices we actually employ.

So the formation-rules of a system, which rigidly proscribe certain combinations of expressions as nonsense, have genuine connexions with those grammatical rules which yield no more than a presumption against certain kinds of combinations of words making sense. They both reflect very general necessities of language. The formation-rules of a system are related to their grammatical analogues somewhat as the entailment-rules of a system are related to their analogues in ordinary speech : the former are rigid and systematic, the latter flexible and unsystematic.

5. Now we saw that entailments of sufficient generality to interest the formal logician were not the only entailments to be found in ordinary speech. Similarly, we find that the gram-matical requirements which are analogous to formation-rules are not the only requirements a sentence must satisfy if it is to make sense. No grammatical rule is infringed by saying that the cube root of ten is three miles away or that there is a loud smell in the drawing-room. But to say either of these things would be, if not to talk nonsense, at least to say something which had no literal or straightforward sense. The sentences ' He knows French well ' and ' He knows French slowly ' have the same grammatical structure ; but whereas the first makes sense as it stands, the second can be given a sense only by taking it as bad English for, e.g., ' He is slowly getting to know French ' or ' He can read French slowly ' or ' He can understand French when it is spoken slowly '. Similarly, ' The average tax-payer is dissatisfied with the Budget ' makes straightforward sense, whereas ' The average tax-payer died yesterday ' would be a joke, an epigram, or a piece of nonsense.

It seems, then, that there are additional restrictions, besides those laxly imposed by grammar, on the ways in which words may be combined to make literal sense. We may refer to these as type-restrictions or type-rules; for they rule out combinations of expressions of certain types. Some have been tempted to assimilate violation of type-restrictions to self-contradictions. But this seems a mistake. The reason why 'loud smell' makes no sense is not that smells, like murmurs, are necessarily soft. Referring to something as a smell proscribes as senseless the question whether it is loud or not loud : it does not commit the speaker to one of two incompatible answers to the question. Instead of assimilating non-grammatical type-restrictions to non-formal entailments, we had better recognize a parallel relationship : between grammatical type-restrictions and non-grammatical type-restrictions on the one hand; and between formal entailments (i.e., entailments of the generality which interests the logician) and non-formal (lexicographers') entailments on the other. No one, after all, would want to assimilate grammatical rules to highly general entailments.

6. There is a certain metaphysical view, opposed to the conclusions of the last section, to which a preoccupation with formal logic may incline us. It may be summarily expressed as the view that the only irreducible type-differences are those which formal logic recognizes; that all other type-differences between expressions are ultimately explicable as differences between the logical forms of the sentences which contain them. This requires explanation. Formal logic commits us to a distinction in type between singular referring expressions (values of individual variables) and predicative expressions (values of predicative variables). But obviously the considerations of the last section require us to make further type-distinctions within each of these types. For example, the names of human qualities and the names of individual human beings may alike figure as singular referring expressions. But not everything that can, with literal significance, be said of individual human beings can, with literal significance, be said of individual human qualities; and conversely. To put it very roughly : the ranges of expressions with which the names of men and the names of men's qualities can be significantly combined are different. It can

sometimes be plausibly maintained, however, that a singular statement about a human quality is logically equivalent to a general statement about human beings. In such a case we may be encouraged to say that the difference in type between expressions playing formally similar roles in formally similar sentences has been reduced to a difference in form between sentences about things of the same type (viz., human beings). Sometimes it is said that the translation of the singular into the general statement discloses the ' real ' logical form of the former.

This manœuvre has several interesting features. If we commit ourselves to the last of the steps mentioned, then we are giving to the expression ' logical form ' a quite different *sense* from any in which we have used it hitherto. For why, of the two equivalent sentences, should we choose to say that the general sentence reveals the ' real ' form of the singular sentence rather than the reverse ? Why should we think of the reduction, of the elimination of a certain type of expression, as going in that direction rather than the other ? The only answer can be that we think of expressions referring to individual human beings as more ' fundamental ' or ' basic ' in type than expressions referring to human qualities. For suppose our general sentence is written in the form ' $(x)(fx \supset gx)$ ', with the appropriate values for ' f ' and ' g '. Then the corresponding formula of the form ' fx ' will take, as values of the individual variable, expressions referring to individual human beings. The original singular sentence, equivalent to the general sentence, itself exemplified the formula ' fx ', but had, as the value of ' x ', the name of a quality. So one says that ' $(x)(fx \supset gx)$ ' was the real form of the original sentence rather than ' fx ', only if one thinks of individual variables as somehow basically designed to indicate gaps to be filled by designations of individual people rather than designations of qualities. One can speak, *in this way*, of the real logical form of a sentence or statement only if one has already selected a certain type of expression as the basic type in terms of which ' real logical form ' is to be defined. Thus the real logical form of a sentence S will be given by the formula exemplified by a sentence S' which is (1) equivalent to the sentence S and (2) contains no expressions of non-basic types and no subsidiary formulae such that a variable, free in that formula, would take an expression of a non-basic type as a value. This is a far cry from the sense in which we have used 'logical form' up to now.

Even if we forswear this last step, and hence refrain from introducing new elements into the notion of logical form, it remains true that the general programme of explaining type-differences, other than formal-grammatical ones, along these lines, presupposes the selection of one type of expression as the type *par excellence* of individual expression. This selection will in its turn dictate the selection of one type of predicative expression as the type *par excellence*. This selection of basic types will yield a range of sentences of the form '*fx*' such that any individual expression occurring in any of them can be significantly combined with any predicative expression occurring in any of them. As far as these sentences are concerned, the formal difference in type between individual and predicative expressions will *coincide* with the difference between the two basic types of expression selected. From sentences of this range we can construct (by truth-functional composition, quantification, or any other means recognized in our formal logic) more complex sentences, which will not, however, contain any expression of any further types except those officially recognized in our logic (or our grammar). Now the general programme of explanation of type-differences can theoretically be carried out if, and only if, for every sentence containing expressions of non-basic types there is a logically equivalent sentence in which these expressions are eliminated in favour of expressions of the basic types, together with whatever devices for constructing complex sentences are recognized in our formal logic (or our grammar). If we could show a reasonable presumption that this programme of translations could be carried out, we might reasonably claim to have explained all type-differences in terms of those recognized by formal logic (or grammar), together with the entailment-rules sanctioning the translations.

Much metaphysics consists in the attempt to show that this programme (or a part of it) could theoretically be carried out. Sense-impressions have been among the candidates for the designata of the basic individual expressions; so have material objects. There is, however, no reason for supposing that the programme can be carried out; and there are many good reasons for supposing that it cannot.

When the reductionist programme is combined with belief that the truth-functional and quantificational systems give an adequate analysis of the means of framing complex statements, then the metaphysical pull of formal logic is at its most powerful. For then we have the belief that modern symbolic systems, together with ordinary entailment-rules, give a completely adequate map of the logic of language in its statement-making aspect. In this section I have indicated yet another field—that of distinctions of type—in which this claim is unfounded.

III. THE LOGIC OF LANGUAGE

7. In discussing the logic of ordinary language I have frequently used the word ' rule '. I have spoken of entailment rules, referring rules, type-rules. The word is not inappropriate : for to speak of these and other ' rules ' is to speak of ways in which language may be *correctly* or *incorrectly* used. But though not inappropriate, the word may be misleading. We do not judge our linguistic practice in the light of antecedently studied rules. We frame rules in the light of our study of our practice. Moreover, our practice is a very fluid affair. If we are to speak of rules at all, we ought to think of them as rules which everyone has a licence to violate if he can show a point in doing so. In the effort to describe our experience we are continually putting words to new uses, connected with, but not identical with, their familiar uses; applying them to states of affairs which are both like and unlike those to which the words are most familiarly applied. Hence we may give a meaning to sentences which, at first sight, seem self-contradictory.[1] And hence, though some have incautiously spoken of the violation of type-rules as resulting in sentences which, though neither ungrammatical nor self-contradictory, are nonsense, it is in fact hard to frame a grammatical sentence to which it is impossible to imagine some sense being given; and given, not by arbitrary *fiat*, but by an intelligible, though probably figurative, extension of the familiar senses of the words and phrases concerned.[2]

In speaking of entailment-rules we make use of the distinction between analytic and synthetic (or contingent) statements. In speaking of type-rules we make use of the distinction between

---

[1] See Chapter 1, pp. 6–7.   [2] See Chapter 2, Section 5.

the literal and the figurative use of language.   But we must not imagine these distinctions to be very sharp ones, any more than we must imagine our linguistic rules to be very rigid.   Very often we may hesitate between saying, of two uses of a word, that one is literal and the other figurative, and saying that they are just two different, though equally literal, senses of the word. Sometimes we shall be uncertain whether to say that a word is being used in the same sense, or different senses.   And these notions—of figurative and literal senses, of different senses and the same sense—are, with all their imprecision, indispensable to explaining what we mean by type-distinctions and type-rules. Similarly, we may very often hesitate to say whether a given sentence is analytic or synthetic; and the imprecision of this distinction, as applied to ordinary speech, reflects an imprecision in the application of the notion of entailment to ordinary speech.

This fluidity in our rules, and this imprecision in the distinctions they involve, are things we must be aware of if we aim at a realistic study of the logic of ordinary speech.   But though they make such a study more complicated and less tidy than the study of formal systems, they do not make it impossible.   In a way, the awareness of them makes it easier; for if we realize that we are at best describing only the standard and typical uses of certain kinds of expression, we shall be less disconcerted by untypical cases.

8. Side by side with the study of formal logic, and overlapping it, we have another study : the study of the logical features of ordinary speech.   The second study can illuminate the first, and can by it be illuminated or obscured.   Much of this book is concerned with the inter-relations between the two.   I have given, in outline, some examples of the kinds of distinction we can draw, and the kinds of generalization we can make, in pursuing this second study.   The most important general lesson to be learnt from them is that simple deductive relationships are not the only kind we have to consider if we wish to understand the logical workings of language.   We have to think in many more dimensions than that of entailment and contradiction, and use many tools of analysis besides those which belong to formal logic.   The scope of the second study is further

greatly extended if, instead of restricting our attention to the statement-making use of language, we consider also some of the many other uses it may have. Nor, in this study, are we confined to linguistic minutiae; although the detailed examination of small linguistic differences may be absorbing enough. For in trying to discover the answers to questions of such forms as ' What are the conditions under which we use such-and-such an expression or class of expressions ? ' or ' Why do we say such-and-such a thing and not such-and-such another ? ', we may find ourselves able to frame classifications or disclose differences broad and deep enough to satisfy the strongest appetite for generality. What we shall not find in our results is that character of elegance and system which belongs to the constructions of formal logic. It is none the less true that the logic of ordinary speech provides a field of intellectual study unsurpassed in richness, complexity, and the power to absorb.

CHAPTER 9

INDUCTIVE REASONING AND PROBABILITY

I. SUPPORT AND PROBABILITY

1. OF a piece of deductive reasoning one can inquire : Is it valid or invalid ? Do the premises entail the conclusion, or do they not ? These are questions to which a ' Yes-or-No ' answer is possible. If the sense of the argument is clear enough to admit of an answer it admits of a clear-cut answer : the argument is valid; or it is not. This is not to say that we might not hesitate over the question of whether an argument was valid or not.[1] But this is the sort of hesitation which leads, perhaps, to saying : ' Well, interpreted in this way, the argument would be valid; interpreted in that way, it would be invalid.' It could never lead to our assigning an intermediate status to the argument. The phrase ' moderately valid argument ' has no sense.

Deductive reasoning is not the only kind of reasoning, or even the most common kind. We make deductive steps when we do pure mathematics and, sometimes, when we argue philosophically. We make such steps in less rarefied regions as well : when we do the arithmetic of everyday ; when we turn one form of words into another, when we make a précis, when we try to show that our opponent in argument has contradicted himself. But a good deal of our reasoning does not proceed by steps of this kind, but of another; though a single train of argument may involve moves of both sorts. Thus the detective and the historian, when they draw conclusions from their premises, their evidence, often draw conclusions which are not entailed by those premises. There would often be nothing self-contradictory in accepting the premises, and rejecting the conclusions, of their arguments. But it does not follow from the fact that an historian's or a detective's argument is, by deductive standards, invalid, that it is in any sense unsound. It may be an argument to which deductive standards are inappropriate : it may make no claim to be deductively valid. Deductive

---

[1] See Chapter 8, Section 7.

standards are not the only standards of good argument; for deductive reasoning is not the only kind of reasoning. The reasoning of the experimental scientist, like that of the historian and the detective, is, in differing degrees, non-deductive. Of course, the scientist may make many deductive steps; but if these were the only permissible steps, experimental science would be impossible. For it is a part of the scientist's function to establish conclusions which are not entailed by his data, his evidence. An example of a well-established scientific statement might be one giving the melting-point of a certain metal : ' Under pressure-conditions x, m always melts at y degrees.' The evidence on which such a statement was based might consist of one or two experimental tests, together with the fact that no *known* metal has, *so far as has been observed*, a variable melting-point under constant-pressure conditions. These ' premises ' do not entail the conclusion that m always melts at y degrees under conditions x. There would be nothing self-contradictory in conjoining them with the prediction that the next piece of m, melted under these conditions, will melt at $y + 50$ degrees. Yet the evidence may be quite conclusive, though the ' argument ' is not deductively valid. Of course, one could introduce an argument which *would* be deductively valid. We could introduce as a premise the general statement : ' All metals have constant melting-points under constant-pressure conditions.' This statement, together with that recording the result of just one experimental test, would entail a conclusion of the form : ' Under pressure condition x, m always melts at y degrees.' The general statement introduced as a premise might itself be a consequence of some other theoretical statement accepted as well established. But at some point we should inevitably come to a theoretical statement based ultimately upon the evidence embodied in statements recording the results of particular observations; statements which did not entail the theoretical statement. No number of statements recording particular observations can ever entail a theoretical statement of this kind; for the theoretical statement is, while the particular observation-statements are not, exposed to the logical risk of refutation by statements recording the results of similar particular observations which may be made in the future.

Examples of this sort are perhaps better avoided. For most

of us know little of natural science.   Fortunately, we need go to
nothing so elevated as history, science, or detection to find
examples of non-deductive reasoning.   Ordinary life provides
enough.   Consider

>   (a) He's been travelling for twenty-four hours, so he'll
> be very tired.
>   (b) The kettle's been on the fire for the last ten minutes,
> so it should be boiling by now.
>   (c) There's a hard frost this morning : you'll be cold
> without a coat.

Plainly the statement made by the first clause of each sentence
is regarded as a reason for accepting the statement made by the
second clause.   The second statement in each case is in some
sense a *conclusion* from the first; the first can in some sense be
called a *premise*.   But the premise does not entail the conclusion.   It would not be self-contradictory to say : ' The
kettle has been on the fire for ten minutes, but the water is
stone cold.'   One might be inclined to say that this would be
impossible : but the impossibility is not logical.   On the other
hand, though the premise does not entail the conclusion, it is a
perfectly adequate reason for accepting the conclusion in each
case.   The arguments, though not deductively valid, are perfectly sound arguments.

As before, we might be tempted to explain the apparently
non-deductive soundness of the arguments by saying that they
were *really* deductive arguments with a suppressed premise.
And it certainly is true that we can, for each of the arguments
(a)–(c), construct a corresponding and valid deductive argument
by introducing a fresh premise : e.g., for (a), ' People who travel
for twenty-four hours are always tired afterwards '; for (b),
' Kettles always boil within ten minutes of being put on the
fire '; for (c), ' Anyone not wearing a coat is cold on a frosty
morning '.   But by regarding these general statements as suppressed premises of arguments (a)–(c), we do not get rid of the
general problem of explaining how we can reasonably draw conclusions from premises that do not entail them.   We merely
shift its emphasis to the narrower question : How do we establish
general propositions such as these ?   For these are not logically
necessary propositions.   If they had been, arguments (a)–(c)

9

would have been deductively valid. It is, of course, common experience that constitutes our grounds for general beliefs like these. But the beliefs go beyond the experience. To inquire by what kind of reasoning we are justified in accepting unrestricted general propositions which are not necessary propositions, is merely to put the general problem in a more specific, and less realistic, form. The form is less realistic because these generalizations based on common experience do not often appear in practice as the conclusions of arguments from particular instances. They are less reflectively adopted. But ' p so q ' arguments like (a), (b), and (c) are common.

There seems in fact to be no good reason for limiting the question in this way. We saw earlier [1] that, given a certain *deductive* inference, it was always possible to construct a different inference by introducing, as an additional premise, a necessary statement corresponding to the principle of the original inference. But we saw that the claim that this procedure revealed the real character of the original inference was in general misleading; for our acceptance of the additional premise as logically necessary was the same thing as our acceptance of the original inference as valid. Similarly, in the case of the non-deductive steps in (a), (b), and (c), our acceptance of the corresponding general proposition in each case as true, is the same thing as our acceptance of the particular inference, not as deductively valid, but as somehow sound, or correct, or reasonable. One might say that, as the necessary proposition stands to the principle of the original deductive inference, so the non-necessary general proposition stands to a principle of some other kind of reasoning. We cannot express principles of this kind by the use of the second-order words, like ' entails ', which belong to deduction; but we might express them by the use of phrases like '. . . makes it certain that . . .', or '. . . is a good ground for concluding that . . .'. Thus our acceptance of the non-necessary proposition that all kettles boil within ten minutes of being put on the fire will be the same as our acceptance of the non-deductive principle that the fact that a kettle has been on the fire for ten minutes is a good ground for concluding that it will be boiling; and both are the same as our acceptance of the step in (b) as sound or correct or reasonable.

[1] Cf. Chapter 7, Section 9.

The problem we are to consider, then, is the nature of that kind of reasoning from one non-necessary statement (or conjunction of statements) to another, in which the first does not entail the second. This kind of reasoning is generally called inductive. Sometimes this title tends to be reserved for those cases in which the conclusion is a general statement. But this we see to be an artificial restriction. For the acceptance of a non-necessary general proposition as established is the same as the acceptance of the general correctness of a class of particular pieces of reasoning from premises to conclusions which they do not entail; just as the acceptance of a certain general statement as necessary is the acceptance of the validity of a class of particular deductive inferences.

2. I want now to draw attention to certain further differences between inductive and deductive reasoning. For this purpose, I want a general word for the relation between the grounds for an inductive conclusion and the conclusion itself. The only thing I have said so far about the relation is that it is not that of entailment. Let us say that in an inductive argument the grounds *support* the conclusion; and let us, instead of speaking of the premises of an inductive argument, speak of the *evidence* for an inductive conclusion. Now we saw, at the beginning of the last section, that the premises of a deductive argument either entail the conclusion or they do not. They cannot entail it more or less; there can be no question of *degrees* of entailment. But there can be, and is, a question of degrees of support; there can be, and is, better or worse evidence for inductive conclusions. Thus suppose that $p_1 - p_n$ are statements which support the statement that q. Think, then, of the degrees of support which common speech discriminates: $p_1 - p_n$ may make it *certain* that q; they may make it *virtually certain* that q; they may make it *highly probable* or *quite probable* or *quite likely* that q; they may give *some probability* to q. Or again, in terms of the word 'evidence': they may constitute *overwhelming* or *conclusive* evidence for q; *pretty conclusive* or *good* evidence, *some* evidence or *slender* evidence. Similarly, they may be conclusive grounds or reasons, good grounds or reasons, slender grounds or poor reasons for holding that q. It is important to notice that where we may speak of conclusive or overwhelming

evidence for q, of $p_1 - p_n$ making it certain that q, there also we may speak of *proving, establishing,* or *putting it beyon⌐ ⌐ll doubt* that q, although, since the arguments are inductive, we do not produce as grounds anything that entails q. For it is not a question of support falling generally short of entailment; of entailment being the perfection of support. They are not related as the winner to the runner-up and the rest in the same race. The perfection of support is proof, but not deductive proof; it is conclusive evidence.

A way we have, then, of acknowledging, when support for an inductive conclusion is less than overwhelming, that this is so, is the use of the words ' probable ', ' probability ', ' probably '. These words are the source and subject of many confusions. One which need be mentioned only in order to be dismissed emerges in the statement, sometimes made, that the conclusions of inductive arguments are, *as such*, only probable; perhaps very, very probable, but never certain; for they are not entailed by their grounds. This is to make the mistake of thinking that entailment and support are competitors in the same field. But there are other confusions, more difficult to disentangle, for which the misunderstanding of the words ' probable ', ' probably ', and ' probability ' is responsible. Let us observe these words in their rôle of acknowledging that support for an inductive conclusion is less than overwhelming.

A psycho-analyst might make the following pronouncement : ' On the basis of clinical experience over a good many years, it now seems probable that a very strict régime in the nursery is always followed by aggressiveness in later life.' Let us express the generalization here said to seem probable in the short form : ' All cases of f (very strict nursery-régime) are cases of h (later aggressiveness).' We may suppose that the qualifying phrases are omitted, that someone says simply :

($g1$) It is probable that all cases of f are cases of h.

Here an inductive generalization is declared to be probable. Consider now how this pronouncement might be applied in a particular case. Someone might say : ' Her nursery régime is very strict indeed; so she'll probably develop aggressive tendencies in later life.' We may write this shortly as

($s1$) fa, so probably ha.

The word 'probably' here acknowledges that fa is less than conclusive support for ha. Let us call support that is less than conclusive, *incomplete support*. Then acknowledging, in ($s1$), that fa incompletely supports ha is indirectly acknowledging the incompleteness of the support for the universal proposition that all cases of f are cases of h.

Now compare the use of 'probably' in ($s1$) with its use in the following cases:

> ($s2$) He's been travelling for seven hours, so probably he's tired.
>
> ($s3$) There's a fog to-night, so the train will probably be late.

If someone demurred at ($s2$) or ($s3$) (' I don't see why that should tire him '), the first speaker might back them up with :

> ($g2$) Well, people generally are tired after travelling for seven hours (or)
>
> Most people are tired after seven hours travelling, you know.
>
> ($g3$) Trains generally are late when there's a fog.

What we now have to compare is the relations between ($s1$) and ($g1$) with the relations between ($s2$) and ($g2$), and between ($s3$) and ($g3$). The singular sentences ($s2$) and ($s3$) resemble the singular sentence ($s1$) in that they are all of the pattern ' p, so probably q '. In all three the use of ' probably ' acknowledges the incompleteness of the support which the statement preceding ' so ' (the statement that p) gives to the statement following ' so ' (the statement that q). In ($s1$) acknowledging this is also acknowledging the incompleteness of the support for the universal generalization that all cases of f are cases of h. But in ($s2$) and ($s3$), acknowledging the incompleteness of the support which the statement that p gives to the statement that q is not acknowledging the incompleteness of the support for a universal proposition. We may regard it as beyond question that people are *usually* tired after travelling for seven hours, that trains are *usually* late when there is a fog. If so, what our use of ' probably ' indirectly acknowledges in these cases is not the incompleteness of the support for a universal proposition, but the fact that the generalization is itself not a universal, but a propor-

tional, generalization. It says, not ' all ' but ' most ', not
' always ' but ' generally '. Such statements are sometimes
called relative frequency generalizations : (g2) for example,
asserts that the relative frequency, among people who have just
been travelling for seven hours, of people who are tired, is high.
In this instance the relative frequency is only vaguely indicated ;
but it may be given, with more precision, by a numerical ratio.

So while ' probably ' may be said to have the same role in
(s2) and (s3) as it has in (s1), there are differences in the ways in
which it comes to have that role. It has the same role in each,
in that it acknowledges the incompleteness of the support which
the statement that p gives to the statement that q. It has the
same role in that, while acknowledging the incompleteness of the
support, it nevertheless claims the support to be fairly good.
The acceptance of (s1) and (s2) has parallel effects on our actions.
If we want only non-aggressive people in our school, we rate low
the claims for admission of the person of whom (s1) is said ; but
we do not rule her out altogether. If we want only non-tired
people for the expedition which is about to begin, we rate low
the claims of the person of whom (s2) is said ; though we do not
rule him out altogether. The reason why the candidates for
school and expedition respectively are not ruled out altogether
is that each may be an exception to a general rule. But the
reasons why each may turn out to be an exception to a general
rule are different. In the first case the relevant generalization
(though universal) was said to be only probable and may therefore turn out to be false, i.e., to have exceptions, of which the
candidate may be one. In the second case the relevant generalization (though its truth is unquestioned) is not a universal
generalization, and therefore admits of exceptions, of which the
candidate may be one.

To sum the matter up rather crudely. We use the word
' probably ' in one case because there is incomplete support for
a ' complete ' generalization ; in the other case, because there is
complete support for an ' incomplete ' generalization. Of
course, we might also use it where there was incomplete support
for an incomplete generalization.

It must not be supposed that whenever we utter a singular
sentence of the form ' p so probably q ', we can always point to
just one generalization, complete or incomplete, so simply

related to our argument as $(g2)$ is to $(s2)$, or as the generalization declared to be probable in $(g1)$ is to $(s1)$. For this would by no means be true. It suffices that the simple cases exist, and that, if we understand them, we shall find it easier to understand the more complex ones.

3. A generalization which is, in the above sense, incomplete (as, e.g., one of the form ' Most cases of f are cases of g ') may be more, or less, incomplete. That is to say, the ratio of f . g cases to f cases affirmed in such a generalization may be more or less high. To indicate this ratio with any precision we have to have recourse to figures; to fractions or percentages. Thus we write : ' 78% of f-cases are g-cases ' or ' The ratio of f . g cases to f cases is 78/100 '.[1] Where our use of the word ' probable ' or its cognates reflects the incompleteness of a generalization, it will tend to reflect also the *degree* of incompleteness of the generalization. We talk of degrees of probability, and may express these numerically : we might say, for example, ' Both parents have fair hair, so the probability of their child having fair hair is x/y '. This has encouraged the hope that talk of the probability of something being g, given that it is f (e.g., of a child having fair hair, given that it has fair-haired parents), can be explained simply as talk of the ratio of f . g things to f things (e.g., the ratio of fair-haired children with fair-haired parents to children with fair-haired parents). Up to a point, this is correct. For it is correct, though pedantic, to re-express the generalization ' x out of y children of fair-haired parents have fair hair ' in the form ' The probability of a child of fair-haired parents having fair hair is x/y '; and conversely, the word ' probability ', in this use, can be eliminated in favour of a statement of relative frequencies. But some have been encouraged to go further, and to suggest that an account in terms of relative frequency ratios may provide a complete elucidation of the notion of probability and, with it, of the notion of support; since variations in degree of support can be expressed by the use of the

---

[1] Why not ' the ratio of g cases to f cases is 78/100 ' ? An example will make the answer clear. ' 7 out of 10 children under twelve have an I.Q. below 100 ' does not mean ' The ratio of the number of *people* with an I.Q. below 100 to the number of children under twelve is as 7 to 10 '; it means ' The ratio of the *number of children under twelve* with an I.Q. below 100 to the number of children under twelve is as 7 to 10 '.

word 'probable' and associated words. This is obviously wrong. Only if observed relative frequency ratios offered strong *support* to the generalization that the ratio of f . g cases to f cases was x/y should we be justified in saying, of a fresh case, as in our example, 'Both parents have fair hair, so the probability of their child having fair hair is x/y'. The observed relative frequency explains *the degree of support* which 'Both parents have fair hair' gives to 'Their child will have fair hair'; but only on the assumption that the generalization of the x/y ratio beyond the observed cases is itself *adequately supported* by the evidence of the observed cases. So this second and fundamental sense of support cannot itself be explained in terms of relative frequencies and indeed cannot be expressed in numerical terms at all; it can be characterized only by such expressions as 'strong', 'adequate', 'weak' and so on.

The point is indeed a very obvious one. If we return to our earlier example of the form 'p so probably q' (viz., 'He's been travelling for seven hours, so probably he's tired'), it is obvious that the strength of the support which the statement that p gives to the statement that q is the product of two factors: first, the degree of completeness of the underlying generalization; second, the degree of completeness of the support for the underlying generalization. The first is a matter of relative frequencies; the second is not. The assimilation of the second to the first is perhaps encouraged by the fact that the strength of the support which one singular statement gives to another is a function of both.

4. There is another class of propositions in which we assign numerical probabilities to singular statements; but seemingly not on the basis of statistical generalizations. They may, however, lead to similar confusions to those which we have just discussed. To someone about to cut a pack of cards, one might say that the chances of his cutting an ace or a court-card were $\frac{4}{13}$. To someone about to throw a die we might say that the mathematical probability of his throwing a six was $\frac{1}{6}$. We are in fact more likely to use the language of 'chances' than that of 'probabilities'; but we may waive this point. Here we might seem to be in the position of being able to assign a probability to a statement simply by doing a little calculating. The

first probability-statement seems to be *entailed* by the statement, which we can verify here and now by counting, that there are fifty-two cards in the pack of which sixteen are court-cards or aces; the second probability-statement seems to be *entailed* by the statement, which we can similarly verify here and now, that the die is a cube, of which one side and one side only is marked with six dots. So it might seem that in each case we make an inductive step (for is not the conclusion couched in the language of probability ?), and yet a step of which the correctness depends on nothing more problematical than simple arithmetic. Such cases have excercised an undue fascination over some logicians concerned to elucidate the nature of inductive reasoning. If it could be shown that all probabilities were fundamentally similar to these, then to those obsessed with deduction as the model of all reasoning, there seemed to come hope of relief. For it would then seem possible to exhibit induction, not as a special (i.e., non-deductive) kind of reasoning to conclusions which are not entailed by their premises, but as ordinary (i.e., deductive) reasoning to conclusions which *are* entailed by their premises, but which are conclusions of a special kind, i.e., numerical, or quasi-numerical, probability-statements. This hope of interpreting induction as a kind of calculation, a special branch of the deductive science of arithmetic, is illusory. We may grant that the step from the statement that the object before us is a cube of which one side only is marked with six dots, to the statement that the probability of a six being thrown is $\frac{1}{6}$, is an inductive step. But the fact that the object is a cube provides no logical guarantee of the truth of the statement that there are just six possible ways in which it may lie when it falls. There is nothing self-contradictory in saying that when the cube touches the floor it will explode, disintegrate, or melt. Even the statement that there are just six possible ways in which it may lie when it touches the floor, and that the position in which the six is uppermost is one of these, does not entail the statement that the probability of the six turning up is $\frac{1}{6}$. This is entailed by nothing less than the statement that the six possible ways in which the die may lie are *equally* probable or, as it is sometimes expressed, equally possible. And this will be so only if the cube is a body of a certain kind : of a kind, namely, of which it is true that the number of times that the different surfaces of bodies of that kind turn up in successive throws tend to equality as the number of throws increases. The statement that there are six equally possible ways for the die to fall is an inductive conclusion from the data with which we began; but, although it may be adequately supported by these data, it does not follow from them by a mathematical calculation. The induction is over before the calculation begins. The calculation of chances is not even a species of induction, let alone the whole story about induction. Either the data of the calculation are themselves the conclusions of inductions or induction does not enter into the picture at all.

Of course, we in fact incorporate the relevant provisos about equality of chances in the sense we give to the expression ' true die ' : so that the step from ' This is a true die ' to ' The chance of your throwing a six is $\frac{1}{6}$ ' is a purely deductive step. But this fact is of no help to anyone who wishes to explain degrees of inductive support in terms of arithmetically calculable chances. It shows only that certain steps which we might be tempted to think of as inductive, since their conclusions contain the word ' probability ', are not inductive at all.

5. The notion of support and with it, that of degrees of probability, cannot then be explained solely in terms of relative frequencies or numerical chances. On the contrary, the relevance of chance and frequency ratios to our practical assessments of certainties and likelihoods presupposes the existence of a kind of support which cannot itself be analysed in these terms. For their relevance depends upon our having certain general beliefs which may themselves be better or worse grounded, well or poorly supported. It is because we possess, say, a general belief that a certain proportion of As are Bs, that we take this proportion into account in estimating the likelihood of a particular thing being a B. It is in the light of a general belief, say, that certain chances are equal, that we take into account the mathematical ratio of desired cases to possible cases in estimating the likelihood of an event of the desired kind. General beliefs of this sort, which are the preconditions of particular estimates of probability, need not, however, be explicitly formulated; any more than we need explicitly formulate the principles of particular pieces of deductive reasoning which we

unselfconsciously perform. Forming a general belief may be more like forming a mental habit than arriving at a reasoned conclusion. But, however a general belief is arrived at, it will always make sense to ask how strong the evidence for it is, whether it is well or ill supported.

It is this fundamental sense of ' support ' which must, then, be examined. How do we tell when evidence is good or bad, strong or weak, conclusive or slender, better or worse? This may seem a difficult question. But the kind of difficulty should be noticed. Judges and historians, detectives, biologists, and ourselves every day assess the quality of evidence for conclusions, make judgments of relative probability. The clever do it better than the stupid. But it is not so difficult a matter that some of us cannot do it at all. It is not a specialized skill. The difficulty we are faced with is not the difficulty of doing it, but the difficulty of describing what we do.

The question, then, is : what do we mean by saying of a non-necessary generalization—to the effect, say, that all (or most) As are Bs—that it is well established, or more or less strongly supported by the evidence? Now, in fact, in estimating the evidence for such a generalization, a factor of enormous importance is its relation to the general body of our knowledge and belief : the question of how it fits in with the rest of our every-day general convictions and with accepted scientific theories. The importance of this factor obviously depends on the degree to which the relevant beliefs form a closely knit complex structure. Thus it has maximum importance in the field of physical theory ; minimum importance where we are dealing with the unorganized congeries of rule-of-thumb beliefs by which we are guided in our unspecialized transactions with the world. In general, however, its importance is so great that to neglect it in practice would be absurd. But it is no less absurd to refuse to abstract from it in this theoretical inquiry. A generalization might fit in as well as you please with some wider body of beliefs ; and yet both it and the general theory might be false. The ultimate test of a generalization which applies directly to instances is to be found in the instances to which it applies.

Having abstracted to this degree from the considerations which we in fact take into account in assessing the evidence for a generalization, we can give our question quite a simple answer.

It is this.   The evidence for a generalization to the effect that all As are Bs is good (1) in proportion as our observations of instances of As which are B are numerous, and (2) in proportion as the variety of conditions in which the instances are found is wide; always provided that no instance is found of an A which is not B; for such an instance would, of course, suffice to refute the generalization, if the latter were strictly interpreted.   Conditions (1) and (2) are commonly contrasted : the mere accumulation of instances favourable to the generalization is called ' simple enumeration '; and ' induction by simple enumeration ' is said to be a relatively weak form of argument.   But the contrast is misleading, though it has a point.   If all the instances of A observed had in common not only A and B but also a third feature C, then the assumption that (1) was the only relevant condition would lead to the conclusion that we had at our disposal equally strong evidence for the two logically non-equivalent generalizations, viz., ' All As are Bs ' and ' All ACs are Bs '.   The first of these entails the second, but is not entailed by it : the truth of ' All ACs are Bs ' is consistent with the falsity of, say, ' All ADs are Bs ', and hence with the falsity of ' All As are Bs '.   So evidence that supports to a certain degree the claim that all ACs are B supports to a lesser degree the wider claim that all As are B.   This is the point of the contrast, the reason why condition (2) is required.   But the need for condition (2) does not imply the existence of two fundamentally contrasted kinds of inductive reasoning.   Suppose we frame a higher-order generalization to the effect that all generalizations of the form ' All A—s are Bs ' (e.g., ' All ACs are Bs ', ' All ADs are Bs ', &c.) are true.   Then the truth of ' All ACs are B ' constitutes one favourable instance of this generalization, the truth of ' All ADs are Bs ' constitutes another favourable instance and so on.   By condition (1), the greater the number of such generalizations we establish, the better the evidence for the higher-order generalization.   But the higher-order generalization and the original generalization (' All As are Bs ') have exactly the same force, are logically equivalent.   So, if we were to think of conditions (1) and (2) as describing contrasting methods of induction, we should have the paradox that the application of the second method to the original generalization was identical with the application of the first method to a generalization equivalent to the original generalization. This should teach us to think of conditions (1) and (2) not as describing contrasted methods, but as stressing complementary factors to be weighed in assessing the evidence for a generalization. The essential unity of the process of accumulating evidence might be emphasized by writing the generalization, not in the form 'All *A*s are *B*s ', but in the equivalent doubly general form ' In all conditions, all *A*s are *B*s '.

The case of proportional, as opposed to universal, generalizations presents no important difference in principle. Abstracting from the factors we have decided to abstract from, the evidence that a certain more or less exactly specified proportion of *A*s are *B*s varies in strength with the variety of kinds of instance in which that proportion is found to hold, and with the numbers of instances of each kind.

6. Now I must emphasize, with all possible force, that the preceding two paragraphs, though they say something fundamental about the nature of evidence for general beliefs, are not to be taken as an accurate description of some standard and familiar process of inductive inference. Because we can *count* instances, for example, and because the strength of the evidence is said to be related to the number of favourable instances, we might be tempted to think that we could assess the strength of the evidence for a general belief with numerical precision; or we might be tempted to think that every black crow we see should fortify us in our conviction that all crows are black. In fact, we can never describe the strength of evidence more exactly than by the use of such words as ' slender ', ' good ', ' conclusive ', &c.; it is exceptional that a single favourable instance should make any difference to the strength of our conviction; and when a single instance does make a difference, it may take us straight from ignorance to certainty, as when, in the laboratory, a general fact is established by a single test. Such facts are in part explained by the factors, already mentioned, from which we have abstracted : the relevance of the general background of experience, assumption, and explicitly formulated theory against which we make our assessments of the evidence, whether for a general or a particular conclusion. These background presumptions will determine, to mention nothing else, which

variations in conditions we shall think it necessary to take account of. We have to remember, too, the great complexity of the ways in which background beliefs may be related to foreground problems; how many general beliefs may bear upon the probability of a single event; how important are the analogies between one case and another, as well as the strictly deductive relations between beliefs; how relatively crude many of our ways of classifying phenomena are. When we bear in mind these things, it will not seem surprising either that no precise rules of general application can be formulated for the assessment of evidence or that no precise vocabulary is available for the description of its degrees. There are techniques of limited application (e.g., for collecting and interpreting statistics), but there is no general technique. We say, of a man who is good at weighing evidence in the ordinary affairs of life, that he has good judgment. The use of this very general, non-specialist, word is revealing. The man who is good at weighing evidence has not mastered the instructions for using some particularly intricate scales. His experience must be wide; but he is not, except incidentally, a specialist.

We must remember, moreover, that our assessment of evidence is an activity undertaken not primarily for its own sake, but for the sake of practical decision and action. Our use of words for grading evidence will in part reflect the degree of caution demanded by the action proposed. Evidence which the general public finds conclusive may not satisfy the judge.

II. THE 'JUSTIFICATION' OF INDUCTION

7. We have seen something, then, of the nature of inductive reasoning; of how one statement or set of statements may support another statement, S, which they do not entail, with varying degrees of strength, ranging from being conclusive evidence for S to being only slender evidence for it; from making S as certain as the supporting statements, to giving it some slight probability. We have seen, too, how the question of degree of support is complicated by consideration of relative frequencies and numerical chances.

There is, however, a residual philosophical question which enters so largely into discussion of the subject that it must be discussed. It can be raised, roughly, in the following forms. What reason have we to place reliance on inductive procedures? Why should we suppose that the accumulation of instances of As which are Bs, however various the conditions in which they are observed, gives any good reason for expecting the next A we encounter to be a B? It is our habit to form expectations in this way; but can the habit be rationally justified? When this doubt has entered our minds it may be difficult to free ourselves from it. For the doubt has its source in a confusion; and some attempts to resolve the doubt preserve the confusion; and other attempts to show that the doubt is senseless seem altogether too facile. The root-confusion is easily described; but simply to describe it seems an inadequate remedy against it. So the doubt must be examined again and again, in the light of different attempts to remove it.

If someone asked what grounds there were for supposing that deductive reasoning was valid, we might answer that there were in fact no grounds for supposing that deductive reasoning was always valid; sometimes people made valid inferences, and sometimes they were guilty of logical fallacies. If he said that we had misunderstood his question, and that what he wanted to know was what grounds there were for regarding deduction *in general* as a valid method of argument, we should have to answer that his question was without sense, for to say that an argument, or a form or method of argument, was valid or invalid would *imply* that it was deductive; the concepts of validity and invalidity had application only to individual deductive arguments or forms of deductive argument. Similarly, if a man asked what grounds there were for thinking it reasonable to hold beliefs arrived at inductively, one might at first answer that there were good and bad inductive arguments, that sometimes it was reasonable to hold a belief arrived at inductively and sometimes it was not. If he, too, said that his question had been misunderstood, that he wanted to know whether induction in general was a reasonable method of inference, then we might well think his question senseless in the same way as the question whether deduction is in general valid; for to call a particular belief reasonable or unreasonable is to apply inductive standards, just as to call a particular argument valid or invalid is to apply deductive standards. The parallel is not wholly convincing;

for words like ' reasonable ' and ' rational ' have not so precise and technical a sense as the word ' valid '.   Yet it is sufficiently powerful to make us wonder how the second question could be raised at all, to wonder why, in contrast with the corresponding question about deduction, it should have seemed to constitute a genuine problem.

Suppose that a man is brought up to regard formal logic as the study of the science and art of reasoning. He observes that all inductive processes are, by deductive standards, invalid; the premises never entail the conclusions.   Now inductive processes are notoriously important in the formation of beliefs and expectations about everything which lies beyond the observation of available witnesses.   But an *invalid* argument is an *unsound* argument; an *unsound* argument is one in which *no good reason* is produced for accepting the conclusion. So if inductive processes are invalid, if all the arguments we should produce, if challenged, in support of our beliefs about what lies beyond the observation of available witnesses are unsound, then we have no good reason for any of these beliefs. This conclusion is repugnant. So there arises the demand for a justification, not of this or that particular belief which goes beyond what is entailed by our evidence, but a justification of induction in general. And when the demand arises in this way it is, in effect, the demand that induction shall be shown to be really a kind of deduction; for nothing less will satisfy the doubter when this is the route to his doubts.

Tracing this, the most common route to the general doubt about the reasonableness of induction, shows how the doubt seems to escape the absurdity of a demand that induction in general shall be justified by inductive standards.   The demand is that induction should be shown to be a rational process; and this turns out to be the demand that one kind of reasoning should be shown to be another and different kind. Put thus crudely, the demand seems to escape one absurdity only to fall into another. Of course, inductive arguments are not deductively valid; if they were, they would be deductive arguments. Inductive reasoning must be assessed, for soundness, by inductive standards. Nevertheless, fantastic as the wish for induction to be deduction may seem, it is only in terms of it that we can understand some of the attempts that have been made to justify induction.

8. The first kind of attempt I shall consider might be called the search for the supreme premise of inductions.   In its primitive form it is quite a crude attempt; and I shall make it cruder by caricature.   We have already seen that for a particular inductive step, such as ' The kettle has been on the fire for ten minutes, so it will be boiling by now ', we can substitute a deductive argument by introducing a generalization (e.g., ' A kettle always boils within ten minutes of being put on the fire ') as an additional premise.   This manœuvre shifted the emphasis of the problem of inductive support on to the question of how we established such generalizations as these, which rested on grounds by which they were not entailed.   But suppose the manœuvre could be repeated.   Suppose we could find one supremely general proposition, which taken in conjunction with the evidence for any accepted generalization of science or daily life (or at least of science) would entail that generalization. Then, so long as the status of the supreme generalization could be satisfactorily explained, we could regard all sound inductions to unqualified general conclusions as, at bottom, valid deductions.   The justification would be found, for at least these cases.   The most obvious difficulty in this suggestion is that of formulating the supreme general proposition in such a way that it shall be precise enough to yield the desired entailments, and yet not obviously false or arbitrary.   Consider, for example, the formula : ' For all f, g, wherever n cases of $f . g$, and no cases of $f . \sim g$, are observed, then all cases of f are cases of g.' To turn it into a sentence, we have only to replace ' n ' by some number.   But what number?   If we take the value of ' n ' to be 1 or 20 or 500, the resulting statement is obviously false. Moreover, the choice of any number would seem quite arbitrary ; there is no privileged number of favourable instances which we take as decisive in establishing a generalization.   If, on the other hand, we phrase the proposition vaguely enough to escape these objections—if, for example, we phrase it as ' Nature is uniform '—then it becomes too vague to provide the desired entailments.   It should be noticed that the impossibility of framing a general proposition of the kind required is really a special case of the impossibility of framing precise rules for the assessment of evidence.   If we could frame a rule which would tell us precisely when we had *conclusive* evidence for a generaliza-

tion, then it would yield just the proposition required as the supreme premise.

Even if these difficulties could be met, the question of the status of the supreme premise would remain. How, if a non-necessary proposition, could it be established ? The appeal to experience, to inductive support, is clearly barred on pain of circularity. If, on the other hand, it were a necessary truth and possessed, in conjunction with the evidence for a generalization, the required logical power to entail the generalization (e.g., if the latter were the conclusion of a hypothetical syllogism, of which the hypothetical premise was the necessary truth in question), then the evidence would entail the generalization independently, and the problem would not arise : a conclusion unbearably paradoxical. In practice, the extreme vagueness with which candidates for the role of supreme premise are expressed prevents their acquiring such logical power, and at the same time renders it very difficult to classify them as analytic or synthetic : under pressure they may tend to tautology; and, when the pressure is removed, assume an expansively synthetic air.

In theories of the kind which I have here caricatured the ideal of deduction is not usually so blatantly manifest as I have made it. One finds the ' Law of the Uniformity of Nature ' presented less as the suppressed premise of crypto-deductive inferences than as, say, the ' presupposition of the validity of inductive reasoning '. I shall have more to say about this in my last section.

9. I shall next consider a more sophisticated kind of attempt to justify induction : more sophisticated both in its interpretation of this aim and in the method adopted to achieve it. The aim envisaged is that of proving that the probability of a generalization, whether universal or proportional, increases with the number of instances for which it is found to hold. This clearly is a realistic aim : for the proposition to be proved does state, as we have already seen, a fundamental feature of our criteria for assessing the strength of evidence. The method of proof proposed is mathematical. Use is to be made of the arithmetical calculation of chances. This, however, seems less realistic : for we have already seen that the prospect of analysing the notion of support in these terms seems poor.

I state the argument as simply as possible; but, even so, it will be necessary to introduce and explain some new terms. Suppose we had a collection of objects of different kinds, some with some characteristics and some with others. Suppose, for example, we had a bag containing 100 balls, of which 70 were white and 30 black. Let us call such a collection of objects a *population*; and let us call the way it is made up (e.g., in the case imagined, of 70 white and 30 black balls) the *constitution* of the population. From such a population it would be possible to take *samples* of various sizes. For example, we might take from our bag a sample of 30 balls. Suppose each ball in the bag had an individual number. Then the collection of balls numbered 10 to 39 inclusive would be one sample of the given size; the collection of balls numbered 11 to 40 inclusive would be another and different sample of the same size; the collection of balls numbered 2, 4, 6, 8 . . . 58, 60 would be another such sample; and so on. Each possible collection of 30 balls is a different sample of the same size. Some different samples of the same size will have the same constitutions as one another; others will have different constitutions. Thus there will be only one sample made up of 30 black balls. There will be many different samples which share the constitution : 20 white and 10 black. It would be a simple matter of mathematics to work out the number of possible samples of the given size which had any one possible constitution. Let us say that a sample *matches* the population if, allowing for the difference between them in size, the constitution of the sample corresponds, within certain limits, to that of the population. For example, we might say that any possible sample consisting of, say, 21 white and 9 black balls matched the constitution (70 white and 30 black) of the population, whereas a sample consisting of 20 white and 10 black balls did not. Now it is a proposition of pure mathematics that, given any population, the proportion of possible samples, all of the same size, which match the population, increases with the size of the sample.

We have seen that conclusions about the ratio of a subset of equally possible chances to the whole set of those chances may be expressed by the use of the word ' probability '. Thus of the 52 possible samples of one card from a population constituted like an orthodox pack, 16 are court-cards or aces. This fact we allow ourselves to express (under the conditions, inductively established, of equipossibility of draws) by saying that the probability of drawing a court-card or an ace was $\frac{4}{13}$. If we express the proposition referred to at the end of the last paragraph by means of this use of ' probability ' we shall obtain the result: The probability of a sample matching a given population increases with the size of the sample. It is tempting to try to derive from this result a general justification of the inductive procedure : which will not, indeed, show that any given inductive conclusion is entailed by the evidence for it, taken in conjunction with some universal premise, but will show that the multiplication of favourable instances of a generalization entails a proportionate increase in its probability. For, since *matching* is a symmetrical relation, it might seem a simple deductive step to move from

> I. The probability of a sample matching a given population increases with the size of the sample

to

> II. The probability of a population matching a given sample increases with the size of the sample.

II might seem to provide a guarantee that the greater the number of cases for which a generalization is observed to hold, the greater is its probability; since in increasing the number of cases we increase the size of the sample from whatever population forms the subject of our generalization. Thus pure mathematics might seem to provide the sought-for proof that the evidence for a generalization really does get stronger, the more favourable instances of it we find.

The argument is ingenious enough to be worthy of respect; but it fails of its purpose, and misrepresents the inductive situation. Our situation is not in the least like that of a man drawing a sample from a given, i.e., fixed and limited, population from which the drawing of any mathematically possible sample is equiprobable with that of any other. Our only datum is the sample. No limit is fixed beforehand to the diversity, and the possibilities of change, of the ' population ' from which it is drawn : or, better, to the multiplicity and variousness of different populations, each with different constitutions, any one of which might replace the present one before we make the next draw. Nor is there any *a priori* guarantee that different mathematically possible samples are equally likely to be drawn. If we have or can obtain any assurance on these points, then it is assurance derived inductively from our data, and cannot therefore be assumed at the outset of an argument designed to justify induction. So II, regarded as a justification of induction founded on purely mathematical considerations, is a fraud. The important shift of ' given from qualifying ' population ' in I to qualifying ' sample ' in II is illegitimate. Moreover, ' probability ', which means one thing in II (interpreted as giving the required guarantee) means something quite different in I (interpreted as a proposition of pure mathematics). In I probability is simply the measure of the ratio of one set of mathematically possible chances to another; in II it is the measure of the inductive acceptability of a generalization. As a mathematical proposition, I is certainly independent of the soundness of inductive procedures; and as a statement of one of the criteria we use in assessing the strength of evidence of a generalization, II is as certainly independent of mathematics.

It has not escaped the notice of those who have advocated a mathematical justification of induction, that certain assumptions are required to make the argument even seem to fulfil its purpose. Inductive reasoning would be of little use if it did not sometimes enable us to assign at least fairly high probabilities to certain conclusions. Now suppose, in conformity with the mathematical model, we represented the fact that the evidence for a proposition was conclusive by assigning to it the probability figure of 1 ; and the fact that the evidence for and against a proposition was evenly balanced by assigning to it the probability figure $\frac{1}{2}$; and so on. It is a familiar mathematical truth that, between any two fractions, say $\frac{1}{6}$ and $\frac{1}{5}$, there is an infinite number of intermediate quantities; that $\frac{1}{6}$ can be indefinitely increased without reaching equality to $\frac{1}{5}$. Even if we could regard II as mathematically established, therefore, it fails to give us what we require; for it fails to provide a guarantee that the probability of an inductive conclusion ever attains a degree at which it begins to be of use. It was accordingly necessary to buttress the purely mathematical argument by large, vague assumptions, comparable with the principles designed for the role of supreme premise in the first type of attempt. These assumptions, like those principles, could never actually be used to give a deductive turn to inductive arguments; for they could not be formulated with precision. They were the shadows of precise unknown truths, which, if one did know them, would suffice, along with the data for our accepted generalizations, to enable the probability of the latter to be assigned, after calculation, a precise numerical fraction of a tolerable size. So this theory represents our inductions as the vague sublunary shadows of deductive calculations which we cannot make.

10. Let us turn from attempts to justify induction to attempts to show that the demand for a justification is mistaken. We have seen already that what lies behind such a demand is often the absurd wish that induction should be shown to be some kind of deduction—and this wish is clearly traceable in the two attempts at justification which we have examined. What other sense could we give to the demand? Sometimes it is expressed in the form of a request for proof that induction is a *reasonable* or *rational* procedure, that we have *good grounds* for placing reliance upon it. Consider the uses of the phrases ' good grounds ', ' justification ', ' reasonable ', &c. Often we say such things as ' He has *every justification* for believing that *p* '; ' I have *very good reasons* for believing it '; ' There are *good grounds* for the view that *q* '; ' There is *good evidence* that *r* '. We often talk, in such ways as these, of justification, good grounds or reasons or evidence for certain beliefs. Suppose such a belief were one expressible in the form ' Every case of *f* is a case of *g* '. And suppose someone were asked what he meant by saying that he had good grounds or reasons for holding it. I think it would be felt to be a satisfactory answer if he replied : ' Well, in all my wide and varied experience I've come across innumerable cases of *f* and never a case of *f* which wasn't a case of *g*.' In saying this, he is clearly claiming to have *inductive* support, *inductive* evidence, of a certain kind, for his belief; and he is also giving a perfectly proper answer to the question, what he meant by saying that he had ample justification, good grounds, good reasons for his belief. It is an analytic proposition that it is reasonable to have a degree of belief in a statement which is proportional to the strength of the evidence in its favour; and it is an analytic proposition, though not a

proposition of mathematics, that, other things being equal,[1] the evidence for a generalization is strong in proportion as the number of favourable instances, and the variety of circumstances in which they have been found, is great.   So to ask whether it is reasonable to place reliance on inductive procedures is like asking whether it is reasonable to proportion the degree of one's convictions to the strength of the evidence.   Doing this is what ' being reasonable ' *means* in such a context.

As for the other form in which the doubt may be expressed, viz., ' Is induction a justified, or justifiable, procedure? ', it emerges in a still less favourable light.   No sense has been given to it, though it is easy to see why it seems to have a sense.   For it is generally proper to inquire *of a particular belief*, whether its adoption is justified; and, in asking this, we are asking whether there is good, bad, or any, evidence for it.   In applying or withholding the epithets ' justified ', ' well founded ', &c., in the case of specific beliefs, we are appealing to, and applying, inductive standards.   But to what standards are we appealing when we ask whether the application of inductive standards is justified or well grounded?   If we cannot answer, then no sense has been given to the question.   Compare it with the question : Is the law legal?   It makes perfectly good sense to inquire of a particular action, of an administrative regulation, or even, in the case of some states, of a particular enactment of the legislature, whether or not it is legal.   The question is answered by an appeal to a legal system, by the application of a set of legal (or constitutional) rules or standards.   But it makes no sense to inquire in general whether the law of the land, the legal system as a whole, is or is not legal.   For to what legal standards are we appealing?

The only way in which a sense might be given to the question, whether induction is in general a justified or justifiable procedure, is a trivial one which we have already noticed.   We might interpret it to mean ' Are all conclusions, arrived at inductively, justified? ', i.e., ' Do people always have adequate evidence for the conclusions they draw? '   The answer to this question is easy, but uninteresting : it is that sometimes people have adequate evidence, and sometimes they do not.

---

[1] This phrase embodies the large abstractions referred to in Sections 5 and 6.

11. It seems, however, that this way of showing the request for a general justification of induction to be absurd is sometimes insufficient to allay the worry that produces it. And to point out that ' forming rational opinions about the unobserved on the evidence available ' and ' assessing the evidence by inductive standards ' are phrases which describe the same thing, is more apt to produce irritation than relief. The point is felt to be ' merely a verbal ' one; and though the point of this protest is itself hard to see, it is clear that something more is required. So the question must be pursued further. First, I want to point out that there is something a little odd about talking of ' the inductive method ', or even ' the inductive policy ', as if it were just one possible method among others of arguing from the observed to the unobserved, from the available evidence to the facts in question. If one asked a meteorologist what method or methods he used to forecast the weather, one would be surprised if he answered : ' Oh, just the inductive method.' If one asked a doctor by what means he diagnosed a certain disease, the answer ' By induction ' would be felt as an impatient evasion, a joke, or a rebuke. The answer one hopes for is an account of the tests made, the signs taken account of, the rules and recipes and general laws applied. When such a specific method of prediction or diagnosis is in question, one can ask whether the method is justified in practice; and here again one is asking whether its employment is inductively justified, whether it commonly gives correct results. This question would normally seem an admissible one. One might be tempted to conclude that, while there are many different specific methods of prediction, diagnosis, &c., appropriate to different subjects of inquiry, all such methods could properly be called ' inductive ' in the sense that their employment rested on inductive support; and that, hence, the phrase ' non-inductive method of finding out about what lies deductively beyond the evidence ' was a description without meaning, a phrase to which no sense had been given; so that there could be no question of justifying our selection of one method, called ' the inductive ', of doing this.

However, someone might object : ' Surely it is possible, though it might be foolish, to use methods utterly different from accredited scientific ones. Suppose a man, whenever he wanted to form an opinion about what lay beyond his observation or the observation of available witnesses, simply shut his eyes, asked himself the appropriate question, and accepted the first answer that came into his head. Wouldn't this be a non-inductive method?' Well, let us suppose this. The man is asked: 'Do you usually get the right answer by your method?' He might answer: 'You've mentioned one of its drawbacks; I never do get the right answer; but it's an extremely easy method.' One might then be inclined to think that it was not a method of finding things out at all. But suppose he answered: Yes, it's usually (always) the right answer. Then we might be willing to call it a method of finding out, though a strange one. But, then, by the very fact of its success, it would be an inductively supported method. For each application of the method would be an application of the general rule, 'The first answer that comes into my head is generally (always) the right one'; and for the truth of this generalization there would be the inductive evidence of a long run of favourable instances with no unfavourable ones (if it were 'always'), or of a sustained high proportion of successes to trials (if it were 'generally').

So every successful method or recipe for finding out about the unobserved must be one which has inductive support; for to say that a recipe is successful is to say that it has been repeatedly applied with success; and repeated successful application of a recipe constitutes just what we mean by inductive evidence in its favour. Pointing out this fact must not be confused with saying that 'the inductive method' is justified by its success, justified because it works. This is a mistake, and an important one. I am not seeking to 'justify the inductive method', for no meaning has been given to this phrase. *A fortiori*, I am not saying that induction is justified by its success in finding out about the unobserved. I am saying, rather, that any successsful method of finding out about the unobserved is necessarily justified by induction. This is an analytic proposition. The phrase 'successful method of finding things out which has no inductive support' is self-contradictory. Having, or acquiring, inductive support is a necessary condition of the success of a method.

Why point this out at all? First, it may have a certain therapeutic force, a power to reassure. Second, it may counteract the tendency to think of 'the inductive method' as something on a par with specific methods of diagnosis or prediction and therefore, like them, standing in need of (inductive) justification.

12. There is one further confusion, perhaps the most powerful of all in producing the doubts, questions, and spurious solutions discussed in this Part. We may approach it by considering the claim that induction is justified by its success in practice. The phrase ' success of induction ' is by no means clear and perhaps embodies the confusion of induction with some specific method of prediction, &c., appropriate to some particular line of inquiry. But, whatever the phrase may mean, the claim has an obviously circular look. Presumably the suggestion is that we should argue from the past ' successes of induction ' to the continuance of those successes in the future; from the fact that it has worked hitherto to the conclusion that it will continue to work. Since an argument of this kind is plainly inductive, it will not serve as a justification of induction. One cannot establish a principle of argument by an argument which uses that principle. But let us go a little deeper. The argument rests the justification of induction on a matter of fact (its ' past successes '). This is characteristic of nearly all attempts to find a justification. The desired premise of Section 8 was to be some fact about the constitution of the universe which, even if it could not be used as a suppressed premise to give inductive arguments a deductive turn, was at any rate a ' presupposition of the validity of induction '. Even the mathematical argument of Section 9 required buttressing with some large assumption about the make-up of the world. I think the source of this general desire to find out some fact about the constitution of the universe which will ' justify induction ' or ' show it to be a rational policy ' is the confusion, the running together, of two fundamentally different questions : to one of which the answer is a matter of non-linguistic fact, while to the other it is a matter of meanings.

There is nothing self-contradictory in supposing that all the uniformities in the course of things that we have hitherto observed and come to count on should cease to operate to-morrow; that all our familiar recipes should let us down, and that we should be unable to frame new ones because such regularities as there were were too complex for us to make out. (We may assume that even the expectation that all of us, in such circumstances, would perish, were falsified by someone surviving to observe the new chaos in which, roughly speaking, nothing foreseeable happens.) Of course, we do not believe that this will happen. We believe, on the contrary, that our inductively supported expectation-rules, though some of them will have, no doubt, to be dropped or modified, will continue, on the whole, to serve us fairly well; and that we shall generally be able to replace the rules we abandon with others similarly arrived at. We might give a sense to the phrase ' success of induction ' by calling this vague belief the belief that induction will continue to be successful. It is certainly a factual belief, not a necessary truth; a belief, one may say, about the constitution of the universe. We might express it as follows, choosing a phraseology which will serve the better to expose the confusion I wish to expose :

> I. (The universe is such that) induction will continue to be successful.

I is very vague : it amounts to saying that there are, and will continue to be, natural uniformities and regularities which exhibit a humanly manageable degree of simplicity. But, though it is vague, certain definite things can be said about it. (1) It is not a necessary, but a contingent, statement; for chaos is not a self-contradictory concept. (2) We have good inductive reasons for believing it, good inductive evidence for it. We believe that some of our recipes will continue to hold good because they have held good for so long. We believe that we shall be able to frame new and useful ones, because we have been able to do so repeatedly in the past. Of course, it would be absurd to try to use I to ' justify induction ', to show that it is a reasonable policy; because I is a conclusion inductively supported.

Consider now the fundamentally different statement :

> II. Induction is rational (reasonable).

We have already seen that the rationality of induction, unlike its ' successfulness ', is not a fact about the constitution of the world. It is a matter of what we mean by the word ' rational ' in its application to any procedure for forming opinions about what lies outside our observations or that of available witnesses. For to have good reasons for any such opinion is to have good inductive support for it. The chaotic universe just envisaged, therefore, is not one in which induction would cease to be rational; it is simply one in which it would be impossible to form rational expectations to the effect that specific things would happen. It might be said that in such a universe it would at least be rational to refrain from forming specific expectations, to expect nothing but irregularities. Just so. But this is itself a higher-order induction : where irregularity is the rule, expect further irregularities. Learning not to count on things is as much learning an inductive lesson as learning what things to count on.

So it is a contingent, factual matter that it is sometimes possible to form rational opinions concerning what specifically happened or will happen in given circumstances (I); it is a non-contingent, *a priori* matter that the only ways of doing this must be inductive ways (II). What people have done is to run together, to conflate, the question to which I is answer and the quite different question to which II is an answer; producing the muddled and senseless questions : ' Is the universe such that inductive procedures are rational ? ' or ' What must the universe be like in order for inductive procedures to be rational ? ' It is the attempt to answer these confused questions which leads to statements like ' The uniformity of nature is a pre-supposition of the validity of induction '. The statement that nature is uniform might be taken to be a vague way of expressing what we expressed by I; and certainly this fact is a condition of, for it is identical with, the likewise contingent fact that we are, and shall continue to be, able to form rational opinions, of the kind we are most anxious to form, about the unobserved. But neither this fact about the world, nor any other, is a condition of the necessary truth that, if it is possible to form rational opinions of this kind, these will be inductively supported opinions. The discordance of the conflated questions manifests itself in an uncertainty about the status to be accorded to the alleged presupposition of the ' validity ' of induction. For it was dimly, and correctly, felt that the reasonableness of inductive procedures was not merely a contingent, but a necessary, matter; so any necessary condition of their reasonableness had likewise to be a necessary matter.   On the other hand, it was uncomfortably clear that chaos is not a self-contradictory concept; that the fact that some phenomena do exhibit a tolerable degree of simplicity and repetitiveness is not guaranteed by logic, but is a contingent affair.   So the presupposition of induction had to be both contingent and necessary : which is absurd.   And the absurdity is only lightly veiled by the use of the phrase ' synthetic *a priori* ' instead of ' contingent necessary '.

INDEX

REPRINTED BY LITHOGRAPHY IN GREAT BRITAIN
BY JARROLD AND SONS LIMITED, NORWICH